W9-BMI-519

In Memoriam

Patricia Gail Carpenter
(November 4, 1949–April 15, 2000)
A violet by a mossy stone
Half-hidden from the eye!
Fair as a star, when only one
Is shining in the sky.
    –William Wordsworth
She helped to make the world a better place.

People Worth Meeting
and
Stories Worth Repeating

Also by Robert L. Williams

*100 Practically Perfect Places in the
North Carolina Mountains
Faces of the Snow
Mad Dog's Tooth
The Thirteenth Juror
50 Hikes in the Mountains
of North Carolina
Gaston County: A Pictorial History
Starting Over
English Clarified (co-author)
Cuttin' the Corners (ghosted)
The Gallows Birth
Fingers of the Rain
The Eye of the Cockatrice
Brain Dead*

Robert L. Williams

PEOPLE WORTH MEETING
and
STORIES WORTH REPEATING

Southeastern Publishing Corporation
3613 Dallas-Cherryville Highway
Dallas, North Carolina 28034

People Worth Meeting and Stories Worth Repeating
Published by Southeastern Publishing Corporation, Inc.
3613 Dallas-Cherryville Highway
Dallas, North Carolina 28034
Copyright ©2000 by Robert L. Williams

All rights reserved. No parts of this book may be
reproduced in any form, electronically or otherwise, without per-
mission from the publisher.
Published in the United States of America by
Southeastern Publishing Corporation
Library of Congress Cataloging-in-Publication Data

Williams, Robert L. People Worth Meeting and Stories Worth Repeating, a collection of short biographies, folk heroes, travel stories, and
narratives of notable people and descriptions of notable places.
ISBN 1-893330-04-4
Printed in the United States of America
10 9 8 7 6 5 4 3 2 1

The ballads of the People are the bulwarks of the State.

–Eugene Fitch Ware

O brave new world, that has such people in it.

–William Shakespeare, *The Tempest* V, i, 183

We all like people who do things, even if we only see their faces on a cigar-box lid.

–Willa Cather, *The Song of the Lark*

If you want a cause to celebrate living, learn what the Good People of the nation have done, and then do likewise.

–Leonard Trebor, *Thoughts in Passing*

Davie County Public Library
Mocksville, North Carolina

Dedication

This book is dedicated gratefully to all the Good People who have been the inspiration for this work. Among these Good People are the Carpenters: Dean, Jackie, Anna and Adrian; Barbara Wright, Joyce Paulin, and, always heading any personal list I make, Elizabeth and Robert III–people who make the world a better place and my life a special celebration for having known them!

Contents

Preface

The Good People described in these pages came to me (or I went to them) while I was contributing human interest stories on a regular basis to several newspapers and magazines. In other words, I was free-lancing stories to anyone who would buy them while I finished out my years as a teacher. It started out as a means of supplementing an income, and quickly the free-lancing became sort of a steady way to make a fairly good living.

Something else happened along the way: I fell madly in love with the stories I was writing. I met a preacher whose faith placed him in more dangerous situations than most soldiers experience. I met a man who carried his house down a mountain, a man who jogged while carrying an automobile engine strapped onto his shoulders, and men and women who in a thousand ways made their world a better place.

Some of these people I met by accident and later wrote about them. Some of them I sought out for the express purpose of telling their stories. It stands to reason that I never met some of these people; they were long dead before I ever heard of them. But that biological fact has not kept me from visiting with them and telling their stories through research and memories. With the help of a great library or dusty old books, I located these people and their stories, and I enjoyed my visits almost as much as I could have if we had been able to sit and converse over a cup of coffee.

Back in the years when I had a brief fling at playing pro baseball I met Lord Salisbury, and I found it impossible to forget him. Robert Eng was a student in a college class I taught. Dr. Cecil Barrier and his wife Lou belonged to the same church I attended. Once I bought a boxful of books at an estate sale, and in one of the ancient volumes I found a wealth of information about Marshal Michel Ney. At old cemeteries I found the story about Lorenzo Ferrer and other fascinating characters. I met some of the people on hiking trails deep in the mountains, and I found others sitting on park benches or in museums.

Others I met while walking the streets of a strange town. Often friends brought me stories, and frequently I found the beginnings of stories buried in the narratives of other sagas.

People wherever I go ask me the same question: where do you locate super stories? I always respond, "Where can you go that you do not find these stories? Everyone I know has a good story, if I can just find a way to encourage him to tell it to me."

I have uncovered good stories in barber shops, at service stations and old country stores, at a chain saw repair shop, at the end of a long and dusty country road, in a line of customers waiting for service at a department store, in churches, hobby shops, and Rotary Club luncheons. Once I found a story lead while I was in a rest room at a park. And the story was printable in a book like this. See if you can decide which story had its origin there.

The stories and the people in this book are inseparable; they are one and the same, with this distinction: while some of the people featured here are still very much alive, others have fallen victim to Time. But the stories, and the people featured in them, will never cease to exist. You can visit them the same way we visit great writers and the notable figures in history: by reading about them. The Bigger-Than-Life personalities will never cease to exist and amaze us.

Not as long as hearts thrill to the sagas of people who have not appeared in the history books but whose stories will one day be a huge part of folk history and legend. Not as long as brave souls are willing to fight City Hall, beat the odds, and somehow win the victory. Or at least win their share of fame while losing honorably and bravely. Not as long as they can hold on and, if not winning the battle, then make it possible for others to win it. Not as long as the Good People celebrate each other and by doing so celebrate History and Life itself.

As long as there are people, there will be champions and these champions do not always lead armies into battle or guide followers to national triumphs. Sometimes they simply conquer themselves, which may, after all is said and done, be the greatest victory anyone can win.

If you never meet any of these people, except through the pages of this book, then this book was worth the writing. Who knows? Your story may be in the next one. I hope so!

I need to add a handful of other thoughts. First, I have taken a few liberties with geography. The stories are as true as they would be if I had been fastidiously correct, but I wanted to spare some relatives and innocent people in some of the more sensational stories. I could find no justification for opening old wounds that had begun the healing processes.

Second, I changed names in two or three stories. I do not want people calling the people involved and asking them to reveal information that I promised to keep secret. No storyteller tells all. Something must be left for you readers to wonder about, to use your imagination in an effort to fill in the blanks. I omitted last names in a couple of instances to avoid producing unwarranted publicity for those involved with the narratives.

Third, there are many stories that have been handed down for generations, and there is no way to guarantee their complete truth. But the stories are good enough that they should be included. After all, Napoleon supposedly said that history is fiction that has been agreed upon. If I were to limit my materials to only those facts that can be proved conclusively, this book (and nearly all history books and biographies) would be roughly the size of a book of matches.

Fourth, I have not quoted everyone precisely. In an interview a person will often start and restart sentences or thoughts, and he will grope for words or use ungrammatical (and in some cases unprintable) language. I have retained the gist of every quote that I used, but I admit to having cleaned up quite a few of them.

Finally, these stories are included for fun, for enjoyment, for recreation, for learning more about our state or our legends or even our neighbors. There has been no intent to harm, embarrass, or to damage reputations or characters. This book has been done in the spirit of telling good stories about good people (for the most part) who taught us valuable lessons about how to live our lives better. If there have been any incorrect or inappropriate inclusions, I apologize for them. I included a couple of travel trips because each location described has its own unique and lasting legends, which are too long to be included in a book such as this. Later, perhaps, I shall tell the stories in their complete form. I hope you enjoy these stories as much as I enjoyed researching and writing about them. And I hope you want more of them. I have lots more to tell.

Let me add a note abut the photos in this book. With only a few exceptions, the photos were the work of me, my wife Elizabeth, and our son Robert III. Some of the photos are, of necessity, old, frayed, faded, and poorly reproduced. When I talked with the publisher about the quality of some of the pictures, I asked for his opinion. His response was immediate. "Poor photo, if that's all we have," he said.

I agree. You will notice that some of the photos are simply photos of old paintings or drawings. It was all we had, therefore, the best we had.

I mentioned earlier that I took a few innocent liberties with the quotations of a few people. I also took the liberty to withhold names of people whose lives peripherally linked with some of the central characters in the book.

I went to an old cemetery to photograph the tombstone of a man who murdered a woman who was also a poet and balladeer as well as an expectant mother. When I arrived, there were fresh flowers on the grave and a note in a childish scrawl that said, "We love you and miss you, Papaw."

There is no way I am going to tell a child that the grandfather or great-grandfather she deeply loved and still misses was a scoundrel and a cold-blooded murderer. If she ever learns that her Papaw was a killer, she will have to find the information in another book.

This book contains some controversial material. The people who are described in these pages were not invariably angels. They had most if not all of the weaknesses that afflict us all at one time or another, but they also had the strengths and virtues that enable men and women to rise above the commonplace and create a plateau of their own where their standards and ideals and accomplishments can be examples for the rest of us.

But if all the people depicted here are not angelic, some of them definitely are. You will find in these pages stories of some of the finest men and women you ever expect to meet on your best days. They are what all of us at times aspire to be. So you will see a mixture of good and bad, people who have faced their worlds in vastly different ways. I did not decide who was heroic and who was cowardly. Instead, I relied upon research and documentation that I found in a wide variety of sources. That is, except for the events I personally saw unfolding.

Concerning the less-than-admirable people in this book, I refer you, the reader, to a line of poetry from Edwin Arlington Robinson who wrote that if some of us were not so far behind, the rest of you could not be so far ahead.

There are two deathbed confessions in this book, and while we cannot know that every word spoken there is true, we can assume that a dying man had very little to gain–and perhaps a lot to lose–by ending his existence with a falsehood. What would I do if another man or series of men made their deathbed confessions which flatly contradicted what the earlier men said? Would I again assume that the deathbed utterances were the truth and the previous confessions false?

I honestly do not know. Happily, to this point, at least, I have not had to face that particular problem. I'll jump off that bridge when I come to it.

Concerning one of the stories in this book, you are implored not to jump to hasty and unfounded conclusions and decide that the unnamed murderer was someone you remember from public life and fame. Do not damage the reputation and honor of an innocent man or woman simply because that person was on the scene and had both motive and opportunity. Such evidence may carry weight in a court of law but not in honest and ethical human relations.

The last thoughts here are notes of appreciation. With any book or long-range project, the efforts of many people play huge roles. The author may have written the words, but it took much work on the part of many people before those words could be written and the book could reach the publisher.

Joyce Paulin, a longtime friend and wonderful human being, is also one of the most efficient persons I have had the pleasure of knowing. She agreed to proofread the pages of this book and did a superb job of it. My wife Elizabeth helped, as she always does, at every turn. She took photos, proofread pages, and accompanied me on the trips necessary to gather material for this book. Our son, Robert III, also took photos, hiked many miles through rugged terrain alongside us, and helped in countless other ways. My family accepted the fact that for long days at a time I would spend my time in the office. They understood that I would not be available to help them as I often did under normal conditions.

And I wish to thank you, the reader, for your interest in my efforts, Without readers, books and authors are doomed. Most of all, I thank God that I enjoyed the health, the life style, and the strength and energy to finish this work. I hope it pleases.

Robert L. Williams, Belwood, North Carolina

Jim Bob and Dotty Tinsley have for decades been superior performers, educators, researchers, writers, and composers. They are known far and wide for their talent, energy, insights, knowledge, and eagerness to help preserve their (and our) heritage. They have performed for or with some of the finest personalities of this century.

One
Singing and Dancing Through Life

When you are visiting in Brevard, one of the most attractive towns in Western North Carolina, you can make your visit even more pleasant by visiting the Jim Bob Tinsley Museum and, if you are lucky, meeting two of the most beautiful people you can ever expect to know. Dotty and Jim Bob Tinsley are not just fabulous entertainers; they are exceptional people in every positive way. Their story and their accomplishments are among the finest I have encountered in my years of writing about interesting people.

Dotty Tinsley (then Wilson) was born in a three-story farmhouse in Laurens County, South Carolina, and after her parents moved to Rosman, just a short hop from Brevard, Dotty became a Tar Heel. And while she and her husband have traveled across the nation and worked in a number of states, she is still a Tar Heel at heart.

"I attended the Brevard Elementary School and then completed my public school education at Brevard High School," Dotty says. "And then I enrolled in Brevard Junior College. Later I finished my formal education by doing graduate work at the University of Florida. Right after junior college work I received a telegram from J. Edgar Hoover and after that I went to work for the FBI."

That's the way you get to know the Tinsleys. You are talking about the most mundane topics, and then, out of the blue, you learn something absolutely astonishing.

"I still have that telegram around here somewhere," she said. "He offered me a reasonable salary per month, and I was off to see the world. More accurately my mother and I were off together."

She added, "She did not want to see me traveling by train from the mountains to the nation's capital."

The date was April 19, 1943, and the United States was deeply involved in a struggle for this nation's very survival as the armed forces around the world fought the Axis powers. Train travel, under the proper conditions, could be delightful; this trip, however, did not fall into the delightful category.

"The train was so packed with servicemen that there wasn't a seat to be found anywhere," Dotty recalls. "We had to ride between the cars, and when we arrived we were covered with soot. When we reached Washington I was terrified of going out on the streets, which were filled with soldiers, sailors, and marines. The country was at war and nothing seemed stable. But I found a place to stay, one that I could afford at $40 to $50 per month for both room and board. After my mother went back home, the only way I'd go out would be if the eight girls in the house attended a movie."

After she returned to Brevard months later, she met, or re-met, the man with whom she would spend her life. Here is her story.

"I really met Jim Bob when I was eight years old and had won a bicycle at the local skating rink. I rode my new bike to the service station to have extra air put in the tires, and the young man who helped me was the man I would later marry. The second time I met Jim Bob came while I was working at the drug store here in Brevard where Opie Taylor is now located. No, not *that* Opie Taylor. There was a bus station stop across the street, and occasionally some of the local servicemen would get to come home on leave, and when that happened, the girls in town would surround the soldier or sailor and hug and scream in excitement. Well, one day the bus stopped and a little sailor stepped out of it. It was Jim Bob, of course, home on leave, and we got to know each other fairly well. The next time he came home we started dating. That was about the time I nearly died from meningitis."

See what I mean about the bombshells out of the blue?

"We were at a dance one Saturday night in 1946," Dotty says, "and that next Tuesday I became severely ill. Bob was enrolled at the University of Georgia and he hitchhiked home to be near me. But I was semiconscious or unconscious for several days and couldn't have visitors. When I became fully alert, I turned to look outside so that I could look out the window. What I saw warmed my heart!"

"There," she said, "under a huge oak tree, sat Bob."

It was a beautiful sight, Dotty recalls, and she had no idea how long he had been sitting under the tree while he waited for news from the doctors. She also had no idea how sick she had really been and what the lingering effects, if any, of the illness might be.

"The country had just completed a terrible war, and now I was in my own personal battle," she said. "The doctors told me that I might have permanent damage to the retinas of my eyes and that I might lose my sight altogether. They also told me I might die within a very short time. Wonderfully, penicillin had just been made available to civilian doctors, and they used it on me. I haven't been sick a day since that time. But at that time, I weighed seventy-eight pounds, I was weak, and we had no idea what the future held for us. It was not the best time to elope to South Carolina to get married."

Another thunderbolt! She explains: "My mother was a Baptist until she married my father, who was a Methodist. So I was a Methodist, and Jim Bob was a Baptist. I had been deathly ill, Jim Bob had just returned from the war and had not found his career yet, and everything seemed to be against us, except that we were totally in love and wanted to get married as soon as possible. So we eloped to Greenville and were married in, of all things, a Presbyterian church that had been beautifully decorated. For another marriage, not ours."

That, too, needs a word of explanation. The church had been decorated for the marriage of a Greenville couple, and when Jim Bob and Dotty arrived, the decorations were still in place, and they were married there, amid the beauty.

"And I learned later that my mother and father had eloped to Greenwood, South Carolina, and they, like us, had been married in the Presbyterian church there," Dotty recalls. "Then, after we were married, we moved to Gainesville, Florida, where I did some graduate school work and started teaching. Bob enrolled as a freshman, eleven years after his high school graduation. He majored in journalism and he was eager to get started on some of his books that he wanted to write. He spent as much as thirty years researching one book! He wanted to get it right, and he did."

After they had completed their studies, the two moved to the Southwest where they taught and Jim Bob delved into the songs of the cowboys. He never has lost his love for the West and its people. He also retains his love for the mountains of both regions.

She continued, "I don't think I have ever seen a human being so dedicated to his work than Bob was. It's that quality that made him such a good writer. Now let Jim Bob to tell you how he sang a duet with Winston Churchill while President Franklin Roosevelt applauded."

When Jim Bob was in Casablanca during World War II, with the Fleet Air Wing of the United States Navy, he spent much of his time in North Africa and Sicily. The Casablanca Conference of world leaders was held there in 1943 and Jim Bob was asked to sing.

Churchill requested "You Are My Sunshine," and as Jim Bob sang, Churchill joined him for one of the most remarkable duets in Jim Bob's history.

Back up a few years to see how Tinsley found himself singing with one of the great leaders in world history. When he was thirteen years old, Tinsley made his radio debut as a folk singer and musician on the Bascom Lamar Lunsford radio show in Asheville, and in 1950 he appeared on the Youth Opportunity Program on CBS.

He also performed on the Grand Ole Opry out of Nashville, Tennessee, and he had his own radio program weekly on the First American Expeditionary Station in French Morocco in 1943. In the late forties, after the war, Jim Bob and the Drifters appeared with cowboy superstar Gene Autry on a number of occasions.

Living as a working cowboy, Tinsley learned firsthand the rigors and the beauties of the Old West, and he later put what he had learned into a series of books. One of these books was *He Was Singin' This Song*, for which he received the National Cowboy Hall of Fame's Wrangler Award in 1982. He was the first person who was not a composer ever to win this award.

When Tinsley wrote another book, *For a Cowboy Has to Sing,* Roy Rogers and Dale Evans wrote in the preface, "Reading the histories Jim Bob has gathered on each of the 60 songs is like saddling up a good cow horse and riding back along the Western music trail."

The *New York Times* designated this book as one of the notable volumes published in 1992. Tinsley, incidentally, was the second person inducted into the National Cowboy Song and Poetry Hall of Fame.

"He researched one book for fifteen years," Dotty said. "He has to be totally certain he has all his facts right. He is impatient with shoddy scholarship, and he did not want to add to the problem."

Tinsley never left a topic until he was certain he had gathered all the facts within reason. He then organized his material meticulously. He has also written such books as *The Sailfish: Swashbuckler of the Open Sea, The Florida Panther, the Puma, Legendary Lion of the Americas, The Florida Cow Hunter, The Hash Knife Brand,* and *The Land of Waterfalls: Transylvania County, North Carolina.* You can purchase autographed copies of Tinsley's books at the museum.

Tinsley's book on waterfalls features terrific photos, detailed and clear directions, and the folklore behind the falls. If you plan to make your own waterfall search, this book is essential for your trip.

While you are in the area, plan to allow yourself at least a couple of hours to enjoy the Jim Bob Tinsley Museum & Research Center at 20 West Jordan Street in Brevard. Inside the museum (there is no admission charge, although donations are cheerfully accepted) you will see memorabilia collected by the man who, in addition to the previous honors, received the Pioneer Award of the National Radio Heritage Association, the Cowboy Cultural Award, and many other honors. Collections include western music, recordings, posters, sheet music, records, and tapes of cowboy music, original art, photos, and a collection of cowboy history, bronze sculptures, saddles, spurs, branding irons, horns, weaponry, and other outstanding attractions.

Some days you can catch Dotty and Jim Bob Tinsley at the museum in Brevard. However, they live part of the year in Florida. Recently Jim Bob played the guitar there and sang while Dotty clog danced. After all these years, they are still a fantastic team. At the museum, in addition to the occasional picking and singing, you may also be treated to some super stories about the Old West as well as anecdotes from the North Carolina Mountains. If you get the chance, ask Jim Bob about his impressions of Gene Autry and Roy Rogers. Or ask him about his cowgirl sweetheart Patsy Montana. Or ask about the cougar he killed in hand-to-claw battle.

One of his favorite stories is about one-time cowboy star Rex Allen who was performing for an audience of senior citizens. One lady in the crowd was not impressed by the star of the show, and Allen walked over to speak to her personally. He asked the lady if she knew who he was.

"No," she said, "but if you will ask the lady at the desk, she'll be happy to tell you who you are."

The Tinsley fame is not that way. In Brevard, everyone knows them.

Jim Bob and Dotty Tinsley have been partners on the stage and in life for decades, and they have retained their enthusiasm for life and music.

Jim Bob Tinsley, legendary singer, writer, and performer

Marshal Michel Ney as he appeared at the peak of his military career. After his "execution" he sailed from France to the United States and taught school for decades in the Cleveland, North Carolina, area.

Two
The Man Who Wouldn't Stay Buried

On December 7, 1815, Marshal Michel Ney was executed by a firing squad composed of his own men. Death was instantaneous, the result of eight wounds in the chest, three in the neck, and one in the right arm. The attending physician approached the body, which lay in a pool of crimson, and examined him for signs of life. There were none. The funeral service was held the following morning, with no members of Ney's family present.

Ney was buried in Luxumbourg Gardens, just outside Paris, in an unmarked grave. And when the simple ceremony ended, so did the history of Marshal Ney, the man who led Napoleon's troops in a series of campaigns culminating in the disastrous battle of Waterloo.

Or did the most incredible part of the Ney saga begin when the firing squad destroyed the brilliant military commander whom Napoleon had called "the Bravest of the Brave"? Let's take a closer look.

There was no sun on the morning of execution. Clouds hung like a pall over the countryside, like the same clouds of war and defeat and glory and infamy that had hovered over France for years.

A slow rain had started to fall shortly after midnight and continued until daybreak, when Ney was taken from his cell and, accompanied by one priest and two guards, rode in a simple fiacre to the place of execution which, for unexplained reasons, had been changed at the last minute. He was led to the wall, and the firing squad prepared to kill the marshal.

No sooner was the funeral over than the questions began to fly. Why did Ney's family not attend the funeral? Why was Ney, one of the most celebrated soldiers in Europe, buried in an unmarked grave, like a pauper? Why was the execution site changed? Who authorized the change?

Third Creek Presbyterian Church is a serenely beautiful place of worship located in the small town of Cleveland between Statesville and Salisbury. Marshal Michel Ney is buried to the left of the church. The cemetery is open during daylight hours.

Here is the final resting place of Marshal Ney, the Man Who Wouldn't Stay Buried. The plaque on the corner states emphatically that the man inside the grave was the commander of Napoleon's army.

Let's permit the facts, as we know them, to speak for themselves.

On the way to the wall Ney rode silently in a fiacre to the Plaine de Grenelle where a small crowd of about thirty men waited for him. As soon as it was fully light, Ney's former soldiers led him to the wall and then retreated into a military formation. The commander of the firing squad approached Ney and offered him a blindfold.

Ney refused. "Do you think that I have not known death, that I fear it?" he asked.

The officer returned to the firing squad, gave the commands, and the cold air was filled with the crash of gunfire. At the same moment, Ney jerked spasmodically, then, after sagging against the rain-darkened wall, he pitched forward and was still. His body lay stretched across the narrow ribbon of pebbles that lined the wall.

The only words spoken, except those to the firing squad, were simple and dismal: "Twenty years of glory–wiped out by one day's blunder." The speaker abruptly turned and walked toward Ney's body where the man collected souvenirs, doubtless to display to friends at the tavern later: several bloodstained rocks, which he deposited into a small bag and carried away with him.

A second military detail removed the body from the widening red circle beneath him and collected the remainder of the bloody rocks and dropped them into a larger sack.

Twenty years of glory wiped out by one colossal blunder! And at that moment began the second life of Marshal Michel Ney.

Born in 1769 in Saar, the coal-mining region between France and Germany, Ney lived in obscurity in the small town until he was an adult, at which time he joined Napoleon's army. In his early life he had not distinguished himself in any way. He clerked in a store, dabbled at law, and earned his living by manual labor before he decided to leave Saar and enlist in the Hussar regiment nearby in France.

The decision was a good one for Ney, even though it violated his father's commands, and in the army Ney found what he had been searching for all his life. Instantly he loved the excitement, the glitter of sabers, the noise of battle, the danger, and most of all the glory that resulted from victory. Within weeks, Ney found himself embroiled in some of the fiercest fighting in Europe, and he loved it. Within a dozen years he had risen from the lowest ranks to the top.

Start with Ney's rank as marshal, the equivalent of general in today's military. More important, he had by his abilities and performance attracted the eye of the Little Corporal, Napoleon Bonaparte, who quickly recognized Ney's ability to ferret out and utilize the abilities of others. And, most important, win battles.

In rapid succession Ney was elevated to the title of Prince of Muscova, Duke of Elchigen, and finally Marshal of France. He was one of only eighteen officers to hold the final title.

By September 7, 1812, Napoleon was ready to strike deep into Russian territory. Almost instantly Ney led the attack on Borodino, which resulted in a masterful victory for the French and left 80,000 enemy casualties. Later, when the Russian winters had done what no army could accomplish, the French were forced to retreat from Smolenske, and Marshal Ney maintained order and kept the withdrawal from becoming a complete rout.

In appreciation of Ney's performance, Napoleon ordered a French goldsmith to strike a medal especially designed to honor Ney. But the Bravest of the Brave could not win the most important victory of his life— to that point. Weakened by fatigue, hunger, and exposure to the elements, Napoleon's army of 180,000 troops tried to rally to meet the combined forces of Prussia, Russia, and Austria.

It was a hopeless effort. In 1813 Napoleon suffered a disastrous defeat. Returning to Paris, Napoleon was compelled to sign the abdication agreement that removed him as head of the French nation. On April 11, 1814, Napoleon retired in disgrace to the island of Elba.

Ney, left without a leader, joined the forces of the Bourbon King Louis XVIII, and there he served loyally and admirably until the worst possible event occurred. Ney had to choose between king and friend.

Napoleon, leaving Elba, had reassembled a small army and was marching toward France. Ney was ordered by King Louis to take his own troops and march to meet Napoleon, conquer him, and bring him to Paris in an iron cage, like some savage animal.

Europe held its figurative breath as the distance between the two armies narrowed to only a few miles. Ney, the superb military genius, marched his men toward his former comrades in arms. When the two armies met, Ney dismounted from his horse and marched on foot until he faced Napoleon.

There was no doubt about it: Ney was on his way to one of the most important decisions of his life, and he was ready for the role.

When Ney reached his old commander, instead of placing him under arrest, he knelt before Napoleon, offered him his sword and services, and the two old soldiers were reunited once more. And again Europe trembled as both Ney and Napoleon marched toward Paris.

For one hundred days the world watched and waited as the Little Corporal and the Bravest of the Brave fought their way across Europe to a small town that was to go down in history as the universal symbol of defeat. The Duke of Wellington, the Iron Duke, met Ney and Napoleon at the Battle of Waterloo. On June 18, 1815, just outside the town of 10,000 inhabitants, Napoleon indeed met his Waterloo.

So did Ney. The defeated marshal found himself in an iron cage, much like the one in which he was to have imprisoned Napoleon to take him back to Paris. Now Ney suffered the indignities of defeat as he was trundled back to the city that had honored him highly.

The trial began in the middle of summer in 1815. The charges were simple: treasonable activity against the throne of France. The fate of Ney would be, if he was found guilty, the firing squad. There were no appeals and higher courts to save him.

As the trial opened, Ney's defense team offered Ney a loophole that would likely have freed him: to testify that he was born in Saar and was not a Frenchman; therefore he could not have committed treason against France.

"No!" Ney thundered when the opportunity was put to him. "I have lived as a Frenchman and fought as a Frenchman, and I am prepared to die, if necessary, as a Frenchman."

His one line of defense demolished, Ney was found guilty and the sentence was handed down. All that remained was for the firing squad to follow the orders to kill the former commander.

After the execution, the body of Ney was taken to a nearby hospital where a doctor pronounced the marshal dead. After the burial in the unmarked grave, the life and history of Michel Ney of France ended.

And the history of Peter Stewart Ney of Scotland began.

The history of the new man began in the city of Bordeaux, in the southwest corner of France, where a vessel prepared to sail from France to Georgetown, South Carolina. Few if any of the passengers or crew of the ship had any notion of the identity of the newcomer who boarded at the last minute. The new life of Marshal Ney was taking shape.

As the ship left the city known for its wines, a passenger met a man who looked vaguely familiar. The second man was rather short, had reddish hair, and his face was scarred with reminders of the smallpox that had ravaged France earlier.

"I know you," the passenger said to the pockmarked man. "You are Marshal Ney of France."

"Don't be absurd," the scarred man responded. "Marshal Ney is dead and buried."

With that, the man turned abruptly and returned to his cabin, where he isolated himself for the remainder of the voyage. He even took his meals in the tiny cabin, and when the ship docked in Georgetown, the man left quickly and disappeared into the crowded mass of people on the waterfront.

But the stay in Georgetown was not uneventful. Almost as soon as the red-haired man found living quarters, someone started the rumor that Marshal Michel Ney was alive and well and living in the city. The pockmarked man departed quickly and headed to the larger city of Charleston to lose himself in the crowds.

History repeated itself, and the man left the coast and traveled inland, north to Charlotte and to a tiny community where there was a small college located. One popular story coming out of the visit was that the college was seeking a design for a seal or logo of sorts, and the strange and mysterious man sketched one that the college liked and accepted.

Much later a goldsmith in France, so the story continues, saw the letterhead and demanded to know how the college obtained the design which was, he insisted, an original rendering that he had done at the request of Napoleon Bonaparte. The design was used on a special medal to be awarded to Marshal Michel Ney, the Bravest of the Brave.

The stranger left the area and shortly afterwards found himself in the town of Statesville, which was little more than a stagecoach crossroads. But the tiny town was the scene of many notable visits, largely because of the crossroads. One day a French dignitary was in town, and the locals held a parade in his honor. As the parade passed before the crowd, the ambassador gasped in horror, clutched at his heart, and collapsed in a dead faint.

"I saw a ghost," he babbled when he regained consciousness.

"I saw a dead man," he repeated in near-hysteria. "I saw Marshal Michel Ney of France."

Again the pockmarked man disappeared into the crowd and did not appear again until he surfaced in the even smaller community of Cleveland, east of Statesville and halfway to Salisbury in Rowan County, today just off US 70.

Here the newcomer introduced himself as Peter Stewart Ney, a schoolteacher from Scotland. He quickly laid claim to a small fame in the community. He was a fiery-tempered teacher who had a good appetite for ale. Often he would sit in the local tavern and drink his ales and at the same time explain to his cronies the little-known facts of history.

When he was inebriated, he would use salt shakers and mugs to represent the various military units, and he would move these about the table to explain what *really* happened during key battles. Later, when sober, he would deny his statements of the previous evening, or he would sheepishly explain that he was not thinking lucidly and that he had no firsthand knowledge of battle at all.

He was, he repeated, only a simple schoolteacher from Scotland and knew nothing of Continental politics and battles except what he had read in books. And, four thousand miles from Paris and the glory he had once known, Peter Stewart Ney met his classes dutifully and with almost as much enthusiasm as he had once marched into battle.

The new teacher, everyone agreed, was special. First, he was impressive in his attitude and appearance. Despite being short, he was swarthy, muscular, and temperamental. Even the truants agreed that he was a superb teacher, despite his awesome temper which caused him at times to rip a history textbook to shreds and rant to the class that the author knew nothing of what really happened in a particular battle.

He had his drinking companions, but there were no really close friends. Typically, he spent his days in the classroom or in the nearby tavern.

But he had visitors. Not just neighborly callers but questionable men of intrigue. These visitors always arrived after darkness had settled in over Cleveland, and they were gone before morning.

Then there were the letters which arrived mysteriously, always with strange handwriting and stamps or seals from foreign countries. And the teacher's accent, all agreed, was not from Scotland.

He lapsed into French, in fact, when he became very angry or agitated. And sometimes German. Or so the local people thought.

The man lived in an atmosphere of intrigue and wonder, and the scene with the Home Guard did not quieten the rumblings. Students in that day were expected to take part in military drills and other activities that were part of a soldier's life. On one particular morning the drilling consisted of the finer arts of swordsmanship.

Jokingly, the fencing master, after having shown up the ineptitude of the students, approached the aging teacher, who was sitting under a tree and watching the proceedings. The fencing master asked Ney if he would like to learn to defend himself.

"I have no interest in fencing," Ney is reported to have said. He lay back on the grass and continued his reverie.

"Anyone can learn," the fencing master continued. "Even an old and untrained schoolteacher can learn."

Ney again shook his head and declined.

"Anyone can learn," the fencing master cajoled. "Anyone, that is, but a coward."

With a roar, Ney leaped to his feet, grabbed a nearby broomstick, and with such a clumsy weapon proceeded to disarm the fencing master repeatedly. Having totally vanquished his tormentor, Ney again lay down on the grass under the huge oak tree.

"I told you," he said, "that I have no interest in fencing."

Immediately, rumors buzzed around the town. According to some of them, Ney was a royal prince in hiding because of the danger to his life. In another, he was a monarch of a tiny European nation who had abdicated and fled in terror from his homeland.

More fuel was added to the flames when Ney became ill and had to have the aid of a local physician, who as part of his efforts to help the aging man, had to undress Ney. The doctor couldn't wait to get to the settlement where he told anyone who would listen what he had seen: the teacher's body was a mass of scars and obvious remainders of ancient wounds. The doctor insisted that Ney had unmistakable saber cuts and bullet wounds on his chest, arms, and legs.

But this was nothing compared to the reaction on the day that the student made his regular trip to buy the teacher a newspaper. When the teacher read the headlines, he dismissed classes instantly.

Ney was visibly shaken, students recalled, as he threw the paper to the floor and dashed from the one-room schoolhouse without saying a word to anyone. He rushed to his cottage and slit his throat from ear to ear.

One student picked up the paper and read the headline that had so unnerved the teacher. The message was simple and ominous.

NAPOLEON IS DEAD, the headline screamed. The students alerted adults in the community who rushed to Ney's cottage.

They found Ney lying in a blood-soaked bed. Miraculously, the blade had somehow missed the jugular vein and Ney was still alive. The doctor who had arrived shortly after Ney was discovered told the old man that the wound must be stitched in order for it to heal.

Ney nodded, and in a whisper he instructed the doctor to rub salt in the wound to quicken the healing processes. The doctor shook his head and told Ney that the pain would be unbearable. Ney insisted.

"Do you think that I am a stranger to pain?" he said. "Do you think that pain can be stronger than my will?"

The doctor did as he was told, and within a very short time Ney had recovered to the extent that he could again teach his classes.

One by one, however, rumors continued to arrive in the tiny town. One stated that for unknown reasons the site of Ney's scheduled execution in France had been changed at the last minute and that the bullet marks on the wall where Ney had stood were all to the left and right of Ney. Another rumor held that something like an animal bladder had been found at the execution scene and that the bladder had held a bright red fluid, such as a dye. The scene of the man who collected pebbles was explained by the obvious idea that the stones were covered not with blood but with the dye.

The "doctor" who signed the death certificate never existed. He was an imposter who wanted people to believe that Ney had died at the hands of his former soldiers.

Another story, this one verified, revealed that Ney's wife, who had not attended the funeral and had never demonstrated grief in any way, had somehow become so suddenly and inexplicably wealthy that she could afford to have servants carry her bed alongside her when she went for a walk, in the event that she became tired and needed to rest. The servants would then carry her and the bed back to the house.

How did the old teacher respond to the rumors? With complete silence. He never honored the stories by denying them. Or, if he did honor the questions, he answered by saying that he was Peter Stewart Ney, a schoolteacher from Scotland.

How convincing are the arguments that the teacher was actually Marshal Ney of France? Governor Clyde R. Hoey, having read one of the publications about the controversy, wrote these words: "I would like to publicly commend your splendid book.... It is not only a most interesting story but also a convincing argument that Peter Stewart Ney, the school teacher whose body lies in an inconspicuous grave in Salisbury, was Marshal Ney of France.

"I confess that I had always considered the Ney story more interesting than accurate, but...I have been convinced that the mysterious, battle-scarred old martinet of Rowan County schoolrooms, was undoubtedly the man whom Napoleon had described as 'the bravest of the brave.'"

The governor, who was also a brilliant attorney, concluded that even though scholars might disagree with the conclusion that the old teacher and the youthful soldier were one and the same, "...I cannot say, but as a jury lawyer I can say that you have presented a case that will leave but little doubt in the layman's mind."

As added evidence, it must be noted that handwriting experts who saw and examined the writing of Marshal Michel Ney and Peter Stewart Ney were of the opinion that the two men were in fact one and the same. One of the men who made the examinations was Henry E. Thomas of the United States Secret Service. The man's expert opinions were sufficient to impress and convince the judges and juries of the federal courts.

Arguments to the contrary, the old teacher lived for three decades in the Cleveland community, and for many of those years he taught his classes. Then, in November of 1846, Ney became ill again. He had complained to his few friends that he had not felt well for days. The final illness began as a nagging cough and sore throat and then a lung congestion that would not respond to the crude medical treatments known in that day. Quickly the discomfort grew into pneumonia, a condition which in those days was often fatal among older citizens. It was very clear to those closest to Ney that he could not survive this latest challenge to his health and life. He had no more new lives to live. He had somehow managed to avoid death on the battlefield, at sea, and from smallpox and typhoid epidemics, but no more. He had given all his strength and courage to life and now he was depleted. The old man was obviously only minutes from the end of his life.

"Mr. Ney," the doctor told him, "there is nothing more that I can do for you. You cannot last through the night. Do you have anything that you would like to tell us?"

Ney remained silent. For hours the sounds of his labored breathing filled the room. Then, shortly before dawn, the doctor, who had remained with Ney during the ordeal, again questioned him. "The end is here," he said. "Won't you tell us who you really are?"

The old soldier struggled to rise from his bed in one final and heroic effort to regain his feet. He did not want to die helplessly in bed; his life had been one of action and heroism, and he wanted his death to be the same. But he lacked the strength to rise again; he managed to elevate himself to one elbow before his strength and breath failed him.

"Before God," he managed to gasp, "I am Marshal Ney of France."

Then he fell back, dead.

That night an old chest that Ney had owned for years disappeared from the cottage. It was later recovered in New York City and was returned to Cleveland to be opened. That first night, however, the cottage caught fire mysteriously and burned to the ground. Thus ended the story of the stranger who moved into a tiny rural area and kept the town alive with questions about his previous life. The tombstone in the church cemetery tells the story in brief eloquence:

In Memory of
Peter Stewart Ney
A native of France and
Soldier of the French Revolution
under
Napoleon Bonaparte
who departed this life
November 15th, 1846
aged 77 years

Fred Beal, center, wearing tie, came to North Carolina to organize the mill workers as communist party activists. He and several other men were convicted of second-degree murder and jumped bail to accept political asylum in Russia. Beal later returned and served his prison term here.

Chief Orville Aderholt   The infamous wax dummy

Three
The Dummy That Shook the South

The Dummy made its appearance in the Charlotte trial of the so-called Loray Seven more than seventy years ago, and its effects will be felt in the North Carolina Piedmont and the entire South for decades to come. In brief, the Dummy managed, without saying a word or moving a nonexistent muscle, to convict seven people of murder and send them, indirectly at least, to Russia, where they became honorary members of the Communist Party and the Soviet Socialist Republic.

Not bad for a wax concoction put together hurriedly by a high school student in Gaston County.

The story began, locally, on New Year's Day, 1929, but it had its real origin much earlier and hundreds of miles away.

When Fred Beal was growing up in the vicinity of the immense textile mills of Lawrence, Massachusetts, his mother begged him never to go to work in one of the jails, as the workers referred to the mills. But when Fred was old enough he, like nearly all of his friends, dutifully went to the mill to ask for a job. Within hours he saw why people hated the mill: he saw brutal mistreatment of workers, rapes, and inhuman hours of work under horrible conditions.

Beal witnessed a boss forcing a young girl into unwilling sex acts, and Beal attacked the boss man and left him for dead. He fled home and hid, awaiting the law officers. Instead, another boss, one with a strong streak of humanitarianism, persuaded him to return to work. He did not know what to expect, but he respected the new boss, and when the two entered the mill a few minutes later, Beal realized that he had made the proper decision.

The Loray Mill in 1929 was known as the largest mill under one roof in the entire world. The communists selected the mill for their union efforts because they knew the mill had a reputation nationwide for the exploitation of workers, miserable working conditions, and low pay. When Fred Beal and associates arrived, trouble began immediately. Daily news stories appeared around the world as the strike that began in April dominated the news for weeks. The Gastonia police chief was murdered, and a seven-months pregnant balladeer was shot to death before the strike ended.

The National Textile Workers Union liked to select women and children and dress them shabbily and then take them to New York and other large cities to "prove" how bad conditions were in mill villages. There was, of course, some truth to the allegations.

After a quick meeting the boss assured Fred that he would not be punished; on the contrary, he offered him a raise in pay.

So Fred Beal staged a one-man walkout and labor strike–and won! He was hooked at that moment on union activities, and he regretted his association with one particular union for the rest of his life.

As the labor wars continued in New York and New England, Beal saw a young woman cross a picket line despite police warnings that she would be shot. The young woman wrapped herself in the American flag and marched across the line, while the police held their fire.

"You people are too soft," one striker yelled. "That's why you'll never win."

"No," the policeman answered. "We value human rights and human life. That's why we'll never lose."

Later, another woman in another strike tried the same trick, and this time the police gunned her down in cold blood.

In yet another incident, strikers were picketing what was at the time the largest mill in the world, and as women holding their small children walked the picket lines, black vans swooped into their midst and masked men leaped from the vans and pulled the children from their mothers' arms and sped off into the night with them. Later the mothers were told that if they wanted their children back, they'd have to go back to work.

That same day union workers kidnapped the only son of the mill owner, and the strikers issued the same basic warning: if the owner wanted his son back, he'd have to release the children and grant the workers their demands.

Helpless, the owner complied, and after the children were back with their parents, the strikers drove past the owner's house and dumped the murdered body of the owner's son on the lawn of the mansion where the family lived.

And Fred Beal watched and learned how cruel and inhuman the labor wars can be. Shortly afterwards, in a jail cell in New York, Beal learned of two executions that changed his life.

The news was brought to him reportedly by noted poetess Edna St. Vincent Millay. She came to the jail cell where Beal, John Dos Passos, and others were being held prisoner because of their violent activities in a strike. Her message was simple: Sacco and Vanzetti are dead.

The two Italian immigrants, Nicola Sacco and Bartolomeo Vanzetti,

Davie County Public Library
Mocksville, North Carolina

104682

had been arrested years earlier and charged with armed robbery and murder. Despite overwhelming evidence of innocence, Sacco and Vanzetti were found guilty and sentenced to die. After years of appeals and delays, the two men faced the death chamber, and by dying they became symbols of tyranny and corruption.

That night Fred Beal joined the Communist Party. His reasons were simple.

"I joined the Socialist Party because it was the party of peace," he explained. "I joined the Communist Party because it was the party of war."

When Fred Beal arrived in North Carolina on January 1, 1929, he made several important discoveries. First, he learned that weather in the Sunny South could be as bitter as in New England. He arrived in the midst of an ice storm that left him nearly frozen. The union that he fought for could not, or would not, provide him with an automobile, so he had to ride a motorcycle the entire distance.

The second discovery was the same as the first. The coldness of the weather matched the frigid hearts of the union leaders from up in Massachusetts and New York. The organizers, promising whatever Beal needed in his fight in the South, in reality provided him with essentially nothing. They later abandoned him when he was of no further use to their party and cause.

A third discovery was that in the South there were many who hated and feared unions as much as they were hated in the North. And Beal had been in the Tar Heel State only one day before someone tried to kill him. He walked down a lonely road in Charlotte when the driver of a huge and powerful automobile attempted to run down Beal and destroy him and his efforts.

Later, while eating at a restaurant, Beal received a telephone call, and the caller said that Beal could either leave town on the train or in a pine box. If he stayed, the caller said, he would be killed on sight.

On April 1, 1929, Beal ordered the workers who had joined the union to walk out of Gastonia's Loray Mill. Instantly the fights began: men and woman, young and old, battled bitterly in alleys, on the main streets, and in vacant lots. Police were kept busy in their efforts to maintain law and order. Workers who had joined the union were evicted from their homes during an early spring sleet storm. Leaders hastily set up a tent village not far from the huge mill. Hoodlums, hit men, and hired guns arrived from

New York, Chicago, and New Jersey, and local authorities countered by forming a vigilante group known as the Committee of One Hundred, Black Hundred, or the Flying Squadron.

The fighting continued sporadically and at times seriously until the first week in June when Chief Orville Aderholt and Gastonia police officers visited the tent city in response to a call they had received earlier. As the officers approached union headquarters, the armed strike guards met them. Angry words were exchanged.

The union leaders had what they considered ample reason to distrust the officers. Earlier, masked men attacked the union storehouse and destroyed blankets, food, and other supplies and then burned down the building. To add insult to injury, strikers on the scene later found eyeglasses belonging to a prominent attorney who later would be a key player in the courtroom trial.

As the officers confronted the guards, someone fired gunshots, and all hell broke loose. It was like a small war as guns blazed and fists flew.

The battle lasted only a few minutes, and when the smoke cleared, Chief Aderholt lay on the ground, fatally wounded. Other officers received gunshot wounds. As the fighting reached its most furious point, witnesses testified, they could hear the shrill voice of Vera Bush screaming for the men to kill the police.

"Do your duty, men!" she called out again and again. "Do your duty."

After the shooting, union leaders fled in all directions. Fred Beal made his way to Spartanburg, South Carolina, while others found temporary refuge in homes of friends in Gaston County and in nearby Charlotte. In the home of a friend, Beal contacted the union leaders in New York and asked them to send money. They promised to comply, and when he went to the telegraph office to get it, officers arrested him.

Nobody ever learned who tipped off the officers that Beal was in the vicinity and would appear at the Western Union offices, but it was obvious that a sincere if crude espionage system was at work. When officers transported Beal back to Gastonia, a caravan of cars, many of them driving without headlights, surrounded the police car.

The driver left the highway and took a rural road to the home of a Kings Mountain man. The reason for the detour was that the driver was hungry and wanted a sandwich, according to one report. They left Beal in the car, and a man emerged from the darkness and aimed a gun at Beal.

For some reason, he did not shoot.

In jail in Gastonia, along with some of his coworkers, Beal later wrote, the jailer entered the cell freely and made no effort to keep the workers from taking his weapon and breaking out of jail. When the strikers did not attempt to escape, the jailer later even took his loaded revolver out of its holster and allowed the men to examine it.

During this time, someone opened the back door of the jailhouse, and Beal could see several cars parked in the alley. He could also see the shotguns and rifles of the men in the cars. It was clear that the men wanted Beal and his cohorts to make a break so they could shoot them down in cold blood as they escaped.

As the men sat in the cells, one of them found that he could remove the cover of an electrical socket, and the men took turns poking their fingers into the socket and feeling the electricity course through their arms.

"We're just getting used to what it's going to be like in the electric chair," one of the men said.

Originally there had been seven men and several women placed under arrest, but the prosecution dropped the charges against the women because, as one of them put it, "There's no way the state will execute a woman, and if the women aren't killed, the men won't be either."

As Beal awaited trial, he reflected on the broken promises of the union organizers and their betrayal of him and his fellow workers. They had originally promised to provide enough food and clothing and shelter to keep the strikers safe from cold and hunger for as long as the strike lasted. The organizers also promised manpower, legal aid, and massive strikes in neighboring towns so that when the strike ended, the entire country would be controlled by the Communist Party.

It was not that wild a dream. According to reports issued at the time, there were 300,000 textile workers in the South alone who had joined the Party. A report out of Detroit stated that the nation had been divided into thirteen districts, and the takeover would consist of about seventeen basic steps. When the first step was achieved in the Gastonia area, then strikers in the surrounding areas would implement the same step, and in ripple effect the steps would in turn flow across the county, the South, and the entire nation.

The master plan called for the communists to take over the mills and manufacturing generally, then shipping, and finally food production. At this point the bloodless revolution would end and the United States would be a communist nation.

Little was left to chance. Teachers set up schools where children were taught to hate the Stars and Stripes and to revere the hammer and sickle of Russia. Children barely twelve years old were trained to go to Russia to take part in the ongoing revolution there, and kids from Gastonia did indeed make the journey to Russia.

The money was another matter. At a meeting Beal told the people in attendance that they would be fed and sheltered as long as the strike lasted. A wizened old mountain man who had come to town to work in the mills asked how much money the union had at its disposal. Beal answered that he did not know but that it was enough to last as long as the strike endured.

"Do you have fifty million dollars?" the man asked. Beal replied that the union did not have that kind of money.

"Do you have one million dollars?" the man asked.

Again, Beal replied that it was not quite that much.

"How many people do you plan to have on strike, here and in other places?" the man continued. "Are we supposed to fight this battle all by ourselves?"

Beal assured him that he would not be alone, that people all over the state and all over the South would join the Loray strikers.

"How many?" the man demanded. "A thousand? Ten thousand?"

"More than that," Beal replied. "A hundred thousand at least."

The man did some rapid calculating. He did not like what he concluded.

"Do you have half a million dollars?" he asked Beal.

"Not that much," Beal replied. "But enough."

The man then said, "If fifty thousand people go on strike, and if each family has two children to support, that will be two hundred thousand people. If each person needs only one dollar a week to keep them in food and shelter and clothes, in three weeks the union would need more than half a million dollars. And there's no way in hell we can win this strike in three weeks."

With that, he rose and walked out. Others followed him.

One of the women from New York met with wives of the mill workers. She unwisely decided to ridicule the workers.

"I understand some of you people have never been on an elevator or escalator," she said. "You've never seen a skyscraper or attended a Broadway show or been inside a hotel. You've never eaten in a real restaurant, and you have never ridden a streetcar. Many of you cannot read, and you are superstitious enough to believe that if you put a horsehair in a tub of water overnight it will turn into a worm."

One of the uneducated mountain women spoke up at once.

"You are right," she said. "We are guilty of everything you have said. But have you ever seen a waterfall? Have you ever been to a barn dance? Did you ever ride a horse or mule? Did you ever eat wild strawberries and blackberries right off the plants? We can't read, maybe, but can you read a trail in the woods? And while we might believe that about the horsehair, you people think you can put a good honest American in a union meeting for an hour and she'll turn into a communist."

Even Beal's most trusted helpers proved untrustworthy. George Pershing came to town and announced that he was a nephew of General Black Jack Pershing, the World War I hero, and that George was himself a decorated war hero.

The staff of the Gastonia *Daily Gazette* did a little research and learned that Pershing was in no way kin to General Pershing. Nor was George Pershing a war hero. In fact, he did not serve at all in the war. The truth was that during the war Pershing was in a California prison where he served a sentence for child molesting.

The Amalgamated Bank of New York was another matter. At one point Beal had boasted that the bank held a million dollars for the strike expenses. The *Daily Gazette* reported that there was no escrow account because there was no such bank in New York.

To add to Beal's woes in jail, he learned that there had been a shooting in which the wife of the mill owner had been killed. That was bad enough, but then a corrected report came. The dead woman was not a boss relative at all but the poetess and balladeer Ella May Wiggins, the leading working woman of the strike. It was Ella May's ballads and her plaintive voice that inspired strikers when all else failed.

And now she was dead, shot down in the middle of the road as she and others were on their way to a giant union meeting. Their truck had been halted at a barricade, and armed men appeared from everywhere, it seemed. Strikers fled in all directions, but Ella May, seven months pregnant, was unable to run and was murdered in cold blood.

Worse, there were seventy-five to three hundred witnesses to the broad-daylight murder, and not one of them could identify the killer. Her murder is still officially unsolved.

And as Beal awaited trial, little good news came his way. The bad news was that the prosecution had lined up some of the greatest talent in the area. Clyde Hoey, later United States senator and governor of North Carolina, and one of the most striking men in the entire nation, agreed to assist in the prosecution, which was led by John Carpenter, a highly competent attorney. Other local notables joined the team.

The only good news to reach Beal was that the attorneys for the so-called Loray Seven would be Arthur Garfield Hays, regarded by many as the second-best defense lawyer in the country. Only famed barrister Clarence Darrow had greater prestige. To make matters seem better, the core staff of the sensational Scopes Monkey Trial of Dayton, Tennessee, agreed to join the defense team.

And it was here that the Dummy had its origin. When it was over, many people thought that there were two dummies, one of them being Hays, in the courtroom battle. It happened like this.

Ann Harding, a Broadway actress and a client of Arthur Garfield Hays, was trying to get out of a New York contract so that she could go to Hollywood to star in movies. Her producer agreed that if Miss Harding would agree to star in *The Trial of Mary Dugan*, he would release her from her contract.

Hays assured Miss Harding that the play would be a flop, and she agreed to star in it throughout its Broadway run. To everyone's shock, the melodrama became a super hit.

The play itself had an absurdly unrealistic ending in which a wax dummy, during a courtroom scene, took justice into its own hands and destroyed the villain.

As Beal and codefendants prepared themselves for trial, Hays and his team prepared their defense, while almost across the street from the courthouse there stood a movie theater in which a former Hollywood stage hit was playing.

The movie, of course, was *The Trial of Mary Dugan*.

Beal, unfortunately, was oblivious to the background of Hays, and he had no way of knowing that the dummy would move dramatically from the Broadway stage into Beal's own life and future.

The setting was perfect. The courthouse custodian flatly refused to work after dark because of the mysterious "ghost" of Chief Orville Aderholt that roamed the courthouse halls at night. The fears of the janitor had infected others, and the ghost became a daily topic of the conversation of those working inside the courthouse.

Then there was the juror who was preoccupied with his own death and eternal fate. He asked other jurors again and again to read certain passages of scriptures to him, and he seemed to find the most serious elements of the case wonderfully funny. Like the old cartoon characters, the juror had actually once climbed far out on a limb and then had sawed the limb off behind him. He crashed to the ground as he for the first time realized the error of his ways. Two of his brothers committed suicide, and others in his family were "mentally unstable."

Add to the scene the recent murder of Ella May Wiggins and the constant turmoil in town as a result of the killing, and you have the ideal scene for a bizarre drama that made the melodramatic scene in the stage play seem realistic by comparison.

Hays never caught on to what was happening, not until it was too late for him to avoid the damage. During the early hours of the trial, Hays had dealt effectively with the state's case. He was winning on all counts, and so were the Loray Seven.

The first moment that Hays realized that he had been sucker-punched came when the courtroom doors opened wide and a huge object, covered with a sheet (exactly like the one in the drama and movie) was wheeled to the front of the courtroom and positioned precisely between the daughter and the widow of Chief Orville Aderholt.

Only hours before the trial started there was another disturbance in the courthouse. The custodian there refused to work after dark because, he said, of what he had seen in the hallway: the Living Dead!

The ghost of Chief Orville Aderholt!

As the trial began, both prosecution and defense struggled to put the right jury in the box. Hays, despite his courtroom experience, somehow allowed J. G. Campbell on the jury. Campbell had earlier caused the court to erupt into laughter when he, when asked about his occupation, said he was a newspaperman. When pressed for more details, he tipped his imaginary hat and said to the customer who had just bought his evening newspaper, "Thank you, sir."

During the actual trial Campbell had been a constant source of worry for the other jurors, for the judge, and for the defense staff. The prosecution, logically enough, didn't mind that the man was obviously mentally disturbed and in need of psychiatric help. The state felt that the juror could easily be persuaded to vote in their favor. The defense apparently hoped to use the juror as grounds for a mistrial in the event the verdict went the wrong way for them.

Then it all happened: the terror of the janitor, reports of the ghost of Chief Aderholt roaming the courthouse halls at night, the mental instability of the juror, the presence of Arthur Garfield Hays on the scene, and the movie, *The Trial of Mary Dugan,* all came together in a few moments of horror and sensationalism that lasted for years.

Hays watched helplessly as court officers yanked the sheet away from the huge object and everyone in the room saw the life-size wax sculpture of Chief Aderholt, whose wax body still wore the chief's uniform, complete with his own blood still much in evidence.

The results were beyond belief. The chief's widow screamed in horror, and her daughter collapsed into a dead faint. Judge M. V. Barnhill banged his gavel furiously and without effect. The electric emotional wave swept over the spectators as Hays was on his feet and shouting his unheard objections.

The ghost mystery was clarified now: the custodian had seen the state's team as they carried the wax dummy into the courthouse and concealed it in a closet near the courtroom. The dummy itself was created by a local high school student who had been hired by the state's prosecution team.

The real drama, now, was taking place in the jury box as J. G. Campbell, already a pathetic and addled person, experienced a total mental collapse. He began to scream for Jesus to forgive his sins, and it took half a dozen people to subdue him and eventually lace him into a straitjacket. Court officials had the tragic figure taken back to his hotel room where he tried to hide under the claw-legged bathtub and begged for a gun so that he could kill himself. He told witnesses that he wanted to be buried facedown at a crossroads.

The next day the headline in the local paper told the story with direct language that left no one in doubt as to the case: JUROR IS CRAZY; MISTRIAL IS DECLARED. Hays was destroyed; he cited urgent business in New York and left the South forever.

Later, when the final trial occurred, Beal's defense was too weak to combat the state's artillery, although earlier, before the mistrial, a poll of the jury showed that to a man they were ready to acquit Beal and his friends–and no defense witnesses had taken the stand.

In the new trial, this one held in Charlotte, the state produced witnesses who testified that Vera Bush and others had screamed to the guards, "Do your duty, men! Do your duty." That "duty," of course, was to kill the policemen. The solicitor reenacted the death of Chief Aderholt, and even fell to the floor and simulated the dying cries of the slain chief. It was like shooting fish in a rain barrel.

As he concluded the state's case, John G. Carpenter reminded the jury that Gaston County had been a virtual Eden before the horrible serpents of communism had invaded, their fangs ready to poison the entire populace of the county. Carpenter reminded the jurors that the yarn produced in the county could reach to the sun and moon and other heavenly bodies and back to circle the earth several times.

He concluded by mimicking the voice of Vera Bush. "Do your duty, men!" he pleaded with the jury. "For God's sake, do your duty!"

The jury almost instantly returned with a verdict of murder in the first degree, and Judge Barnhill had to admonish them that the men were not charged with first-degree murder. The jury retired again for a few minutes and rendered an acceptable verdict. The seven defendants were released on bail to await the results of their appeal. While they waited, Beal and the others fled the county and the state and arranged a voyage to Russia, where they would be named honorary Russian citizens. They were given the task of building the Russian textile empire.

Russia, however, was not the workers' paradise the men had expected, and they soon became horribly disenchanted with communism. Some of the men died there, but Beal was one who was smuggled back into this country where he was arrested and taken to prison.

"I'd rather be a prisoner in this country than a free man in Russia," he told reporters as he entered the New Caledonia prison.

Several years later Clyde Hoey, one of the prosecutors who sent Beal to prison, reduced his prison sentence so that later the state could parole Beal. Beal traveled about the Gaston County area and apologized to the local citizens for the harm he and his cohorts had done. He died of a heart attack a short time later in New England.

The strike was crushed, but the effects of it remain even today. Unions, respectable ones, have appeared in the county, and cotton is no longer king. But the memory of the strike, of the terrorism created by the Black Hundred, and the tragic deaths of two good people will never be forgotten. Neither will the memory of the Dummy That Shook the South ever be forgotten.

Incidentally, later one man on his deathbed asked that a judge, an undertaker, and a preacher come to his hospital room. He asked them hypothetically that if a man murdered a pregnant woman, had the man committed one murder or two. When they asked why he was asking the question, he replied, "Because I killed Ella May Wiggins."

Earlier the man had told friends that he had experienced horrible nightmares during which Ella May reproached him, and jerked out handfuls of hair. In real life the man lost his hair as rapidly as the Nightmare Ella had pulled it out. His health failed with astonishing rapidity, and quickly he was at death's door. That was when he made his confession.

Later, a man in North Georgia made a deathbed confession to his family. He told them shortly before he died that he had killed the chief of police in Gastonia and had let seven innocent men take the blame. The men's lives had been ruined, he said, because of his act, and he did not want to die without confessing it.

The confession came too late to help the Loray Seven. Most of them died abroad, remained in hiding, or lived secretively in other parts of the country. One man, still wanted and still alive as late as 1980, lived under an assumed name in San Francisco. His marriage had been destroyed and his personal life remained in shambles, and half a century later he lived in fear that confession could alleviate.

The damages done in the Loray Mill strike and the other strikes that erupted almost simultaneously across the South did irreparable damage to the cause of organized labor, and it has been only within recent memory that unions have made their way into some of the textile mills. If you find yourself in Gastonia, even today, it would not be a good idea to bring up the subject of the strike, unless you pick your company carefully. Feelings still run high, and understandably so.

As one mill owner said, "We will not outlive the memory of that strike. At any time we could see repercussions in some parts of the county. Ella May Wiggins is gonna walk tonight!"

    Fred Beal commented that he left the socialist party because it was the party of peace and joined the communist party because it was the party of war. On another occasion he stated that he did not own a gun and would not know how to use one if he had it. He said that there would be no violence in the strike, but many of the strike guards who arrived from Chicago, the New Jersey mob scene, and New York City did not share Beal's peaceful philosophy. In fact, strike guards often boasted that they were neither afraid nor reluctant to use their guns. The photo above shows clearly that the guards were heavily armed and that their attitudes were belligerent.

Grave marker of Ella May Wiggins in Bessemer City

In the Episcopal Church cemetery in Lincolnton you can see a grave marker shaped like a table. The inscription on the marker says that the deceased was Lorenzo Ferrer, a native of Lyon, France, who died at age 96. Many people are convinced that Ferrer was the infamous pirate Jean Lafitte, one of the heroes of the Battle of New Orleans during the War of 1812. At the extreme western boundary of the cemetery you can find a black stone with the name Louisa on it and the information that the stone was erected by Lorenzo Ferrer. Lafitte also had a mistress named Louisa.

Four

The Peaceful Pirate of the Piedmont

Many years ago there was a comic book that proclaimed that the stories inside were cold, hard facts rather than the wild fiction that so often intrigued readers. The slogan of the magazine was "Truth is stranger and a thousand times more thrilling than fiction."

There may be more than a grain of truth to the claim. Many of history's mysteries challenge the most imaginative of Hollywood's epics and legends, and few are more interesting than the story of the peaceful pirate of the Piedmont.

The hero of the story is a man about whom very little was known during his lifetime. Lorenzo Ferrer (there are several spellings of his name) arrived in the small foothills town of Lincolnton, North Carolina, several years after the War of 1812 ended. Ferrer told no one much about his background, but his actions suggested mystery.

The stranger bought a house behind the ancient jailhouse in Lincolnton (the old jail has since been replaced by a newer one) and lived there peacefully. He shrugged off questions about his past, and he volunteered no answers to the many queries of how he earned his living. But the man had a liking for children, and he loved to tell them stories about piracy. He told them about bloody battles, pieces of eight, and the skull and crossed bones.

He even allowed the children to see pirate gold and to handle and play with jewels that were obviously expensive. Ferrer would come to town and sit in the Court Square, and the boys, who called him The Pirate, looked forward to his daily visits.

At his home Ferrer kept several chests filled with gold and other valuables. He did not mind showing these trinkets to his friends.

On one occasion Ferrer had a visitor named Peter Stewart Ney. Yes, this was the same man described in an earlier part of this book, a man who was undoubtedly Marshal Michel Ney, commander of the troops of Napoleon Bonaparte. When Ney met the peaceful pirate, the tempers of both men flared almost instantly. One report stated that the two men were on the brink of a sword fight.

Imagine! In the tiny Piedmont town, far removed from the battlegrounds of Europe and the drama of the high seas, two men engaged in a near-fight over their political ideologies. What makes the story even more incredible is that the combatants very likely were not only the top soldier under Napoleon but also the famed pirate Jean Lafitte, the hero of the Battle of New Orleans.

Impossible? Don't be too certain. Look at the possibilities.

During the battle of New Orleans (fought, ironically and tragically, after the war had ended), Lieutenant General Sir Edward Pakenham landed near the mouth of the Mississippi River and engaged in battle the troops of Major General Andrew Jackson, whose army was not considered a match for the superior English forces.

Help came from two unexpected sources. First, Cherokee Indian Chief Junaluska came to Jackson's defense at the Battle of Horseshoe Bend and reportedly saved Jackson's life in two different ways. First, Junaluska's men swam the river and stole the canoes of the Indians fighting on the side of the British; second, an enemy warrior had raised his war hatchet to slay Old Hickory and Junaluska killed the Indian and saved Jackson's life a second time.

Then, on January 8, 1815, Pakenham's men met Jackson's army, and this time Jean Lafitte led his pirates into the fray. Pakenham's army suffered heavy losses, and for Lafitte's heroism at New Orleans, President James Madison pardoned him and his men.

But Lafitte was not the sort of man to settle down and live a domestic life: not yet, at least. Shortly after the pardon was issued, Lafitte and his men chose a hideout on the site of modern-day Galveston, Texas, and Lafitte appointed himself governor of the port.

Lafitte's second piracy career lasted only a short time. Hamilton Cochran of Pennsylvania insists that Lafitte was killed in 1816. The information is a little like the Mark Twain's response to the rumors that he had died in Europe. He wired to his publisher that "reports of my death have been greatly exaggerated."

So did Lafitte die? According to Cochran, Lafitte's ship battled a British cruiser in the Gulf of Mexico, and Lafitte was shot in the chest and grapeshot crushed the bone in his right leg. Still, Lafitte fought until he was unable to stand, at which point the British killed him.

In a family Bible one of Lafitte's acquaintances wrote that Lafitte had gone to be with Dominique You, said by many to be the brother or cousin of Lafitte. From this inscription it was assumed that Dominique You was dead. But he was very much alive and operating just off the South Carolina coast for a brief time. Some think that Lafitte simply moved his operations to the Palmetto State coastline. It was rumored widely that Theodosia Burr, daughter of infamous Aaron Burr, the brilliant man who killed Alexander Hamilton in a duel, was captured and killed by Lafitte or by some of his pirates.

Returning to New Orleans, Lafitte took up residence with a quadroon woman (a person with one-fourth African blood; that is, a person with one black grandparent) named Louisa. The couple who "lived on the square like a true married pair," as Kipling put it, had a son believed to have been named Vatinius. (Some say that Lafitte met Louisa in Charleston, incidentally.)

For the record, the *Encyclopedia Britannica* states that Lafitte died in 1826, a full decade after the date given by Cochran. And the tombstone in Lincolnton at St. Luke's Episcopal Church states that Lorenzo Ferrer died in 1875 at age 96.

When Federal troops neared Lincolnton during the Civil War, Ferrer (Lafitte) asked Wallace Reinhardt to help move some iron chests to the Lincoln County Courthouse. The story is that when the chests were moved, Ferrer opened one chest and scooped up a double handful of gold coins for payment. He later added a "massive gold watch attached to a heavy gold chain." Ferrer reportedly in his will left large sums of money to Lincoln County friends.

And at the very edge of the cemetery at St. Luke's Episcopal Church in Lincolnton (on the corner of Cedar and Pine streets) there is a dark tombstone bearing the name Lorenzo Ferrer, but my wager is that it is Lafitte buried there. This much is certain: anyone who died three different times in three different years was one tough old bird.

Five
Mille-Christine: the Ebony Nightingales

Mother Nature can often be unspeakably cruel; at other times she is generous to a fault. And, sandwiched between the two extremes, are the benevolence and brutality of mankind.

As an example of the best and worst of Nature and Man, think of the wonderfully beautiful and horribly tragic case of Mille-Christine, the Ebony Nightingales. Born into slavery, Mille-Christine first saw the light of day on the plantation of Jabe McCoy in Columbus County, North Carolina. Mille-Christine was the daughter of Jacob and Monemia McCoy, slaves on the Jabe McCoy plantation.

Mille-Christine was neither one person nor two. The Siamese twins, who were joined near the waist and shared one liver, always spoke of themselves as one person, and it is indeed rare to think of any two persons who could have been closer in every way than were these twins. Or this *person*, depending upon your viewpoint.

The twins were born on July 11, 1851, and at birth they weighed seventeen pounds. They were joined at the hips by an eighteen-inch cylinder of flesh. Otherwise, they were nearly normal in every way.

They were beautiful, everyone attested. They had a wonderfully sweet disposition, and they seemed to love everyone. They were also one another's best friends, and for more than sixty years they enjoyed a supremely rewarding friendship, unlike the original Siamese twins, Eng and Chang, who fought bitterly and frequently. So similar were the natures of the girls, their friends thought of them as one person and spoke of Mille-Christine as "she" rather than "they."

And, in a medical sense, they were one person. They shared the same nervous system, and separation would have been fatal to both, just as any illness to one was serious to both.

For example, if someone touched Mille's hand, Christine did not feel the contact. But if someone touched the leg or foot of either twin, the other instantly felt the touch.

At the same time, each twin had her own mentality, emotional outlook, creative energy, and intellectual capability. Despite their individuality, however, the girls agreed upon nearly everything: their tastes and appetites and attitudes were almost invariably attuned.

The world, however, did not see the dignity, the grace, and the beauty of the twins. To men like John Purvis of Chesterfield County, South Carolina, the girls were biological misfits, and as such they could be used to appeal to the twisted minds of mankind and earn a profit.

So Purvis bought the twins for $1,000, plus one-fourth of all the twins earned as sideshow attractions that Purvis arranged. Purvis was not astute financially, however, and soon he sold the twins to a Doctor Maginley for $200.

Dr. Maginley's plans failed, also, along with his health. He took the twins to Philadelphia, where he died, leaving the twins helpless and bewildered by this strange new world. It was not until years later that W. J. Millar found the twins, who had somehow made their way to Boston, and he became their manager and made immediate plans to take the twins on a world tour where they would demonstrate to the world that they were not freaks in any sense of the word; in truth, they were wonderfully talented singers.

The twins were owned, as despicable as the word is when used in reference to a human being, by Joseph Smith of South Carolina, and Millar became their manager. But Smith was not at all the prototypically brutal person normally associated with servitude.

Smith was, apparently, a very humane and wise person who was also very generous and considerate. Under his guidance, Mille-Christine became truly happy for the first time since they had left their parents in North Carolina. They made a name and a career for themselves because of their talents, not for their physical condition.

Others, however, were not as humanely disposed as Smith had been, and twice the girls were kidnapped for the purpose of showing them as

Nature's abnormalities across the country. Once the kidnappers were burly and aggressive professional prizefighters who abducted the twins for pay. On another occasion hoodlums took the girls to show as accidents.

Smith died in 1860, shortly before the outbreak of the Civil War, and his son, Joseph Pearson Smith, took the twins to Spartanburg, South Carolina, for protection. When the younger Smith granted the twins their freedom, they chose to remain with him so that he could act as their manager and book their singing engagements throughout Europe (in every country on the continent) and in the United States.

Under the auspices of Smith, the twins joined a circus as a singing act and toured all but two states in the Union. One of the great fans and admirers of the twins was Queen Victoria, who frequently requested them to sing at a command performance. By this time Mille-Christine was (were) billed as the Ebony Nightingales, the African Twins, or the Carolina Twins.

The number of admirers grew astonishingly, and not only for the sublime musical talents of the twins. They were highly intelligent, articulate, charming, and fascinating conversationalists. They spoke five languages fluently and others capably.

Money poured in, and Mille-Christine bought the land where they had been born as slaves and hired a construction crew to build them a fourteen-room house there. They also bought other farms or building lots to give as presents to their friends of both races in the American South.

Then, almost as fast as their good fortune came, it vanished. In their huge house they had stored their antiques and mementos from around the world so that their residence had become a showplace in itself. It was also their treasure house.

And one night it burned to the ground. It was suspected that arsonists, resentful of the twins' success, torched the house. Rushing from the house into a rainstorm, the twins sat on a salvaged trunk and watched their life's work go up in flames. Because of the prolonged cold and exposure, Mille became ill with what was diagnosed as a simple cold. But the cold grew worse and soon she realized that she was suffering from tuberculosis.

Christine remained healthy and strong, but it was apparent that she could not live if Mille died. A Doctor Crowell contacted Johns Hopkins Hospital to determine if surgical separation was possible. The response was that Mille should be given massive doses of morphine but that it would be impossible to separate the twins.

The fire had occurred in 1909. Mille lived until 1912, and on the afternoon of October 8 of that year she died. It was said that Christine knew of her sister's death even before Dr. Crowell knew.

Christine knew that she, too, had died, essentially, when her sister did. Although still healthy and strong, she realized that life was impossible without her sister.

It is uncertain how long she lived. Some said that she lasted only eight more hours; others argued that she survived for seventeen hours after Mille died. Those friends who remained by Christine's side remembered that she spent her final hours in prayer and in singing hymns. News of Christine's death came on October 10, 1912. Because medical records were not kept carefully, there is no time of death available.

News of Christine's passing spread across the world, and huge numbers of condolences came in from everywhere. The world joined in mourning for the deaths of the Ebony Nightingales, whose voices were stilled after so many years of creating beauty and spreading joy to all who heard them.

A carpenter constructed a double coffin from cypress wood, and Mille-Christine were buried following a funeral service at a Baptist church near the home.

But even in death the beautiful twins with the glorious voices were not safe from the scavengers who had earlier tried to market the exceptional and delightful twins as curiosities. Armed guards kept watch over the grave to be certain that the human ghouls did not steal the bodies in order to sell them to carnivals.

In 1969 the grave of Mille-Christine was opened, and the remains of the world-famous twins were moved to a cemetery near Whiteville, North Carolina, on the shores of White Lake, one of the most beautiful bodies of water in the South.

The inscription on the grave marker, in part, tells a major part of the life of Mille-Christine. The message says, "Mille-Christine...lived a life of much comfort owing to her love of God and joy in following His commands. A real friend to the needy of both races...."

Perhaps a better commentary is found on the original grave marker: "A soul with two thoughts. Two hearts that beat as one."

Mille-Christine was born into a cruel world. By their lives they made it a much more beautiful one.

Charles Keyes: the Parson of the Hills

Six
Preacher to Chickens and Outlaws

When Charles Keyes was four years old, he said, he desperately wanted to become a mountain preacher. He would go out into the barnyard and stand on a chicken coop while he preached to the chickens. When he was five, he was preaching to anyone in his native mountains who would listen.

Preaching came as naturally to Keyes, better known as the Parson of the Hills, as breathing does to some people. He said that his preaching career started, in a sense, before he was born.

"In 1918, just before I was born," Keyes said, "my mother fell upon her knees and begged God to call me to the ministry. I was not the only one in the family with a religious calling. My father was ready to start his religious studies at Emory and Henry College in Virginia when he met my mother, and the two were married soon afterwards. Three of my uncles were presidents of huge banks, and my sister taught language in Hawaii; other family members were successful in business, and my mother's father was mayor of West Jefferson for more than a quarter of a century. My great-uncle, a preacher, collapsed and died in the pulpit while he was delivering his last sermon. One of my maternal ancestors married the outlaw Jesse James before he went west and into the history books."

But the center of family attention was not only outlaws or bank presidents. Charles Keyes, at age four and later at five, attracted people from miles around to hear the boy preacher delivering sermons.

"I couldn't read," Keyes said, "so I had to preach from what my mother and grandmother read to me from the Bible. But I preached."

When he was still a child, Keyes found a particularly beautiful location in the woods near his home, and he dragged sections of old logs to the woods, aligned them like pews in a church, and then he stood on a stump to preach to the rough and tough mountaineers who came into the forest to hear the Word.

One man in particular came forward one day and asked the boy preacher to pray for him. The man added that he had been very wicked and needed all the forgiveness he could find.

"That man went through a listing of all the crimes and sins he had committed," Keyes recalled in an interview many years ago, "and I think he must have done every criminal act possible in this world."

Others were equally evil in their former lives. "I preached on a regular basis to outlaws, bootleggers, and the old mountain people who wanted to hear what I had to say," he told me one evening during a visit to his special camp in Hickory, North Carolina. "When one of the mountaineers wanted to be baptized, I had to get two men to help me, because I was so small I couldn't handle the grown-ups."

Not all who heard the Boy Wonder were sympathetic, however. Once Keyes entered a restaurant to ask for a drink of water, and the owner reached under the counter, pulled out a hammer, and hit Keyes in the head, knocking him unconscious. Later Keyes learned that the man was angry because of comments Keyes had made about the liquor business in the mountains.

But neither were all the listeners antagonistic. Keyes recalled one man who was in his eighties and who needed a large-print Bible so that he could read it. Keyes managed to get the Bible to the man, as well as some new clothes to replace the rags the man wore, and one day the old man walked seventeen miles to hear Keyes preach.

Even during his early years Keyes had started to help people in need, and his fame spread across the mountains. He accepted money from those able to pay, and he worked (at times by selling roasted peanuts) to earn extra money. He then used the money to help the poor in the pockets of poverty in the mountains.

Make no mistake about it. The mountains the tourists see today bear little resemblance to the same areas decades ago. Today there are tourist attractions everywhere, but during the early decades of this century poverty was apparent nearly anywhere you looked.

Keyes recalled that in his early ministry he went into parts of the mountains that were, as he put it, "true wildernesses." There were often no churches, no schools, no real civilization except for hovels and barns and a little livestock or gardens. In these backwoods areas Keyes would clear away underbrush, set up a brush arbor, and preach his sermons to anyone who would listen.

Often, he told me, he preached at night because the people needed to work during the daytime. Some of the local residents would provide lanterns or old bottles filled with kerosene, a lit twisted rag for a wick, as the only light in the wilderness.

Often, as he traveled on foot among the mountain people, Keyes accepted food and shelter from the residents far from the modern world, and he admitted that he knew many of the people earned a large part of their incomes from the production and sale of moonshine liquor.

"They often told me that I was welcome to preach as much as I liked, but they didn't want to hear me come down too hard on their way of life," Keyes said.

The Boy Wonder was now in his early adulthood, and he saw everywhere the ravages of whiskey on the otherwise fine people. He grew to hate liquor, but he said that he never had turned in a moonshiner and never would. His logic was that if he did not win their confidence, they would never come to hear him preach, and if they never heard preaching, they would never be won to God's ways. On the other hand, he reasoned, if he could convert them, they would give up their moonshining and drinking.

Still, his hands-off policy did not convince all of the moonshiners in the mountains, and often after a revival service he would go to the car he had recently purchased and find that someone had let the air out of tires or, worse, slashed the tires. At other times the bootleggers scratched and dented the car, and on occasion they resorted to putting dirt or sugar in the gas tank.

Gone now was the Boy Wonder nickname, and in its place was the title "Sledgehammer Charlie." This latter name came from Keyes' vicious attacks on the whiskey industry in the mountains.

As he continued his travels, Keyes remained in a state of almost constant amazement at how far removed from the world the people were. Many knew little or nothing about Christianity.

He told me one day of a young man who had come to a service, and at the end of the sermon the young man, an adult, wanted to know if Jesus was killed while he was cutting down a tree or whether a tree fell on him one day. All the man knew was something about the man who died on the tree. He could not read, and his family owned no Bible or other religious literature.

While he delivered his messages to the mountain people, Keyes found himself facing loaded pistols, backwoods gangs armed with shotguns and rifles, and constant threats and vandalism. Once he was staying with a friend when the friend's dogs began to bark. Keyes and his friend rushed outside just in time to see Keyes' automobile rolling toward a high cliff. They saved the car but the would-be destroyers made their escape.

In another instance, Keyes had used all the money he could raise to buy a brand-new large revival tent. After a service he went to the home of his host and in the night vandals had slashed the tent to shreds and had hacked the tent poles into firewood.

On one occasion a man was shot and killed just outside the arbor where Keyes preached. On other nights Keyes faced the snake-handling ceremonies.

The snake-handling cult members often said that you cannot get full religion unless you hold onto the rattles of a snake, and as Keyes sat in the church during his first visit he saw people arriving with boxes under their arms or with sacks hanging from their hands.

During the service people indeed held the venomous snakes and exposed themselves to mortal dangers, all the while proclaiming that if a man's life is "right" he has nothing to fear from the snakes. During his stay among the snake-handlers Keyes learned of several people who died from fatal snake bites.

The explanation was always the same: if people had fasted and prayed as they should have, the snakes would not have bitten them.

In his long ministry, Keyes encountered child-brides, marriages based on the ancient ceremony of jumping over a broomstick, and other practices of the backwoods people. He counseled, persuaded, and helped the people in any way that he could. When he told one man that he needed a marriage license, the man said he had a license but it was on his car.

After several years of helping people in all walks of life, Keyes outgrew the Sledgehammer Charlie nickname and became the Parson of the Hills. In his modified capacity, he began to collect money, canned food, clothing, toys, books, and whatever else the people in the remote mountain coves needed. He traveled through the mountains of North and South Carolina, Tennessee, Kentucky, and Virginia as he delivered his truckloads of help to the needy.

Soon he became one of the most famous men in the South, and his trailers could be seen in the months before Christmas in nearly every town in the area. When the trailers were full, he and his drivers pulled the trailers into the mountain pockets of poverty and delivered the only Christmas that many of the people would ever know.

But he still wasn't finished. Using money collected from the faithful, Keyes established a camp for boys and girls who would never otherwise know that a better life for them was possible. For years the Parson of the Hills ministered to anyone who needed his help. Keyes died several years ago, but his work goes on. And each Christmas (and into the late spring months) the Good News and the goodies arrive in the distant reaches of the North Carolina mountains.

In trailers like the one shown above, Charles Keyes, the Parson of the Hills, spread Christmas cheer all year round to the unfortunate members of society who could not afford food and clothing for their children. The parson visited homes in the Carolinas, Tennessee, Virginia, and Kentucky, and the original Christmas trips soon became year-round excursions to spread Christian goodwill throughout the mountains.

Vicki Thompson and her mother Marie Thompson of Dellview

Onie Dellinger, left, is the only mayor Dellview has ever had.

Seven
Everybody's All-American Town

There's no truth to the rumors that Dellview is going to the dogs. Far from it! In fact, it would be more accurate to say that Dellview came *from* the dogs. At least, the dogs in their own way caused the town to exist.

It happened in a rather pedestrian way. But before you hear the explanation, you need to know a little about Dellview and its people, its heritage, and its past and future.

First, the town was legally incorporated in 1925 and has remained a legal town ever since. During the more than seven decades of its existence, the town duly elects a mayor, a board of town commissioners, a fire chief, a police chief, and all the other key persons needed in any other town in the United States.

But from the time the town was chartered until this writing, the police chief has never answered a call, never arrested anyone for any reason, and never written a ticket or investigated a crime.

The fire chief has never answered a call, either, and even if he did, he'd be very little help because the town does not own or even have ready access to a fire truck, a hose, or even a helmet. Happily, there has never been an unintentional fire in the town's history.

The tax rate is as remarkable as the rest of the government of the town. There simply are no taxes of any sort levied for any reason by the town of Dellview.

Inside the city limits, there has never been a crime, a wreck, or any other form of disturbance that warranted police or civic action. And everyone in town, as a rule, holds one or more political offices.

Dellview, however, is not a totally inert place. In one decade, the population increased to four times the inhabitants in the previous decade. But the town limits did not expand by even a single inch.

Look at the statistics. When Dellview was chartered, it had about eight citizens in the town that is the smallest in the state and, it is thought, in the nation. By 1970 the population was down to two, but by 1980 it had leaped again to eight people. At the peak of its growth, Dellview reportedly had seventeen people, but then some of the kids went off to college and others moved away. A few have died since 1925. There are three houses, not counting chicken houses, and at least one dog, unless the pooch has gone to dog heaven in the last few months.

But there were, in the mid-eighties, twenty-three cats and an unspecified number of opossums and garter snakes.

There are no industries of any sort in Dellview, no stores, no service stations, no civic buildings, and no jobs, unless you count the small machine shop in one of the two brick buildings in the town. The other brick building was for a long time the chicken house, and it was the chickens (not these, but the ancestors of the present fowls) that led to the town's existence.

The town's fathers, the Dellingers, owned chickens, and some of the nearby neighbors (in the suburbs of Dellview) owned dogs, which loved to snack on the chickens. Gaston County law (the town of Dellview is located in western Gaston County about eighteen miles from Gastonia and a little more than a mile from Cherryville) did not permit the chicken owners to kill the dogs, and the only apparent solution to the problem was either to give up chicken-farming or find a way to control the dogs.

So J. Henry Dellinger, the area's top chicken grower, engaged his uncle, David Dellinger, an attorney, to make a visit to Raleigh for the purpose of having the town chartered. The 1925 charter states that Dellview can contract for electrical power with the local providers, to buy and operate a water system, and to allow the police chief, if there happens to be one at the appropriate time, to arrest wrongdoers.

One of the first laws observed in the town is that it is illegal for dogs to kill chickens. It is unclear what the town laws say about the rights of cats and their desire for fowl play. The townspeople have a right to shoot and kill any dogs that are molesting chickens. A second law provides the right to restrict size and shape of hog pens.

It is said that there were once two other laws, but no one seems to remember what they were or why they were needed in the first place. And the chickens, too, have gone the way of all flesh.

At one time Dellview had the distinction of having one of the longest mayoral tenures of any place in the world. Mrs. Onie Dellinger, wife of the town's founder, became the first mayor of the town in 1925 and was reelected mayor every year since that time until the time of her death in 1981.

To make her record even better, Onie Dellinger was elected by unanimous vote every year but one. During one election one of the residents reportedly voted for himself and spoiled an otherwise perfect record.

Local residents claim that Dellview is only four inches wide. They point out that the four-by-four post on Delview Road (note that the name of the road is not spelled the same as is the town) has the town name on both sides of it, and the space between the signs is the width of Dellview.

This is not true. Dellview is basically a square, with each side running 1,500 feet. The town is not likely to grow much, because the land bounding the town is already part of another municipality or is owned by farmers whose families have owned it for years.

Not only that, the residents of Dellview want to remain small, simple, and essentially perfect as a town. There's not much chance that you would buy a vacant lot inside the town limits and build your own house there.

But if you'd like to visit Dellview, drive west of NC 150 through Cherryville until you pass through the main part of the town and head toward Shelby. As you pass a series of hamburger shops and service stations and quick-marts, look on the right for Delview Road. Follow the road slightly more than a mile and you will be in downtown Dellview, where automobile advertisers missed out on a golden opportunity for a television commercial because everyone in the town who could drive owned the same kind of car.

Think of the commercial: the town's residents standing beside their vehicles while the off-camera announcer proclaims, "In Dellview, everybody drives a Dodge." And there are no dogs to chase them!

As you enter Dellview, you will see that there are businesses that spell their name as Delview. That's to keep you from mistaking the suburbs with the real McCoy, and that's what Dellview is.

By general agreement, Old Bill Williams was the greatest of all the mountain men. He began his life in Rutherford County in Western North Carolina, but when he was a young man he crossed the Mississippi to attempt to convert the savages to Christianity. He was also the first white man, as far as can be determined, to see the Grand Canyon and other landmarks of the West.

Eight
The Greatest Mountain Man of Them All

Near the entrance of the Grand Canyon is a statue of Old Bill Williams, sometimes referred to as Wild Bill Williams or simply as Old Bill. Whatever the title, the meaning is the same: this was the man who, everyone agrees, was the greatest mountain man of them all. And that's quite a claim, keeping in mind such stalwarts as Jim Bridger, Jedediah Smith, John Colter, and Carolinas legend Daniel Boone.

These mountain men were among the toughest and most daring of all the human beings recorded in history. Their feats go beyond the heroic into the realm of the impossible: running forty miles to warn and save a fort; after being speared in the back, reaching around one's body and whittling off the spear shaft and carrying the huge spear head in his back the rest of his life; enduring cold so intense that the mercury in the thermometers froze; fighting Indians and wild animals and wilder white men. These were part of the life of the mountain man.

As you near the Grand Canyon, you will see the town of Williams, Arizona, and nearby you can find Mount Williams and Williams Fork River. Annually the Bill Williams Society of the Old West holds its rendezvous, and hundreds of modern mountain men gather to pay their respects to the Tar Heel who was, at one time or another, a Baptist minister, an Easterner, a passive man of understanding and patience, and a longtime advocate of brotherly love.

Yet this same man was a savage who outdid his Indian tutors in the arts of savagery, a cruel and almost sadistic man who killed with a vengeance and morbid satisfaction, and perhaps a cannibal who resorted to eating human flesh in order to survive the Rocky Mountain winter.

Billy Williams, son of Joseph and Sarah Williams of the Horse Creek community in Western North Carolina near Columbus in Rutherford County, was born on January 3, 1787, several years after his father returned from his duties as a soldier during the Revolutionary War. Years later the family left Horse Creek and headed for the wide open spaces of the St. Louis area.

Billy, now Reverend Bill Williams, accompanied them, but, unlike his family members, he had a dream, an ambition, and a calling. His plan was for him to enter the wilderness of the West and carry with him the doctrines of Christianity to the heathen Osage Indians of Missouri, and he would guide the people, whom he regarded as savages, into a cultural marriage with Christianity and brotherly love.

A strange thing happened on the way to converting the Indians to Christianity: the Osage converted *him,* and he returned from the wilderness with his Osage wife, a beautiful young girl whom he called Wild Blossom.

By this time Williams had an Indian name: Pah-hah-soo-gee-ah, meaning "the Redheaded Shooter." Bill Williams was also a folk hero by the time he was in his early twenties. During a buffalo hunt, Bill had saved the life of Little Eagle, an Osage chief. Caught up in the excitement of the hunt and the rescue, and with his adrenaline flowing madly, Bill Williams killed bison, slashed open their carcasses, and gnawed the raw liver of the beasts.

As a young man he had heard the call of Christianity; as an adult, he heard another calling: the call of the wild. But the Divine Spark of Christianity had not been fully extinguished inside the mind and heart of the Red-Headed Shooter, and when war broke out between the Cherokees and the Osage, Bill volunteered to act as a peace emissary, and when he did not fully succeed as peacemaker, he headed for the mountains where he fasted for thirty days in his own personal attempt at a transfiguration.

Ultimately, he renounced the Osage way of life in order to follow another dream. He headed west to help mark the original Santa Fe Trail, the famed wagon trail leading from Independence, Missouri, to the city of Santa Fe in northern New Mexico. For more than half a century, from 1821 until 1880, this trail was the major thoroughfare for families and adventurers heading west.

For his work on the trail, Williams was paid the princely sum of

$132.67. But the pay was not a disappointment; the adventure simply opened the way to the greater heights Bill was to scale.

One of the high points in his career came when he was appointed spokesman for the president of the United States as he negotiated treaties with the American Indians. But now he had added another name to his growing list: he was Lone Elk to the Utes, and as he moved deeper into the West, the settlements were filled with the stories of Lone Elk, his mule Flap-Ear, his horse Santa Fe, and his infamously and deadly accurate rifle, Old Fetchum.

To the other mountain men, including Jedediah Smith, Thomas "Broken Hand" Fitzpatrick, Milton and William Sublette, Henry Frabe, Hugh Glass, and the mulatto Jim Beckworth, Bill Williams was Old Solitaire. The Utes described him as "the eagle in the heaven and the panther in the mountain."

Whatever his name, Bill's destinations did not change. He delved deeper and deeper into the West, and in his travels he stumbled across the Petrified Forest, the Painted Desert, and the greatest marvel of them all, the Grand Canyon. He was the first white man, it is generally assumed, to witness the Grand Canyon, and he was also the first white man to see Yosemite.

It is beyond imagination what Old Bill thought when he first saw the Petrified Forest and the Grand Canyon, but one fact seems certain: when he was later asked what astonishing and incredible forces created these wonders, without hesitation Bill replied, "God Almighty!"

But he still hadn't made it as far as he wished, and he pushed on toward the Pacific Ocean. Along the way he was ambushed by a raiding party of Blackfeet Indians who took Old Bill's horses and would have taken his life if it had not been for the deadly accuracy of Old Fetchum.

Rather than admit defeat, Bill decided that he liked his odds: himself on foot versus more than two dozen Blackfeet on horses. So he set out to track down the Blackfeet. It took him days to locate them, but when he did he launched his own raid, and when it was over he had recovered his own horses and had taken several of the horses belonging to the Blackfeet as interest on the loan. And in the process he served notice that he would not tolerate such infamous activities.

In the San Joaquin valley he and some fellow marauders stole five hundred horses, and the owners of the horses, angered beyond reason, formed a huge posse and rode in pursuit of Old Bill and their ill-gotten livestock. Bill and his friends rode furiously away from their pursuers, until the posse members had judged that it was fear that drove the horse thieves.

Then, without warning, Bill turned and rode wildly into the posse, scaring the daylights out of them and causing them to flee as if the very Prince of Darkness was after them. And Bill calmly took the horses of the posse riders in addition to those already stolen and calmly rode away with double the prize he had originally taken.

His fame–or notoriety–increased with each tale that was taken back to civilization. His feats were the talk of campfire gatherings, military men, and Indians alike. And facts supported the claims, with a few notable exceptions not meant to be taken for truth.

Bill, for example, loved to tell tall tales, and he enjoyed telling how he once attempted to leap across a gorge in the vicinity of the Petrified Forest. The gorge was a thousand feet deep, and if Bill failed in his leap, he'd fall to his certain death.

He leaped, he told his wide-eyed audience, and fell short of the opposite side of the gorge. He knew he was a goner and he prepared for his death. But, to his shock, he discovered that Gravity itself had become petrified along with the trees, and he was able to walk on thin air across the gorge.

But the tall tales could not compete with the real-life stories of Old Bill Williams. Once, for instance, he and forty-three trappers were attacked by three hundred Bannock Indians. Rather than turning to retreat, Old Bill and the trappers charged the enemy, killing nearly half of them and losing only one man.

Old Bill, the Native Americans said, and their white counterparts agreed, was invincible.

When trapping became unprofitable, Old Bill decided to put together a team of transplanted Tar Heels to explore and help settle the Old West. It was an All-Star team of some of the greatest North Carolinians in the state's proud history.

Bill, it must be noted, did not accomplish the organization alone: he was aided by a number of people, including James K. Polk.

President Polk, himself a North Carolinian, had urged fellow Tar Heels to meet at the center of western civilization, Taos, New Mexico, the site of one of the leading art centers in the nation today. On the "team" was Lew Wallace, author of classic novel *Ben-Hur*, who lived at the famed Esmeralda Inn near Lake Lure while he completed the dramatized version of the novel for Broadway. General Lew Wallace of Civil War fame later became the first provisional governor of New Mexico.

Kit Carson, whose relatives lived in the North Carolina Piedmont, became one of the noted scouts and military leaders of the Southwest. And James Pinckney Henderson, of Lincoln County in North Carolina, became the first governor of Texas.

Part of the master plan of these transplanted Easterners was to join John C. Fremont in his efforts to explore the Rockies. But from the start the plan seemed totally wrong. Old Bill, for example, warned the Pathfinder not to enter the Rockies wilderness in winter. He warned that the climate was too extreme for man or beast.

Fremont, true to his nature, refused to accept advice from anyone he considered his inferior, and he rejected Old Bill's advice and discounted the famed Mountain Man's experience. He was soon to regret the choice.

During the exploration, the Fremont expedition found itself trapped in a blizzard that threatened to destroy them all. Snow fell so thickly and furiously that the men could see only a few feet ahead of them, and the fallen snow packed six inches deep on the hooves of the horses and pack mules.

So Fremont finally did what his pride would not allow earlier. He asked Old Bill and two others to rescue him from his own folly.

But it was not a simple plea for help. Bill and his friends had to hike 160 miles to the Rio Grande area, where they could obtain needed supplies.

Along the way the men had to eat their belts, their boots, and their holsters. Their animals became part of their menu almost from the time the ordeal started.

But Old Bill somehow made the trip, although one of the men who started with him died along the way. How the man died remains a mystery, but there were those who said that Bill may have had a hand in it.

No one ever accused Old Bill of having murdered the man: that in itself would have been suicide. The reports that filtered back to Taos were that the man died of exposure and malnutrition, and Old Bill, facing death every minute of the hour himself, saw no reason to let the body of the deceased friend become food for wolves.

Did Bill engage in cannibalism? No one seems to know, but if he had, it would not be the only time such desperate actions occurred. On another ill-fated expedition, members of the Donner Party ate the bodies of those who died in the blizzard. They even went so far as to butcher the bodies and to label the sections by name so that members of the family would not eat their own flesh and blood. The same was done in New England during the "starving time," and cannibalism was not unheard of in other parts of the nation. In recent years, in fact, survivors of a plane crash admitted that they resorted to cannibalism in order to survive until help arrived.

Whatever the story, Old Bill survived. When he and the others emerged from the woods, and when Fremont's group had been rescued, Bill joined United States army troops in a battle against his former blood brothers, the Utes.

This move was one of the worst mistakes Old Bill ever made. During his life as a Native American, Bill had married two Indian princesses and had become chief of at least one Indian tribe. He was, in the eyes of the Southwest Indians, a Ute, once and always. And for him to join the army to fight against them was unacceptable in every sense.

In 1848, not long after the battle, Old Bill was sent to rescue the cache of goods left by Fremont in the mountains. One night as he was setting up camp, a band of roving Utes rode through his campsite and fired point-blank at him. One of the rifle balls struck Bill squarely in the forehead, killing him instantly.

The news traveled fast, as tragic news always does. The story soon reached other mountain men, army troops, and civilians that the Invincible Bill had been murdered.

Mountain men grieved around their campfires, and they told stories that grew more detailed and awesome with each telling, about Old Bill, the greatest of them all. One of their favorite stories was that Old Bill who, after being paid for his pelts, spent the money on one huge spree and never looked back.

"You go through life only once," they quoted Bill as saying, "and I never saw a shroud with pockets."

John Marion, an Old West newspaperman, wrote a tribute to Old Bill Williams, Old Solitaire, Lone Elk, and Reverend Bill, which said, in part, "Thus died Bill Williams–a fair specimen of the old mountaineers–a set of men now nearly extinct; a set of men who possessed as warm hearts, as noble purposes, and as courageous spirits as could be found in any state of society. Rude and unpolished but tender and true, firm in fight but gentle as a woman to misfortune and distress–true Paladins of the mountains and plains."

It was an unofficial epitaph that Old Solitaire would have fully understood–and appreciated.

During his lifetime Old Bill, whose statue stands at the outskirts of town in Williams, Arizona, ranged at will, exploring from Oregon to Old Mexico. He saw wonders no white man had ever before seen, and he experienced rigors and hardships that would have been fatal to virtually anyone else in the nation. From his birth in 1787 until his death on March 14, 1849, Old Solitaire packed more living in his sixty-two years on this earth than most people could have amassed in centuries.

He was schooled in the ways of the civilized world and in the world of the Outdoors. But when he visited family members from time to time, he found that he could not stay long in one place. The call of the wild still echoed in his brain and heart, and he had no choice but to follow the call.

The fact that he lived for more than sixty years was in itself a minor miracle. He faced death almost daily in a dozen forms, from enemy warriors to rattlesnakes to the weather. He endured the worst that life has to offer, and he faced the ordeals without medical aid and without help, much of the time.

Old Bill was buried, some say, in southern Colorado, near where he was killed. But death did not end the legend; it only increased it. Today, all that remains to remind us of the fantastic career of this state's wildest son is a roadside marker just outside Columbus in Polk County. Nothing else is needed. Men like Old Solitaire do not need statues and fame. They created their own legends, and their lives will forever remind us just how much we are capable of doing–when circumstances and ambitions and abilities drive us sufficiently.

Sammy Price points to where members of his family spotted Knobby. The location is in the South Mountains, near Casar. Below, Price holds hair thought to have come from Knobby.

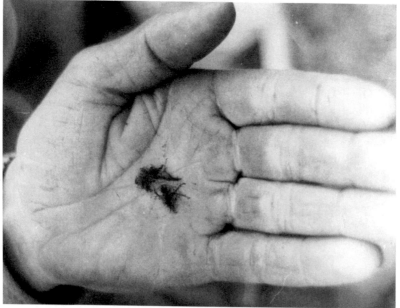

Nine
Gentle Bigfoot of the South Mountains

Back in the days when I wrote stringer news, I made it a point to stop at a series of local hangouts in order to learn the latest news and get leads on potential stories. It was a mild October morning in 1978 when I approached one of my informants.

"Anything interesting happening?" I asked him, expecting to learn about some local resident who had an interesting history or hobby. One of our neighbors, for example, whittled beautiful walking canes and sent these to his favorite political personalities. Everyone from presidents of the United States to governors and senators had one of the special canes among his souvenirs.

"Not a thing," my informant said. "People can't talk about anything but that strange creature they've been seeing around here."

"Strange creature?" I asked. "What kind of creature are we talking about? Is it an alien life form, or an escaped monkey from some traveling show?"

"No," he said with resignation. "It's some kind of bigfoot. Sort of like that thing people claim they have seen out in Washington or in the Himmalayas. You can find out more about it up at the grocery store on Highway Ten. Sorry I don't have anything good for you."

Seconds later I was on my way, and what I learned has to rank up near the top in strangeness of all the stories I have ever done. During that morning I talked with half a dozen people, all of whom said they had seen the creature on or near Carpenter's Knob.

My sources included a preacher's wife, a banker, a traveling salesman, a high school kid, an elderly retired woman, and a grocer.

Their stories did not vary in terms of what they had seen; only the locations differed. The strange animal had first been seen by the wife of a local preacher and two of her friends as they drove home from an evening church service. As they neared the home of one of the members of the congregation, one of them pointed to what she thought was a cow grazing along the edge of the highway. Thinking that the cow had managed to work its way through the fence, the woman slowed down to see if they could determine who owned the animal.

When they pulled up beside it, the creature, which had been down on all four feet, or on two hands and two feet, suddenly rose in mild alarm, looked into the car, then nimbly leaped the fence and made its way across the pasture to nearby woods.

The women were so astounded that they drove back to the church to tell the preacher and the others who had lingered after the service. Carloads of people left in search of the animal, but no one spotted it again that night.

The animal, which I immediately named Knobby because of the proximity of Carpenter's Knob in the South Mountains, stood well over six feet tall when fully erect, the women said. He had human features, and his face was, they all agreed, gentle, friendly, curious, and compassionate.

Weight of Knobby was estimated at more than two hundred pounds, and his body was covered with short brown hair. His arms were slightly longer than a human being's arms, in relation to body size and height, and his fingers were long and tapered, not at all like those of a chimp or monkey.

The only sad aspect of the creature, they said, was that he had a fresh cut down his face, as if his flesh had been ripped by barbed wire or a similar material. The women again agreed that Knobby did not seem unreasonably frightened of them, and he did not show any signs of fear. He simply exercised the good judgment to depart the scene before someone produced a weapon.

I rushed home, wrote my story, and mailed it to the paper. Two days later the story was spread all over the front page, and Bigfoot hunters appeared from everywhere. But in the interim, after mailing the story and before it appeared in print, more sightings occurred. A 90-year old woman was the next to see the Bigfoot.

When I visited the woman, I carried with me certain notions about her mental acuity. I reasoned that her eyesight might be poor, that her imagination might have run away with her, and that she might have been caught up in the excitement around Carpenter's Knob. I was wrong on all counts.

First, there was not a problem at all with her eyesight. I learned this as soon as I began talking with her.

"Where did you first see Knobby?" I asked.

"Just across the road," she told me, pointing to a tree and a mailbox about three hundred feet away. "Do you see the maple tree? And the mailbox right beside the tree? The one where the mockingbird just lit."

I looked, and surely enough the tree, the mailbox, and even the bird were clearly visible, although I was not certain I could have identified the bird as a mockingbird at that distance. I assured her that I saw the objects and the bird.

"The animal was standing between the tree and the mailbox," she said. "It was about seven o'clock in the morning, and it was just getting light enough to see pretty clearly. I watched him for several minutes, and then I called my son, and he drove up to see for himself. The animal heard the pickup truck coming and it kind of shuffled off into the trees across the pasture. I never saw it again after that."

I talked with the woman for about two hours, and during that time she never repeated herself, never became confused or, as they say in the mountains, addled, and she was never at a loss for a word. Her mind was as sharp as that of many people half her age.

The next sighting was by a banker who was driving through the South Mountains in the early morning, shortly after eight o'clock, and he saw Knobby emerge from a clump of trees, stare at him for several seconds, and then disappear into the woods. The banker stopped at a local store to tell the owner of the strange creature and to ask if there were any reports of circus animals loose in the area.

A day later a farm wife came in from the fields and began to prepare the evening meal. On her way in from the fields she had stopped at her sweet potato patch and dug enough potatoes for the family's meal. She put the potatoes on the porch and then went inside the house. When she came back out, Knobby was eating a potato.

"He was just standing there on the porch," the woman said. "He didn't seem to be scared or upset. He just wanted a sweet potato, I suppose. I didn't know what he might do, so I went back inside and left him to eat all he wanted. I watched him for a few minutes, and then he just walked away, not in the slightest hurry at all."

A day or two later my phone rang one afternoon about four o'clock, and the caller was almost in hysterics. The schoolgirl who called was in her senior year at a local school, and she was literally screaming into the phone for me to come to her house, that Knobby was there and she had taken photos of him.

She finally calmed down enough to give me directions, and I drove to her house where she, her younger sister, and their parents were waiting. The small brick house stood on a rural road only a few miles from Carpenter's Knob. The house sat in a cleared area amid tall growths of loblolly pines. The girl and her sister explained to me that when they left the school bus, they walked up the drive, and as they neared the house, Knobby was standing at the edge of the pines.

Both girls insisted that they had a close-up look at Knobby and that they were totally certain the animal was not a bear. The 90-year old woman had made the same distinction.

"I have lived in the mountains all my life," she said, "and I have seen bears, panthers, bobcats, deer, and whatever else lives in the woods, and what I saw at my mailbox was not anything I have ever seen before in my life."

Now the two girls repeated the claim. "It was not a bear," the older girl said over and over. "He walked on two feet, and he stood taller than any bear in this part of the country. And he had a face just like yours, except that his was covered with short brown hair. If you can wait just a few minutes, you can see for yourself. I took three or four pictures of him before he walked away. My cousin took the film to the store to be developed as soon as I got home. She'll be back in an hour or less."

I cannot describe my disappointment. I have a darkroom in my basement, and I could have developed the film. But I had no choice other than wait. When the cousin finally came home, she had a package in her hand and disappointment all over her face. I knew the moment I saw her that there were no Knobby pictures.

She was in tears as she explained that the photos had been developed by the lab in the drug store and that when she saw the pictures there was not a hint of Knobby. She then took out the negatives and showed me that four shots near the end of the roll were missing. She insisted that she had taken a clear photo of the elusive creature and that someone at the photo lab had seen the pictures and realized what they were and how much money they could bring, if marketed in the right place.

In her defense, a national magazine had contacted me by phone almost as soon as my first story appeared, and the starting price for a photo of Knobby was in the thousands of dollars. And that was only the first offer.

A few days after the thwarted photo episode, I had a call from a man who said that he had never seen Knobby but that he knew where the animal/human was living. He said that there was a cave on his property and that some huge animal had been using the cave as his own private den. I agreed to meet the man the following morning, a Saturday, and together we'd go Knobby hunting.

When I arrived at seven o'clock, there was a light dusting of snow on the ground, and by the time I was out of my car I was surrounded by the man's entire collection of brothers, uncles, and cousins. As I was introducing myself, a missing relative came running and yelling from the barn area.

"Old Bill is dead!" the man screamed. "Something killed hell out of Old Bill."

Horrified, I rushed to the barn and found, to my intense relief, that Old Bill was not Old Solitaire Bill Williams but a huge male goat. The animal lay motionless in the light snow, which bore the marks of some sort of struggle.

Old Bill's neck had been broken, and his body was still warm. There was a chain around his neck, and some of the men theorized that something had spooked Bill and the goat had leaped away from his attacker, and when the chain tightened the force was sufficient to kill Old Bill. We searched the area for unidentifiable tracks and found none. The theory then became one of fear: Bill had smelled Knobby and in his fright had leaped and broken his own neck. But theory was all we had; there was no evidence, of course, to support any ideas presented.

We left the body of Old Bill in the care of some of the family members who had already seen the cave, and a group of us, the others heavily armed, plunged into the deep woods of the South Mountains. I had mentioned that I would be more comfortable if we did not carry guns, but the men insisted, and by this time I was starting to feel a little more apprehension for my own safety.

I had some reason to fear weapons and hunters, which is what I interpreted these men as being. I had no faith that if we happened to see Knobby that they would be content merely to look. I was certain they intended to mount Knobby to display in their den.

Earlier, my wife and I had bought a pre-Civil War plantation house and had hired a company to move it to our property. After we moved into the house, the very first morning there, I opened the front door to enjoy the magnificent view–and someone shot me.

Quail hunters had flushed a covey of birds in front of our house, and one of the hunters opened fire as the birds flew up in front of our new/old house. Some of the bird shot struck me in the lower leg. A little higher and I would have perhaps been blinded. Since that time I did not relish the idea of being in the same state with armed men who lack basic good judgment.

But I had no choice with these men. They were taking their guns no matter where we went. I later realized that many of the people in the area, and incidentally these are some of the finest human beings I have ever known, carried their rifles along with them in the same way that I carried my billfold. Their guns were their American Express cards: they never left home without them.

We found the cave without difficulty, and it was clear that the mouth of the cave was large enough for a fairly big animal to go in and out without difficulty. In fact, a small cow could have entered the cave, if cows could walk on their knees–if cows have knees.

A large root from a nearby tree formed the top part of the cave entrance, and I could see short brown hairs clinging to the bottom part of the root. I raked some of the hairs into my hand and examined them. They were short, perhaps three-quarters of an inch long, about the color of a chocolate lab's hair, and as soft as a newborn kitten's fur.

I had never seen or felt hair like these samples. They definitely were not from a bear or even a panther. Nor were they human.

The hair from a bear's body is generally rather stiff and bristly; a panther's fur is soft but the color is sometimes black and often a dark tan. The root was too high for the hair to have come from a large dog or other domestic animal. I collected a handful of the hair and placed it in an envelope and returned the envelope to my pocket.

Meanwhile, the men stood in a half-circle around the mouth of the cave and dared Knobby to show his face. We had no lights, and there was no way that I was going into that dark cave. We looked around the outside and found more of the hair high on the trunks of trees, as if the animal or whatever it was had rubbed against the tree, either accidentally or to scratch himself. The hairs were about five feet, slightly more, perhaps, from the ground.

Later I took the hairs to a member of the science department of the college where I taught, and the professor examined the hair under a microscope and compared it with samples of other animal hair we had obtained. The conclusion was that the hair was not that of any animal we could use for comparison.

Then, abruptly, Knobby dropped out of sight. No one admitted seeing the creature, and although there were massive hunts, no evidence was found, other than a huge track that could not be identified. And while Bigfoot hunters from all over the world descended upon the tiny town of Casar, North Carolina, no one ever again saw Knobby.

Did the gentle Bigfoot actually exist? I never saw Knobby, and I never saw any real evidence that could convince me. But I know the people of the South Mountains, and they are not habitual liars. In fact, they are as truthful as anyone I have ever met.

So they saw *something*! And it was not a bear, deer, or cow. They saw a creature that they had never seen before. The mystery of Old Bill was never solved, and no one ever learned what had been using the cave near the site of Old Bill's death. I never met anyone with the courage and curiosity to enter the cave to make a real search for whatever made its home there. So the mystery remains.

It will not likely ever be solved. Some people attributed the uproar to overactive imagination. Others insist it was a case of mistaken identity. Still others argue moonshiners attempting to drive people away from their stills, and on and on it goes.

Is there a bigfoot lurking in the forests of the South Mountains? I have no idea, but I like to think there is. He'd have a hard time finding a more beautiful spot in which to spend his time. He'd have clear and clean streams from which to drink, lots of farmers who grow great foods for his meals, and many caves in which to find seclusion and warmth. Knobby could do much worse than live as our neighbor.

Ten
The Fan the Players Came to See

The scene was not a pretty one. The sun was blazing hot and the bunting draped about the speaker's stand had been ripped by wind and angry children whose parents had dragged them to the ball park for a spectacle they would never forget, and the crowd grew more unruly by the moment. It was obvious that there was going to be an ugly scene if someone didn't find a way to practice some major league damage control.

The crowds had come for a once-in-a-lifetime thrill: they were going to see and hear the President of the United States; better still, their children were going to be able to tell their grandchildren about the day the President came to town and they perhaps even worked their way close enough to touch the leader of the Free World.

But the President was a no-show. Earlier a spokesman for the President had called ahead to tell city fathers that Harry S. Truman would not visit their city, after all, because of the urgent need to change schedules at the last moment. And here the legend began, with myriads of versions.

When the announcement boomed over the speaker system, the chorus of boos erupted throughout the municipal ball park. Some of the people on the platform were actually worried about their welfare or even their lives. Too many people had missed a day of work, made a long trip to town, kept the children out of school, and endured the heat and the crowds.

For what? For nothing but sunburn and hunger and irritation.

Then the crowd fell ominously silent, the way the air grows heavy and thick just before a thunderbolt strikes. But the sky was clear and the air was fresh, if hot. There was no storm nearby. There was only the noise of the sullen crowd and the screaming children. Already throngs of people headed for the exits.

Then, at once, they stopped as if they had seen a horror beyond words. Or a miracle! The crowds parted as if they were the Red Sea and the apparition that made its way through the masses was the chariot of Moses. No one spoke. Even the children gaped in wonder, their reasons for crying already forgotten.

"Who is it?" someone finally asked. "Is it the President after all?"

"It looks like a carnival worker," another offered.

"It must be a clown," yet another whispered.

They were all wrong, and in another sense they were all nearly accurate. The vision they had witnessed was George McPoole, better known to people of the Piedmont as Lord Salisbury, the most colorful character in Christendom, as one writer dubbed him. He was, wrote another writer, the fan the players came to see. Here's how some people recall the man.

Lord Salisbury, sedately dressed for the occasion in a blue Prince Albert coat, red trousers, white shoes, a top hat, a necktie that reached below his knees, and blue and white shoes accented by red socks. He made his way through the crowd, motioned for his aides to bring their heavy burdens to the speaker's stand, and waved his hands for silence.

Then, at the walking rainbow's command, the helpers withdrew hot dogs, cold drinks, lollipops, and other goodies for the children and parents alike. While the men served the food, Lord Salisbury began an impromptu magic act, punctuated by clowning around, jokes, and a good time generally. When the entertainment ended, the crowd dispersed reluctantly and Lord Salisbury made his way back to the vehicle that delivered him to the ball park.

He left behind scores of questions. Who was this strange man in the outlandish costume? Why was he there? Who paid him? Where did he learn the magic and the clown's antics? What was his reason for the carnival type of show?

The answers to the questions are not easy. George McPoole was a gentle, quiet man who lived in the Salisbury/Spencer area. For many years he had worked as a railroad man, and before that, when he was still a youngster, he had left home temporarily to work in a traveling show. After he came home to stay, he fell in love with a beautiful young woman and married her, according to the stories that were passed around for years after the mirage first made his appearance in Salisbury. The stories also insisted that the marriage ended unhappily.

Or perhaps it ended tragically. No one seemed to know, and Lord Salisbury wasn't telling. The one constant rumor was that Lord Salisbury, or George McPoole as he was known then, had caught his beloved wife with another man. Another rumor held that McPoole had shot the rival for his wife's affection.

"Did you kill him?" someone asked.

"Well," the colorful man replied with a knowing nod of his head, "he's not alive today."

Another rumor insisted that the errant wife left the area and made her way to Hollywood, where she became a minor decoration in some low-budget movies. No one knows for certain how much truth could be found in any of the rumors.

After his marriage broke up, according to those who knew him best, McPoole went into deep depression. He began drinking heavily, and soon he moved out of his house and into a hotel. He spent his days in solitude and his nights in a stupor.

After months of dissipation, McPoole seemed doomed to end his days as a derelict. Then a friend came to the hotel room and tried to reason with him.

"There are more fish in the sea," the friend said. "So you should not waste your life pining for that particular one."

McPoole shook his head. "There was only one fish for me," he said, "and it is gone forever."

The friend persisted. "You have a unique gift," he said. "You have the ability to make people laugh. You should share your gift with the world. You should bring joy to people, and in doing so, you may find your own happiness."

Later, after the friend had departed, McPoole, so the stories go, left his hotel room for the first time in days, and he made his way down the street to a tailor's shop. There he put in his order for the first outlandish outfit. What happened is part truth, part myth, and part wishful thinking.

Several days later, the outfit delivered, McPoole removed his suit and white shirt and tie and replaced his traditional clothing with the green top hat, purple pants, blue shoes, polka-dotted necktie, red shirt, and the long-tailed yellow Prince Albert coat. He stared in the mirror at the bizarre creature and smiled. At that moment McPoole died and Lord Salisbury was born. And the people who saw him are not likely ever to forget him. He was the kind of person you see once and remember for a lifetime. You could not be indifferent to him. He filled his pockets with hard candy, suckers, chewing gum, and Kits or caramel candy packed in a small cardboard carton. Timidly he made his way to the door of the room, down the stairs, and out into the streets of Salisbury.

He didn't have to wait to see what the reaction of people would be. Instantly a throng of children saw him and started to follow him down the street. With each step he took, the crowd grew larger. Men and women now followed him to see what was going on, and he turned occasionally and tossed candy or other treats to the children.

Later, the day's trip a wonderful success, he placed more orders for more clothing. He added a long watch chain that draped down the front of his pants, and at the end of the chain there was a tiny toilet with a couple of crumpled-up one-dollar bills crammed in what he called the "thunder bowl."

He added three wrist watches for each arm, and then he added more for his ankles, so that he would know the time of day in major countries around the globe. He appended a monocle and walking cane to add extra class to the costume.

It took him several days to make his way to the baseball park, but when he arrived, he was an immediate sensation. One of his first acts upon arriving on the scene was to pull out a roll of bills and offer to bet fifteen yards of money that the Salisbury Pirates would win the game. That was in the days of Manager Tuck McWilliams, hard-hitting Hal Harrigan, and one of the first closers in baseball history, Chief Bennett and his enormous red hanky that he pulled out to wipe his glasses as he stood on the pitcher's mound. The team was already colorful, and Lord Salisbury added his own touches to the already varied palette.

If no one took him up on the bet, he'd remove the wad of money from his coat pocket and roll it down the aisle. The bills were taped together and they would unroll for the promised fifteen yards.

An instant hit at the ball park, Lord Salisbury became the team's official mascot, and so he became the father of a line of creatures that now inhabit every major league park, from the Bleacher Creature to the Philly Phanatic to the San Diego Chicken and other mascots of the past and present. He followed his team from town to town, and it was certain that when Salisbury came to town, the stands would be filled.

But he did not stop at the ball parks. Soon he was taking his act to the orphanages, old folks' homes, as they were known at the time, and to the homes of shut-ins or ill people. Wherever he went, sunshine followed him.

A devout fisherman, he liked to try his luck at the area lakes and ponds, and it was his boast that he never came home without catching at least one fish. Then one day his luck soured, and he walked home in despondency. A friend who managed a variety store saw him on the street and asked what was wrong. Lord Salisbury explained, and the manager took him by the arm and ushered him into the Dime Store (another quaint term gone by the wayside) and back to the aquarium. He invited Lord Salisbury to drop his hook into the goldfish tanks and fish until he had kept his record intact. After that, when he needed to do so, Lord Salisbury fished in the Dime Store.

His fame grew, and when he was in Atlanta for the minor league baseball convention, hotel owners publicly complained that he was unfair to them because he did not stay in a different hotel each night so they all could benefit from his crowd-attracting presence.

I met Lord Salisbury when I was playing minor league baseball, and I shall never forget the hush that fell over the crowd the moment the Walking Rainbow entered the stands. The game invariably halted so the players, too, could enjoy the one-man parade.

Lord Salisbury's health suffered badly many years ago, and when he was drawing near the end of his days, one sports writer said of him, "You are loved because you have the magnetism of a carnival; kids adore you; grown-ups come to the park just to hope you show up. They loved you because you have never used your tremendous popularity to try to make one penny for yourself."

At the peak of his career, Lord Salisbury reportedly would change clothes as often as nine times each day, and each change required from half an hour to a full hour. As his sartorial splendor increased, so did the number of fans. The Salisbury Pirates issued him a free season's pass each year, and he attended nearly all of their games.

More than once he was mistaken for P. T. Barnum. On other occasions people thought he was Judge Kenesaw Mountain Landis. He was baseball's Royal Ambassador at a time when life was simple and uncluttered and people needed a good laugh occasionally.

As he grew older, he had to cut back on his public appearances, but he refused to talk about retirement. He told his friends that when he died, he wanted to be dressed in his usual finery and that he was to lie in state for two days. He left a message for all who had enjoyed him in life to enjoy him in death. "Look, smile, and turn away," he said. That was his parting wish to the world.

At his death, his wishes were granted, at least in part. He lay in state while more than ten thousand people came by to pay their last respects. As expected, he was buried in a gray suit, yellow shirt, and blue tie. The inside of the casket was an eggshell white, the exterior two shades of rich wine.

One editor, in his farewell address to Lord Salisbury said, "God pity the people who go through life never breaking precedent. Solomon in all his glory was never arrayed as Lord Salisbury. It is unnecessary to wish you long life and happiness for one who goes about making the world smile never grows old." The Lord Salisbury philosophy was simple: Never hurt anyone intentionally or say anything that will injure another. Devote as much time to bringing joy as you do to serving selfish interests. When faced with adversity, look, smile, and turn away.

It wasn't only the loud clothing that made Lord Salisbury an outstanding person, but it helped. It was an outward manifestation of the joy that he offered to those around him, although at first he was unable to feel the joy himself. But as he helped others, he helped himself. George Poole, later McPoole, was once asked how he merited the title of a lord. His reply was that he had lived his life honestly and simply, that he had never been guilty of crimes or of taking advantage of the less fortunate. He added that in these respects, he was certainly a cut above the people who had their titles handed down to them through government decrees.

The loudest dressed critter in Christendom is gone, but his legacy lives on in the laughter of children, the deep smiles of total contentment on the faces of those who still celebrate the goodness of mankind, and he lives especially in the hearts of those who find a fantastic thrill each time they go to the ball park and see grown men playing a child's game, with the enjoyment of a child.

The Lord Salisbury legend, one that I had a personal relationship with many years ago, is essentially forgotten. In fact, many of the items included in this story were handed down to me by old sports writers, who could supplement their memories from notes. The legend will be missed.

Well left above ground in Chimney Rock area

The raging flood waters undermined railroads and left wells above ground as the waters washed away entire hillsides.

Eleven

Nature on a Rampage: The 1916 Floods

Mrs. Pearl Alwran and her husband woke in the middle of the night of July 16, 1916, to the noise of shouting outside the house. Neighbors were yelling and hammering on the door, and Mr. Alwran yelled at the people to go away and let them sleep.

"Get out of bed," the night-callers shouted. "The river is rising and you are going to be washed away."

Now wide awake, the Alwrans stepped out of bed and found themselves knee-deep in water. Dressing in panic, they rushed outside to safety. Minutes later their house joined dozens of others that were carried away by the flood waters of the river.

Like thousands of others, the families stood helplessly as the waters continued to rise, as did the damages. Countless millions of dollars worth of property (more than one million dollars in losses to Southern Railway Company alone, back when a million dollars was an incomprehensible amount of money). It was a parlor game back then to try to imagine a million bucks–when a dollar would buy thirty-three large candy bars, ten Turkish towels, or twelve pounds of steak or cheese. Today a million dollars will buy fifty brand-new automobiles fairly well equipped. In 1919 the same amount of money would buy two thousand new cars. Today you can buy four well-appointed new houses with a million dollars. In 1916 you could buy one hundred beautiful houses.

In light of the actual losses, that is, the monetary value at the time as compared to the present, the catastrophe is almost unimaginable. Other businesses and private individuals lost in the thousands of dollars.

Near Chimney Rock the erosion was so great that wells were actually left 12 feet above ground as the rubblestone walls of the wells remained intact as the soil washed away. In Asheville the French Broad River was dotted with houses, barns, and other farm and city buildings washed away. Railway equipment was crushed by debris, and tracks were twisted like spaghetti by the power of the flood. Landslides between Asheville and Chimney Rock left road cuts covered with up to 25 feet of mud, rocks, and uprooted trees.

In some areas the slides were so deep that it looked as if the railroad or the highway had been constructed up to the side of a mountain and then deserted. Near Old Fort 85,000 cubic yards of soil washed out from under railroad tracks, leaving 120 feet of railway hanging suspended in midair. In ancient photos taken days after the flood there are five men standing at arm's length from each other on the tracks, and below them for a hundred feet there is nothing but air.

What caused the devastating floods? The mountains and local rivers had been the scene of heavy rainfalls many times before, and there had been nothing comparable to the damage suffered in 1916. The key to the tragedy was the union of two cyclones that hit the South at almost the same time.

Professor Alfred J. Henry of the United States Weather Bureau wrote that the first storm came inland on the Mississippi coast and veered north. As the storm weakened, it passed into Tennessee and then into the North Carolina mountains.

Then the second storm hit, coming in from the South Carolina coast. Winds in excess of 100 miles per hour toppled trees and forced the low clouds against the mountains, where rain fell in torrents for over two days.

In the early hours of the storm eight to ten inches of rain fell on the mountains to the west of Rutherford and Cleveland counties. Small trickles became creeks, creeks became rivers, and rivers became uncontrollable monsters that demolished everything in their paths.

Then the really heavy rains began. Within 24 hours the rainfall exceeded 22 inches. As the waters funneled down from the mountains, Piedmont and Foothills rivers rose alarmingly. In nearby Gaston County, in the town of Mount Holly, the Catawba River crested at 45.5 feet, a total of 22.5 feet higher than ever recorded before. Waters reached the eaves of mills along the river, and in downtown areas the flood level reached almost to the cross members of the power poles.

In nearby Belmont, uprooted trees and other debris washed up against the bridge over the Catawba River and exerted such immense force that it was apparent that the bridge could not stand unless the trees were cut away. So every available man was sent onto the bridge to try to push or cut away the debris.

Work had to be stopped several times to allow trainloads of peaches to cross the railroad trestle. The delays caused by the market-bound peaches may have been an indirect cause of one of the worst tragedies in the Foothills and Piedmont areas.

As waters rose higher and higher, a 250-foot section of the embankment at each end of the bridge suddenly gave way, and at 5:53 P.M. the entire bridge collapsed. At the time there were 19 men on the bridge, and some of them were killed by the collapsing steel; others were drowned.

Somehow, miraculously, nine of the men were saved. Some clutched boards and clung to them in order to stay afloat, while others swam or were carried by the current to nearby trees where they clung to branches in the tops of the trees, where they remained all night and part of the following day.

By dawn the river had risen 55 feet above normal. When it was light enough for rescue operations to begin, two men in a boat spotted several men in the treetops, and when the boat neared the trees, the current overturned the boat and dumped the men into the river as the boat was swept away.

The two men in the boat, B. M. English and H. T. Verner, joined the men in the treetops and waited for a second rescue attempt, which was accomplished by two other men, Alfonso Ross and Peter Stowe, who managed to maneuver a flat-bottomed boat close enough to the trees for the men to climb aboard.

Eventually all of the highway bridges and railroad bridges were washed away. Buffalo Creek rose high enough that a number of bridges were either washed away or destroyed, and even in the "uplands" part of Cleveland County the waters rose dangerously high as small streams increased in volume and depth and threatened cows in pastures as well as houses and barns.

In northern Cleveland County there still stands a tree with a spike in it, according to local residents, to mark the water level. The First Broad River overflowed its banks and the water spread across pastures and crop lands, and in Rutherford County the Rocky Broad River rose with incredible speed and volume.

Rev. Furman Wright, now 90 years old, was one of the eyewitnesses to the flood who is still here to tell what he saw.

"We lived in Upper Cleveland County at the time, and I don't remember the flood all that well," he said, "since I was only about seven years old. But I remember that my father, who sold Rawleigh goods, hitched up two mules to an old surry and started on a sales trip. He came to a small creek nearby and began to cross the bridge when the waters washed away the bridge, and my father, the mules, and the surry fell into the water. Somehow, my father turned loose of the reins and the mules managed to get free of the surry and swim to shore. My father also swam out of the creek that was by this time a river. I don't remember what ever happened to the surry and the Rawleigh products in it."

Fred and Lillian Mintz, who now live on NC 10 near Delight, have distant memories of the flood. Lillian at the time lived in the northern part of the county and Fred lived in Shelby. Both were very young at the time, but Fred Mintz recalls that his father took him to see the results of the flood.

"Bridges were washed out all along the streams," Mintz recalls, "and the damage was awful. Beyond that, I don't have that many memories of the flood."

In Rutherford County, the damage was also devastating. Because Hickory Nut Gorge is so deep and narrow, the space could not handle the rising waters, and the entire gorge area was damaged severely. In more recent years the gorge sustained great damage, but, according to published reports, the 1916 flooding and damage were more extensive.

A Gaston County native, E. M. Fant, composed a poem shortly after the flooding occurred. The poem in part reads:

"Long and constant poured the rain,/ Till each brooklet, creek, and drain/ Made a torrent deep and wide./ Then Catawba from her head,/ By these dashing waters fed/ Roughly rolled undefied./ Bridge and trestle swept away/ Dams and houses, too, they say,/ Till they reached the Southern Main./ There the railroad called a crew/ To save its trains and trestles, too./ But their efforts were in vain...."

Fant then recounts the tragedy of the 19 men on the bridge which collapsed. But the tragedy in the Piedmont is only part of the story. By today's standards, property loss and damage would run into the billions of dollars, and the loss of lives would have been enormous.

Today it is impossible to imagine the power of the waters that swept through the area in mid-July 1916. At points along the Broad River, the flood level is 4.4 feet. Within little more than one day the level rose to 18.6 feet. It cannot be known for certain, but about 80 persons died.

Standing timber loss was $3 million, and loss of crops was estimated to be, based on an evaluation of $10 per acre, $2.5 million. This does not include business tangible losses and the costs of shutdowns for business or the loss of income, but total losses were estimated at $22 million.

Professor Henry noted that it is extremely rare for cyclonic synchronization to occur, and he stated, mildly, that the floods of 1916 were, indeed, likely to be the storm of the century. But in this particular time period the cyclonic synchronization in fact occurred and left scars that will require decades more to heal.

If you want an example of what the water did, drive or hike into the woods above Morganton or in the Doughton Park area, and you will see where entire towns were washed away. In the Doughton Park forest you can still see huge grinding wheels and other heavy materials that were washed downstream by the small creek that became a raging river in a period of a few hours. Nearly every part of eastern Tennessee and western North Carolina was deeply affected by the flood, and anyone who is not grateful for the many flood-control dams erected along the major streams in the watershed area might want to take a long, hard look at the remaining photos of the floods of 1916. It's a picture that no one wants to see repeated.

Xi Bradley, the first and the last of the initial unit of World War II submarine hunters, spent his early life in Polkville, and after the war he returned to live out his days there. In addition to his military service, he was one of the finest woodworkers in the South. He never attended a reunion in Manteo. He said the pain was too great to endure a second time.

Twelve
The Last of the First Sub Hunters

December 7, 1941, is indeed an anniversary of a day that will live in infamy for millions of Americans old enough to remember the devastating news that the Japanese had bombed Pearl Harbor. For the vast majority of these same people, however, December 8 will be only another day on the calendar.

Not for Xi Bradley of Polkville. Bradley recalled the day with startling detail, because it was the day he returned to the Manteo area on the North Carolina coast, but not for a vacation.

Bradley, less than 24 hours after the sneak attack that launched the United States into World War II, was on active duty as a member of a little-known contingent of this nation's war effort. As a member of the 42nd Wing of the North Carolina Civil Air Patrol (now the Coastal Patrol), Bradley, along with about twenty other volunteers, decided to take the war to the Germans rather than wait for them to come to us.

"We received the news that they were coming," Bradley said, referring to the vicious undersea battle operation known as the "Great American Turkey Shoot" or as Paukenschlag. "We heard the news that German U-boats were on the way to the United States East Coast, and their plan was to sink as many military ships as they possibly could between our coast and England. And our job was to fly over the Atlantic Ocean and spot the submarines."

The task was a formidable one. German Admiral Doenitz had mapped out a brilliant if ruthless military strategy in which a handful of U-boats could terrorize American vessels in the shipping lanes. As many as eight or 10 subs and at times as few as two destroyed ship after ship and killed hundreds of American and foreign sailors or merchant seamen.

"The British spies reported that the Germans had said that if they could whip the United States they would have no trouble with their plan to conquer Europe," Bradley said, "and our job was to locate and help destroy as many U-boats as possible."

For those who have forgotten or have never known just how close the war was to the United States and to this area, it is worth a couple of minutes to stop and reflect that Japanese bombers attacked the West Coast and flew inland as far as Idaho where they dropped incendiary bombs to burn forest lands.

On the East Coast German U-boats lay just off shore and waited for supply ships to sail near them. One German U-boat sank three ships in a period of only seven minutes. It was widely reported that it was possible to sit on the beach at Ocracoke Island and read a newspaper at midnight by the light of burning ships just off the coast.

"Our job was to fly every day all day in our search for the submarines," Bradley explains. "We'd fly out 200 miles and turn at a 45-degree angle and fly 200 more miles. Then we'd make another 45-degree turn and fly 200 miles back toward land. We made flights over the water from the Virginia coast down to Beaufort, North Carolina."

Just how likely were the pilots to spot a German U-boat? Or were the flights only window dressing?

"We spotted four subs in one morning," Bradley recalls. "We saw submarines regularly. One day we spotted a sub that had come to the surface, and we flew as close as we could and dropped a depth charge. We were lucky enough that the bomb went right into the sub's conning tower. We radioed back to the base and had diver bombers fly out to finish off the sub."

One day Bradley was on a flight when he saw a sight that startled him even more than the presence of the subs off the coast. There were two German submarines so close to the Ocracoke coast that the water, Bradley recalls, was only about 10 feet deep on one side of the sub and less than that on the shore side. German sailors had stepped off the sub and had waded onto the beach and were walking toward town.

"We called in our report and the Germans were captured, and I later had the chance to talk to them through an interpreter. One of the men talked openly," Bradley said, "and he told us that he and the others wanted to surrender. He said that Hitler had given them a choice: either man the subs or be killed."

The constant flights became an almost unbearable strain for many people, and several had to leave the patrol.

"We'd fly over the ocean for hours at a time, day after day," Bradley said, "and strain our eyes trying to see through the water. There'd be signs of submarines regularly. There would be an oil slick that told us that subs were nearby. German oil was not like ours. It glittered on the surface of the water, and we'd know the instant we saw it that the sub was near."

The strain was not just the realization that there were enemy vessels just under the surface of the Atlantic. A major part of the stress came from the fact that if the subs were not destroyed, then hours later hundreds of men might die when the sub sank one of the ships carrying supplies to England.

Often the subs tried to hide, but others made a different choice. They fought back.

"The subs had to surface in order to use their machine guns," Bradley said, "and we had them come after us. When they opened fire, we had no choice but to high-tail it out of the area. Our commanders told us that we were observers, not fighters. Our planes were not bombers or fighter planes."

Bradley's memories are understandably painful. He recalls a radio call that came from a friend one day while Bradley was flying on his regular route.

"The memory of that day will never leave me as long as I live," Bradley said. "A good friend named Frank Cook called me on the radio and told me he was going down and needed help. He said he couldn't last long in the rough water. Neither the plane nor the body of the friend was ever recovered."

It's such memories that keep Bradley from attending the reunions of the sub patrol pilots.

"I had a letter a few weeks ago from the person in charge of the reunion," Bradley says. "He told me that of the original group that I flew with, I was the only one left. It's a hard, lonely feeling to be the only one left. We were real friends, and now they are gone."

He adds that there were several members alive from the groups that came later, but, as he put it, "I understand that I am the last of the first sub-hunters. They offered to fly up here and pick me up and take me to the reunion, but I told them I didn't want to face all that heartache again."

Bradley, 82 years old at the time of the interview and suffering from throat cancer in its advanced stages, never saw the monument that was erected near the Manteo airport. Unveiled on April 27, 1997, the memorial is in honor of the World War II personnel of the Civil Air Patrol, Coastal Patrol Base 16. The thirteenth name on the memorial is that of Xi A. Bradley. Bradley died shortly after I had the pleasure and honor of interviewing him.

But there is another memorial that is even larger than the one Xi Bradley never saw. It is not on a hillside near the coast: it is in the heart and mind of Xi Bradley, and it is a tribute to all the men and women who began on December 8, 1941, the fight to preserve this nation. No winds or rains of time will ever dim the tribute.

Men like Xi and his friends, actually boys rather than men in many cases, left homes, loved ones, and the security of their towns and cities far from the noise and deadly atmosphere of the battlefield, and they did so in order to protect the same loved ones and the same homes and towns and cities. They also did it to protect the children who were yet unborn, and to make their world a safer place to grow into manhood and womanhood.

And there should be another memorial, this one in the hearts of those of us who owe an immense debt of gratitude to men like Xi Bradley and all of the other members of the anti-sub patrol and every other American who risked—or lost—their lives in defense of this country. It's not a bad idea to send an extra Christmas card, just to thank these people for their Christmas gift to all of us.

Xi won't be there to read the cards this year or in the years to come, but his friends and loved ones will be. So will the loved ones of all the others who took the war to the Germans, and in so doing they helped to win the war with the Axis. And, in doing this, they made the world a much better place for all of us.

Thirteen
The Tallest Man I Ever Met

Many years ago a friend asked me if I'd like to ride with him over to meet Hilliard Littlejohn. My friend said that I'd come away with a new appreciation for life, health, and living in general if I met Littlejohn.

We made the short drive from the Shelby area to the tiny community of Lawndale, four miles west of NC 18 from Fallston. Littlejohn was working in his yard when we arrived at the tiny house located on a small tract of land alongside a rural paved road. As we drove up, Littlejohn smiled at us, and that one facial expression was enough to drive away all the dark clouds that had hung low in the sky for the entire day. I have never beheld a more beautiful, almost beatific, smile than the one Hilliard Littlejohn beamed at us.

His face was weatherbeaten and strong, like a tree that has withstood numerous storms. As I shook hands with him when we were introduced, I noted that his head barely reached to the level of my belt. I also noted that his long, slender arms were knots of muscle. I don't know that I had ever seen a more incredibly muscled arm in my life. As he moved, thick muscles across his back bulged with the slightest effort he made.

"It's a beautiful day," he told us, and, suddenly, it was. Birds, unheard earlier, now sang almost frantically. There was a sweetness of late-blossoming honeysuckle in the air, and the low clouds had drifted away so that the August sun beat down mercilessly on us, but I don't think we noticed.

I know Hilliard Littlejohn did not notice. I doubt that the fires of blast furnaces would have affected him. He impressed me instantly as the kind of man who could endure intense heat or cold and never be bothered in the least. He was impervious to physical discomfort.

At least, that's the impression I received. He stood there in the broiling sun and beamed his smile and pumped my hand as if I had been the dearest friend he had in the world.

And I suspect that I was. At the same time there is no ego in the thought. Hilliard Littlejohn made everyone he met feel as if that person were the dearest friend on earth. If he didn't become your friend in an instant, then you became his friend.

Littlejohn was not a midget or a dwarf. His feet simply did not develop, and, as incredible as it sounds, he was forced to walk upon his knees wherever he went. In the brief schooling he had, he had to walk upon his knees to and from the schoolhouse. When he worked in the fields, he walked on his knees to and from the fields, and he worked on his knees the entire day.

It hurts to think about the pain and exhaustion he had to endure with each step. You've been there briefly. Think about the times you have had to kneel on a rough surface for a few minutes while you completed some task. Think of the times when, as a child, you walked on your knees across a carpet or hardwood floor.

Now think about walking along a gravel road on your knees. The pain has to be beyond comprehension and endurance. Yet this man did it every day of his life.

Hilliard Littlejohn, during one long period in his life, walked ten to twelve miles each day to work, and while on the job he stood on his knees and used a huge broad shovel to scoop up sand to throw onto the back of a dump truck. The shovels of sand were extremely heavy, and the endless hours of work created the corded muscles in his arms, chest, shoulders, and back.

"I'm not bragging," he said, "but I could stand out there in the heat and throw that sand all day long. I never met a man I could not put in the shade. Some could stay with me for a while, but soon they'd be over under the shade trees and trying to cool off."

When the long work day was done, Littlejohn then walked all the way back home–on his knees! To ease the pain, he fashioned homemade pads to tie around his knees, but these wore out in one short walk. He then used some of his hard-earned money and bought leather pads to buckle around his knees. The pads lasted for several days, and they made his life immeasurably more comfortable while they endured.

When he was a child, Littlejohn never asked for nor received preferential treatment. He knew that he, like every other person in the fields and like every member of the family, had to pull his own weight. There was no room for idlers in the Great Depression era. The meager supply of food came only when everyone contributed. People worked although they were sick, injured, old, or young.

The bottom line was simple: everyone worked. No one shirked.

"I didn't mind the work," Littlejohn said. "My Momma was out there working. So was my Daddy and all the brothers and sisters and cousins and everyone else. I just told them all I'd be all right as long as I was with my family. And when I worked for other people, I was all right there, too, just as long as I was working for a good man. And if I had to work for a man less than good, why, that was all right, too, because I was out there in that big field with God watching over me and loving me. I knew He'd never stop caring about me, just as my Momma never stopped loving me."

Did he suffer in the cotton fields because he had to walk on his knees?

"Not one bit," he said. "All I asked was a wide row and a long-handled hoe."

As he grew from childhood into manhood, Littlejohn held down many jobs, and employers were never happy to see him go.

"I gave the Man a full day's work for a good day's pay," he said, "and if the pay wasn't so good, I made sure the work was."

Eventually Littlejohn found a woman he could love and who could love him, and they were married and reared one son. Then, when the son was just entering the richest years of early manhood, tragedy struck again.

A hit-and-run driver struck the younger Littlejohn almost in front of the family house and killed him instantly. The driver was never identified. Not long afterwards, while the family was still in mourning, a thief broke into the house and stole all the money Mr. and Mrs. Littlejohn had put back for a rainy day. Gone were social security money and the tiny savings of the two.

Littlejohn found a way to smile in the face of this adversity, too. He refused to let life's roadblocks become stumbling blocks. "When you are as low to the ground as I am," he said, "you don't have far to fall. And I learned not to worry about things that can't be corrected or avoided."

Hilliard Littlejohn preparing to till his garden

He added, "And it's never so far back up as it might be for some people. You do the best you can with what you have."

I had to ask the question. I needed an explanation, and my own life's experiences had never prepared me for a man as stoical and as fiercely independent and at the same time so neighborly and loving as was Hilliard Littlejohn.

"How do you continue to smile when your entire world seems ready to end?" I asked him. "How can you take the worst blows that life has to offer and still keep a smile on your face? How can you keep on keeping on?"

He flashed the huge smile again. "My Momma taught me a real lesson when I was just a tiny thing," he said. "She told me that if I ever had my head in the lion's mouth, I must work real easy till I got it out. That's what I try to do: work real easy till I get the problem beat."

Life also taught him many lessons that are not learned in school. When he was a child, the nation was not as attuned to the needs of the special people as it is today. If Hilliard Littlejohn were a child in this age, he'd perhaps have sophisticated surgery to equip him to face the world better. At the very least he'd probably have a car with special gears and accelerator and brake mechanism.

But what he wanted and needed were challenges to be met. If he needed a platform from which to pull the starter cord for his tiller, he built it. If he needed a special railing for the back steps, he built that, too.

He learned what many people never suspect: that there is a world out there that can be unspeakably hard and cruel, not just for a few hours at a time but every waking moment of every day. It's hard for us to realize that there was pain in every step he took, even if the step was on carpet, which he could never afford. We walk across the yard in relative comfort, never realizing that a tiny piece of gravel, a chip, or a sliver of glass can create severe pain for a man like Littlejohn.

When I saw him afterwards, he never seemed to change. Once while I worked as a finder for a network television show, I asked if he'd like to appear on television and show the world what a real man is like.

"I don't think so," he said. "If the world don't know by now, they won't know when they see me."

A few years ago Hilliard Littlejohn died, and although I wasn't there, I have a good idea how he met death: with a smile as broad as a river and as sparkling as meadow frost on a sunny morning. And I think that as he met his Maker, he had already decided how to face that adventure, too. I know how he did it, I think.

By standing tall and looking his Maker squarely in the eye and asking for a long-handled hoe and a wide row. And he'd go to work. I doubt that he'd even ask for feet. A man who has learned how to live fully and deeply here on earth will have no problems hereafter. If he should, by an incredible continued streak of what some people would call bad luck, find himself in the wrong direction, he'd simply work real easy till he got his head out of that particular lion's mouth. And he'd smile while he did it.

But he didn't go that way. Not Littlejohn. Somewhere, Up There, he's the tallest man they've ever seen, and his smile is as beautiful as the most resplendent rainbow. And he's happy. Still!

The old mill at East Monbo jutted out into the Catawba River so that workers could watch their machines and their fishing rods at the same time. At the end of the day the mill "hands" often left with a stringer full of fish as well as memories of a great baseball game.

Lake Norman now covers the original Field of Dreams, and you can catch bass where second base once was. The small mountain jutting up out of the water was once the center field fence.

Fourteen
East Monbo: the First Field of Dreams

Many years ago while I was still in high school, in the tenth grade, in fact, I was invited to pitch for the Phoenix team in the old Tri-County League. The league included teams from Statesville, Long Island, Mooresville Mills, Cascade Mills, Taylorsville, Hiddenite, and a few other bucolic locales. But none of the teams we played could hold a candle to the East Monbo nine, who had, if not the greatest team in the league, the greatest ball park I have ever witnessed.

First, East Monbo no longer exists; it is only a fond, wonderful, exultant memory. It now lies at the bottom of one of the northern reaches of Lake Norman, and fisherman now land bass where once there was second base.

East Monbo was just across the river from Long Island, another of the mill villages that loved baseball, partially because there were many superb players and particularly because there was no other form of recreation in the community, other than fishing and swimming. To say the town was tiny was like admitting the Grand Canyon is special.

To get to East Monbo back then, and this was in the later forties and early fifties, you drove along a quiet, serene, and enjoyable stretch of asphalt until the road ended suddenly and you were in the middle of this dramatically small textile village. So at that point you either turned around or you stayed for the baseball game.

There were houses, many of them surprisingly large, at the top of a steep hill. Just before you turned sharply to the right and started down the hill, you could see the company store which represented the downtown economic life of the village.

The hill was surprisingly steep, and you kept your foot firmly on the brakes as you descended. If you lost control of your car, chances were excellent that you would find yourself eye-to-eye with a huge catfish or carp or bass.

At the bottom of the hill stood the mill, its west walls jutting out into the Catawba River for a hundred feet or more and the entire mill, other than the east wall, actually resting in the water. The mill must have been five hundred feet long, or more, and the Catawba swirled endlessly around the piers.

As workers walked down the hill to the mill, you could see their lunch buckets swinging from one hand. In the other hand there was likely to be either a rod and reel or a cane pole with fishing line attached. As the workers started their shifts, one of the first duties was to see that all the machinery was working properly. The second was to open a window and cast a baited hook and line into the river. As the "hands" continued with their work, the only interruptions came when the tip of the fishing rod or the cane pole began to jerk and dip in a series of quick, spasmodic movements.

Instantly other workers took over machinery that could not be shut down, and the owner of the fishing gear would rush to the window and to the fishing pole and begin to reel in the fish or he would pull in the line, hand-over-hand, until the flopping and frantic fish lay on the floor of the mill. The successful fisherman would then slip the fish onto a stringer that was attached to a nail in the window framing, and the line of fish would be dropped back into the river to remain there until the end of the shift.

At the end of the shift the workers trudged up the long hill, their lunch bucket in one hand and fishing gear–and fish–in the other.

The place was not a paradise; in fact, the mill work was as dull and generally unrewarding as mill work was everywhere else in the county. But when games started in late afternoon and the air was heavy with the scent of the hillside honeysuckle, the river sparkling off the left field foul line, and the birds singing, it was magnificent.

Starting in April and continuing through September, the East Monbo baseball team competed in the Tri-County League, with the players being given time off from their jobs to compete for the league championship. It was essentially true of all the mills that sponsored teams in the league that the players received "benefits" of various sorts.

In my particular case, I was still a high school student when I began to play, and at the end of the first game I pitched the manager of the team presented me with a small brown bag filled with loose change and occasional one-dollar bills or even a fiver now and then. He told me that the money was my "profit" from the concession stand, which I managed, he assured me, during each game.

It was the first I had heard of my new duty, and since I never once set foot in the concession stand, I didn't mind the extra work, which consisted solely of transferring the money from the bag to my pockets. Later, when I actually worked at the mill, the section bosses had someone punch our time card so that we were "on the clock" while we played ball or slept or whatever the occasion demanded or permitted.

My greatest thrill in those days was to play at East Monbo, where the field beside the river presented an incredible sight: flat infield with reddish brown dirt raked as smooth as a tabletop, an outfield of rich green grass clipped as precisely as if a barber had manicured it, and in the outfield a huge mountain erupted shockingly at the end of the outfield grass. The mountain conveniently curved from the right field line and then curved around through center field and to left field until the mountain ended precipitously at the very edge of the river.

During games, it was not uncommon for foul balls to land in the river, and on more than one occasion I witnessed the third baseman or the shortstop doing a header into the Catawba as the fielders chased a long pop fly. On a sultry August afternoon the quick dip, whether the ball was caught or not, was a welcome relief.

Some of the best players in the Tar Heel state performed at East Monbo, and among these were right-handed pitcher Joe Harris of the Scotts community and Efird Gwaltney, a one-eyed and wild-eyed left-handed pitcher and formidable hitter. Both men could throw the ball at speeds estimated to be in the ninety-mile to hundred-mile-an-hour speeds.

In one contest Joe Harris pitched a perfect game, and in another game Gwaltney not only pitched well but hit a pair of homers as well.

Keep in mind that these two men played against each other on many occasions, with Harris pitching for East Monbo and Gwaltney for Taylorsville, Stony Point, or Hiddenite. And whenever the two men met on the baseball diamond, you could expect fireworks.

On one particular afternoon the score was tied as the two fiery competitors matched one another's scoreless innings. Then, as the sun was settling behind the trees across the Catawba, Harris took the mound for what was to be the last inning of the game.

The right field "fence," or mountain, was about 350 feet from home plate. In left field the base of the mountain was approximately 325 feet. In dead center field the mountain base was about 380 feet from home plate.

As Harris fired his final fast ball of the game, Gwaltney, who later played several years of professional baseball, swung from the heels and connected. The ball soared to an incredible height, arcing gracefully over the centerfielder's head, and disappeared into the tops of the trees on the very peak of the mountain.

There's no way to tell how far the ball traveled but there is no doubt that it flew more than five hundred feet and probably far more. In nearly twenty years of organized baseball, I never saw a ball hit so hard or so far.

By the way, players were not the only ones to get preferential treatment. Any of the employees could leave the mill and go outside to watch the game. The only stipulation was that at least one person had to assume the duty of keeping an eye on the machinery.

One day the mill superintendent came to the game and counted noses. It occurred to him that it could not be possible for any of the workers to be inside the mill. He stormed up to the spectators and yelled at them that someone had to keep an eye on the machinery.

At this point one of the workers, a patch over one eye, took the boss man inside and pointed to the worker's glass eye resting atop one of the machines. "If that ain't keeping an eye on the machines, what is?" the worker demanded. The boss had no further questions.

Those days are gone. The mill was demolished and hauled away, and the workers found new places to work. But they never found any place as beautiful as the river, the baseball diamond with the mountain for a fence: the original Field of Dreams.

Fifteen
The Store That Rolled Through History

I f the mountain will not come to Mohammed," the founder of
Islam reportedly said, "then Mohammed will go to the mountain."

That same type of logic prompted John W. Bell, the Lattimore entre-
preneur, to start one of the most innovative and interesting businesses in
the Foothills area. If the customers cannot come to the store, Bell reasoned, then the store will go to the customers.

And it did. Starting in 1938, Bell's Rolling Store, or the Store on
Wheels, began an enterprise that is now legendary in this part of the country. The beauty of the operation was not that John Bell wanted to make a
profit only: those who knew him well pointed out that the driving force
behind the businessman was a spirit of humanity and generosity.

Bell operated a highly successful store in Lattimore, starting in 1930,
and at the central store Bell sold food, hardware, and clothing, among
many other items. While business was good, Bell was aware that few
people in the area owned automobiles, and those with mules or horses and
wagons could ill afford the time needed to make the trip from the outer
reaches of Cleveland and Rutherford counties to Lattimore.

So Bell first opened satellite stores. He then had the original store on
New House Road, the store in downtown Lattimore, and one in Hollis.

But still the needs of customers weren't being met fully. Regularly
during the day people living near the stores called to order food or supplies, and Bell's truck delivered groceries and other commodities to the
nearby residents.

And then Bell came up with the idea of expanding his service to
include virtually every community within driving distance of the main store.
He started by buying a used truck and remodeling it so that he could haul
an enormous amount of merchandise.

The original plan was for the truck to deliver to homes within 12 to 15 miles of the store, with the driver taking a different route each day so that in one week the truck could cover the six major market destinations.

At this point Bell realized that there was another need that his service had not addressed: the farmers who could not drive into town to buy their supplies also could not drive into town to market their crops. At this point Bell arrived at the ideal solution.

He purchased three huge trucks and outfitted them so that the driver could deliver orders to the farmers and at the same time the driver could load up the farmer's produce and bring it into town to sell it. In many cases, because money was in short supply, there was simply a trade.

The three trucks each covered different routes each day of the week. For example, one driver recalls that on Monday he delivered and picked up goods in the Mooresboro-Cliffside area. On Tuesday he covered the Boiling Springs-Number One Township. On Wednesday he drove along the old road past the airport and to Earl and Patterson Springs. On Thursday he delivered and picked up in the Waco area. On Friday the truck covered Belwood, Lawndale, and Casar. And, finally, on Saturday, the driver saturated the Grover area.

Each trip was a 12-hour jaunt which covered up to 100 miles. Because Bell sold his merchandise at bargain prices, the farmers welcomed the delivery truck. And because Bell paid market price or higher for the farmer's goods, the farmers had double reason to welcome the opportunity to have a visit from the Store on Wheels.

On a busy day one driver might haul out 2,500 pounds of goods and return late that same day with 3,000 pounds of farm products that he picked up while delivering his original merchandise.

"My father got into the Rolling Store business because there was a need to be met," says Steve Bell, who owns Bell's Antiques on New House Road, just across the street from where his father's original store once stood. "He got out for an altogether different reason: World War II made gas and tires hard to find, and many of the workers left to go into service."

Bell recalls that when he was a boy he would occasionally ride along with the drivers, sometimes as far as New York City. "My father sold nearly everything people could want," he said, "and he traded for almost anything anyone else would need. Because they were relatively easy to keep, many farmers owned chickens. This meant that there were eggs unlimited as well as surplus chickens. So the drivers traded overalls or cross-cut saws for chickens, and then one of our long-haul drivers delivered the chickens to markets up north. Many of them were taken to Philadelphia, and while he was there the driver would trade the chickens a second time, this time for antiques. That's how Bell's Antiques had its origin."

Bell particularly recalls one trip to New York City.

"We went up there on a delivery, and while we were there we picked up a bell my father had purchased. The bell was to be put on top of the store as a symbol of our family name and also as the national symbol. This bell was made like the original Liberty Bell. It even had a crack in it."

The bell, incidentally, can still be seen atop Horne's Super Market in Lattimore.

And today, half a century after the close of the Rolling Store or the Store on Wheels, Foothills residents recall the delivery trucks with nostalgic pleasure. One such resident is Irene Luckadoo.

"When I was a little girl," Mrs. Luckadoo recalls, "there wasn't much money and there wasn't much way for us to go places. So one of the exciting times came when the Rolling Store came to the house. I remember that my mother bought me shoes for nearly nothing. It was amazing what all that truck carried out to us, and just as amazing what it took back to town after it left us."

Irene Luckadoo wasn't the only one impressed by Bell's innovative idea. Jim Kluttz, who visited the store in 1938, wrote an article that same year for State Magazine in which he said, "His (Bell's) employees have all been very enthusiastic over the work, and they have in a large part been responsible for the success of the 'Store on Wheels.' His customers are behind him 100 per cent, and cooperate with him in every respect. But the main thing standing behind his success in this venture is his complete honesty, and his desire to be of the greatest possible service to the people in the rural communities of Cleveland and Rutherford counties."

One must wonder just how many of the modern megastores in this area that same comment could be made about. Colon Melton, of Boiling Springs, was only a boy when he accepted his first job, but he knew how to work. As part of his duties, he often helped with the grinding of corn meal at John Bell's operation.

"I met Mr. Bell one day, and he immediately asked me if I'd like to come and work for him," Melton said, recalling how he came to accept a position that would be the only job he held during his entire working life.

"I took the job, but when Mr. Bell asked me how I would get from my home to the store, which were miles apart, I told him I'd get there some way or another. But Mr. Bell asked me how I'd like to live with him and his family," he said.

That was the beginning of an exceptional employer-employee relationship. "Mr. Bell was a wonderful man," Melton recalls. "He owned what was the equivalent of a Wal-Mart store today. When I went to work for him, I had no idea I'd never leave the store to look for other work. The only time I was away from the job was when I served as a soldier in World War II."

At first Melton worked in the corn meal and hammer mill part of the store, but eventually he became one of the full-time drivers of the Rolling Store operation. Today, Melton is the only one of the original 50 workers who still survives.

"We had three huge International trucks that were built so there was no wasted space," Melton said. "Each morning I'd leave the store with a load of overalls, aspirin, snuff, cigarettes, cans of Prince Albert tobacco, factory cloth, radios, coffee, flour, mailboxes, and hardware."

He added, "We carried electrical supplies, light farming equipment, oatmeal, metal roofing, saws, shingles, hats, shoes, pots and pans, and nearly anything else the rural farmer might need. We hauled tin cans for the farmers' wives, because many people put up their food in tins rather than in jars, the way they do today. Many people in those days made their own sheets and their own clothes, so we sold flour in sacks that could be washed and bleached, and the cloth was wonderful for household use. Each morning, six days a week, I'd load my truck and then I'd be on the road for up to twelve hours, sometimes longer, and I'd get back late in the day, clean out the truck, and get it ready for the next morning."

The trucks had special containers built under the bed so that the drivers could haul kerosene for lamps for farm families. The kerosene was also used for heating and cooking in some cases. Each truck had its version of a refrigerator in it, so that perishable items could be hauled to or from the farms.

"I stopped at every house on my route," Melton said. "At times I sold the goods I hauled for cash, but other times I traded for hogs, chickens, butter, eggs, molasses, honey, corn, wheat, oats, peas, beeswax, tallow, peanuts, Irish potatoes, cottonseed, onions, tomatoes, and almost anything else people would buy at the store or down the road."

He recalls that many of the farmers did not have telephones and could not call in orders, so it was necessary to work out a system.

"If I did not have what they wanted on the truck, I'd take their order and deliver it the same day the following week," Melton said. "Maybe a man wanted metal roofing for a barn he was building, and I might not have enough to satisfy his needs. So I'd write down his order and, if he was on my Monday route, the next Monday I'd have it for him."

Prices were astonishingly low at that time. In 1938 when Melton began delivering, a good pair of overalls sold for less than a dollar, he remembers. Arm and Hammer Baking Soda sold for three packs for 11 cents. A can of Prince Albert pipe tobacco sold for 11 cents also. The top-of-the-line shoes sold for $1.98 per pair. Sugar was five cents per pound.

At the time there was a standing joke about the cans of smoking tobacco. "Do you have Prince Albert in a can?" the question would be. When the customer was assured that they did indeed have Prince Albert in a can (as opposed to a sack or bag), the response was, invariably, "Then you better let him out before he suffocates."

"We'd sometimes take in grown hogs," Melton said, "and then we'd butcher them and sell sausage and other meats at the store. We didn't like to haul much fresh meat because of the fear that it would spoil, but we always had fatback, which didn't go bad."

Among the more interesting items Melton and the other drivers collected were wild cherry or fire cherry bark and Maypop vines, sometimes known as Mollypop vines. The wild cherry bark was a fine source of cyanide, and the May apple or Maypop was a source of a drug that had medicinal use.

"They covered me up with Maypop vines at Hollis," Melton remembers. "I went up there and they had so much there was no way I could haul it. They baled it up and waited for the trucks to come and get it."

Another crop that had an interesting use was the peach, which had become a popular fruit for area farmers. Melton, not one to give away secrets except by the glint in his eye, said, "They never told me why they grew so many peaches, and on top of that they bought an unusual amount of sugar. Nobody ever explained that, either."

Melton, who started work at a salary of $9 for a week's work of sixty hours and often more, recalls that John Bell always allowed workers to earn more money if they wanted to. "I could work a little harder and earn as much as $50 in a week, which was a lot of money in those days. I was willing and eager to work longer each day in exchange for more than five times my normal salary."

Melton recalls that the truck he drove had four chicken coops, each capable of holding up to 15 chickens. "And often I'd fill all the coops, a total of possibly 60 chickens," he said.

One of the highlights of his career with Bell Stores was that he was allowed to travel occasionally. He remembers that on his first trip to Philadelphia he worried how all those people managed to find food with no fields or gardens nearby. "I also wondered if they had ever been to the country," he said. "I couldn't imagine living in those crowds and never seeing the farmhouses and fields." Now at age 80, Colon Melton looks back happily on his career at Bell's Stores.

"When I went into the army, I was assigned to a weapons company that was sent to fight in the Italian campaign," he says. "It was unlike anything I had ever imagined. We had soldiers on skis, pack mules, rock climbers, and foot soldiers."

At this point he pulls out a history of his outfit, and he turns with justifiable pride to photos of his unit, the 87th Mountain Infantry, in action. See this fellow here," he says, referring to a group photo. "He's the one without a helmet."

The young man is Bob Dole, who had only a short time earlier announced his candidacy for the Presidency. "He was badly wounded later," Melton said. "He was near death, and we were all pulling for him."

I asked Melton what he thought of the modern world.

"My advice," he said, "in case anybody wants it, is for kids to get as far from drugs as they can and as close to a good school as possible. In my day we didn't need an education, but today computers are the rage. Kids need go get in on the ground floor and become experts in something good."

As for the high earnings of rock stars and pro ball players, Melton does not envy them. "I never made as much money in a lifetime as they make in a single night, but I wonder how many of them are as happy as I am. How many cars can a man drive? How many suits can he wear? How many meals can he eat in a single day? How many houses can he live in. No, give me hard work and a satisfied mind any day."

One of the first trucks in the Rolling Store fleet, above, and, below, Conrad Melton, the last surviving member of the Rolling Store drivers.

Robert "Red" Ennis, one of the greatest minor league pitchers

Sixteen
The Nearly Perfect Season

When I was still in high school, the pro baseball player I admired most was a pitcher for the Concord Weavers in the old North Carolina State League. I desperately wanted to meet the pitcher, but I never thought I'd have a chance to do more than yell at him as he mowed down the batters for our local team. That was in 1946, the first year of pro ball in our area after the devastation of World War II.

But in 1996 I rode, along with a busload of others, to Spartanburg, South Carolina, for an evening's entertainment, and on the bus with us was Bob Ennis, my childhood hero. He was delighted that I recognized him and remembered him after all the years in between, and a few days later he came to my home, where the two of us sat and traded stories and memories. I confessed that he had been my hero for that one season, but often heroes have feet of clay, and I dreaded to discover that my new friend was less than I had remembered. But as we talked, I realized that he had been even greater than I had recalled. I knew before he left that day that he had experienced something that every pro player dreams about but seldom attains.

My hero had, for almost five months, a nearly perfect season, one that rewrote at least a part of the record books.

It was time for major league spring training when the two of us sat down, and on the Grapefruit Circuit the same familiar sounds fill the air. Established stars, hopefuls, and future Hall of Fame players assemble to determine who returns home to the farm and whose name will fill the sports pages in coming months.

Bob Ennis, who would not be there, nevertheless felt a sympathetic aching of bone and muscle and a slight twinge in the area of his heart. And in his memory he will be there again and forever.

Robert "Red" Ennis of Boiling Springs once had the kind of baseball season few people have the courage to dream of–a season in which Ennis, rebounding from an injury and from a severe career disappointment, led not only the league or the state in earned-run average but also led the entire nation.

And quite likely the whole baseball world.

"I never played high school baseball," Ennis said. "Instead, I began to play semipro baseball when I was about fifteen years old. In 1941 I agreed to pitch for Kannapolis, which fielded its first professional team ever. I lost my first game, and then got lucky and won twelve in a row. I finished the season 12-1."

Did the major leagues come calling? Not in an age when there were, at one time, 48 professional teams in North Carolina alone, when there were only sixteen major league teams–total– and the odds of a minor leaguer reaching the majors were estimated to be more than 3,000 to 1.

The following year Ennis won 12 and lost seven, and just when it appeared that he might be headed for the Big Leagues, Uncle Sam called and Ennis changed his baseball uniform for a military uniform, and when he was discharged from the army he went to spring training with the Louisville, Kentucky, team.

Now the major leagues beckoned, right? Wrong.

"There were five hundred players trying out for the team," Ennis said, "and soon afterward I, like hosts of others, was given my release. I came home, disappointed. Almost immediately, though, the Concord team called. I was married and had no place to live, and they offered me a rent-free house and a modest salary, and I accepted their offer."

In his first game with the team Ennis faced one of the most formidable teams in minor league history: the old Thomasville team that later sent scores of players to the major leagues. And Ennis lost his first game, 2-1, and it looked as if the string of bad luck would continue.

Then it all came together. He won eleven games in a row, pitched five consecutive shutouts, and won twenty games during the regular season and added three more victories in the league playoffs. He lost only three games that season and compiled an earned-run average that, according to the Howe statistical bureau, was 1.05 earned runs per game.

But the statisticians made a mistake. They forgot to include Ennis's final game which was, of course, another shutout. So rather than an ERA of 1.05 he actually lowered the average to 1.01. The final figure was the lowest in the United States, lower by far than the ERA that won Greg Maddux another Cy Young Award and lower than all but one of the dozens of major league pitchers in the Baseball Hall of Fame.

You want to carry the idea a little deeper into the jungle of statistics? In the history of baseball, the lowest ERA in American League history was 1.04, set by Mordecai "Three-Finger" Brown in 1906. The lowest average in the National League was set in 1914 when Dutch Leonard allowed only 1.01 runs per nine innings.

This means that Bob Ennis of Boiling Springs has at least a tie for the lowest earned-run average in the entire history of the game. In that phenomenal year, Ennis lost the final game of the season to a young whippersnapper who threw a knuckleball that looked like a monarch butterfly migration.

The kid was a fellow named Hoyt Wilhelm.

That was in 1946, and Ennis went on to play higher classes of baseball, eventually pitching for Triple A teams. But the dream of the major leagues never came true. The big leagues never called, and Ennis retired in 1954 and moved his family to Florida.

"Sadie loved Florida," Ennis said, "but when she became ill we felt that it would be better if we came back to North Carolina. We had been married for 53 years when I lost her in 1992. We had a wonderful marriage, and I loved her so much. After I lost her I couldn't eat; I had no will to live. I am positive that I would not be here today if the same woman who cared for Sadie had not helped me regain my sense of direction. Ruth Canipe became such a great friend, and I owe her an immense debt of gratitude."

Now, I wrote later, Red Ennis, long retired from the wars, devotes a large part of his time to gardening, yard work, and some house work. He finds little time for baseball, although he admits that it was hard to give up a game that had meant so much to him.

"Players today are too interested in money," he said. "They don't seem to love the game the way the older players did." Still, there will be more than a casual pang of memory when spring training opens this season. Red Ennis will tune in to the Braves games and relive his memories.

He will never outlive the season when he was the best in the nation, and, perhaps, the best there has ever been.

"Nobody ever enjoyed the game any more than I did," he said, and I wouldn't bet against him. And he's still this kid's hero.

As he started to leave that day, he turned to me and said, his eyes full of tears, "I meant to tell you. You are my hero now."

I later wrote another story, one that I dreaded to tackle. For weeks Bob's health had declined in a frightening manner, and when he entered the hospital, no one doubted that he would never see his home again.

The doctor told the family that Bob had cancer of the liver and that treatment was impossible. I wrote again of how Ennis, playing for the old Concord Weavers of the North Carolina State League (a league which sent scores of great baseball players to the major leagues–including several who are now enshrined in the Baseball Hall of Fame in Cooperstown, New York), had an almost perfect season.

Along the way, Ennis played with or against such baseball greats as Ted Williams, Whitey Ford, Hoyt Wilhelm, Moose Skowron, and scores of others. He faced the best, and he never backed down.

And now, as World Series time nears and after the focus of the nation has been for months on the race to break the single-season home run record of 61 set by Roger Maris in 1961, Bob Ennis faces the toughest battle not just of his career but of his life.

Several months after I met him, Ennis experienced discomforts and weakness, but it was not until late summer that he was diagnosed as having inoperable liver cancer. For weeks he faced powerful medications, pain, and the stark reality of the eventual outcome of his battle.

But as a baseball player Ennis never learned how to quit, to back down from a batter, even one as formidable as Ted Williams, the last player to have a batting average of .400 or higher (he hit .406 in 1941). And he isn't backing down from this fight, either.

As weak as he is, as long as the battle inside him has raged, when Ennis recognizes friendly faces, his own face erupts into a smile, and the hospital room suddenly becomes much brighter. Mention baseball and his face lights up again, despite the pain that daily wracks his body. Mention home-run hitter Mark McGwire and Ennis becomes animated, insisting on sitting up in his bed, despite the oxygen mask that assists him in his respiration. No matter how sleepy, tired, or beaten down he is, he leaps into the topic with all his remaining energy.

Small wonder. A competitor, whether in professional sports or a checkers game, is by definition a fighter. And Bob Ennis was, is, and will continue to be a fighter, no matter what the results of this final encounter.

"I can't believe I had the courage to go straight from the farm into good, strong semipro ball and then into professional baseball," Ennis said. "If I had realized what I was attempting, I doubt that I'd have had the courage to try it. But I guess it's a good thing that kids don't know what's in store for them, or they'd go through life terrified."

When Uncle Sam called, Ennis was disappointed, naturally. He'd had only a taste of pro ball, and he had enjoyed a near-sensational season. Like other ball players, though, he stored his glove and spikes and picked up his rifle and pack and went off to serve this country.

"I had an awfully good team behind me," Ennis said, always giving credit to others, "and they helped me to have a fairly good season."

Fairly good? When you were the best in the nation that year? When you set a record that has never been surpassed in the history of professional baseball?

Looking back, the season was unbelievable. How could one man totally dominate a league made up of some of the finest minor-league players in the nation? Yet Ennis did it. He faced powerful hitters who were the terror of the league, and he recorded one shutout after another. And he won games both with his arm and with his bat.

Look into the volume entitled *The Story of Minor League Baseball* and you will see that Bob Ennis had a winning percentage of .864 and an earned run average of 1.05. But the record book does not tell the entire story. Remember the final game that the news bureau failed to record? And the playoff games were not included in that miracle year.

Factor them in and Ennis has a winning percentage of .892 and an ERA of less than 1.01 for the season, including scoreless relief work.

But what does all this mean in light of the wild cell that is attempting to destroy a man's body and will? It means that Bob Ennis will not see another baseball season, barring a medical miracle. It means that even tough battlers like the old redhead have their limits. They are immortal, not invincible; they are simply eternal.

When the next season rolls around, Bob Ennis will not be there. But this is not a tragedy. Ennis would say, with poet Robert Browning, "I was ever a fighter, so one fight more–the best and the last." He would say, with novelist Ernest Hemingway, "Man can be destroyed, but not defeated." He would say with William Faulkner, "Man will not merely endure; he will prevail."

He said one day that what meant most to him during his career was not the game but the love of his wife, Sadie. His eyes filled with tears as he described her death. He wondered what it all meant.

His death means that all of us have lost–temporarily–one of our dearest friends, a classical gentleman who epitomized good manners, taste, loyalty, and concern for his fellow men. It means that the game of baseball has also lost a great friend, and somehow the bat will not crack against the ball in the future with the sharp clarity it had in the past; hot dogs at the ball park will not smell quite as good–for a long time to come. It means that Bob Ennis will never play baseball again, but he will assuredly become a permanent member of the greatest All-Star Team-ever assembled–where it really counts!

A short time later I wrote the final chapter in my friend's life. Robert "Red" Ennis died quietly and bravely, as he lived. He was buried at Rowan Park Cemetery in Salisbury, beside the grave of his beloved wife Sadie, to whom he had been married for 53 years.

A man who loved baseball as few others have, Ennis had one final wish granted. He often said that he wanted to live long enough to see Mark McGwire break the season home-run record set in 1961 by Roger Maris. McGwire set the mark only hours before Ennis died.

Few will ever know of the marks Robert Ennis set, both on the baseball field and off. When you were in the batter's box, he was a fierce competitor; when he met you on the street, he was as gracious a gentleman as you could ever expect to meet. Wherever you encountered him, you also encountered class in every positive sense of the word.

Robert Ennis died as he lived: gamely, fully, unafraid. His final concern on this earth was who would take care of his dog Max. You see, Bob Ennis was loyal to everyone who befriended him; he was the total and nearly perfect gentleman, respecting all who are respectable; honoring those who were honorable; dispensing kindness and friendship everywhere he went.

Robert "Red" Ennis loved team sports of all types, but above all he loved the Tar Heels of the University of North Carolina. He lived and breathed the success and failures of Dean Smith's basketball team. And if he had been cut, he'd have bled Carolina Blue. Only those who have played sports seriously can really appreciate the records he left.

The house where the murder occurred

Seventeen
A Horse, A Cave, A Killer

This, in a very strong sense, is the first of the most interesting stories I have encountered in my lifetime, and I never wrote about it before because I knew there was no way I could ever get it right. It was far too personal. I don't know that I can do it any better this time, but this is the time to try to exorcise it.

Alf was the killer's name. Prince was the horse. The cave had no name but we called it the Black Canyon because we heard the name in a cowboy movie we had seen. Ernest was the victim.

At the time I was far too young to allow calendar dates to make a difference when the story began to unfold. All I know is that it was in the middle of a long, hot summer, and some horrible virus had kept me in bed for several days. I was ten, and writing this story was the farthest thing from my mind. Living through it was my major goal.

It was August when, as I lay in my bed in the southwest corner of the house on Seventh Street, I saw Alf the Villain sitting in the late afternoon sunlight and heat at the corner of Seventh and Raleigh Avenue. He sat, leaning against the light pole as if the only concern he had in life was letting the heat pass and the cool night arrive.

Across his knees was a shotgun.

He sat there from about five o'clock in the late afternoon until dark, and then rose, cradled the shotgun in his left arm, and walked past our house, and to the corner, where he turned to return to his own home.

The next day he was back at the same time, at the same light pole on the same corner, and he held, apparently, the same shotgun that he had the day before. He stayed there again until the sun had settled behind the trees below Eighth Street. Then he rose, cradled the shotgun in his arm again, and returned home.

This process continued for a full week, during which time I lay in bed, too sick to read, even if there had been books in our house, or listen to the radio, and watched for the story to unfold, but it never did. At first I thought Alf was waiting to sell the shotgun to somebody, a buyer who apparently had reconsidered dealing with Alf, known widely as one of the most insidiously evil men in our town.

Our part of town was where people who had nowhere to go went. It was the dead end for everybody but the lucky few who escaped. The south side was dominated by the huge cotton mill that dwarfed everything around it, by the clatter of the Southern Railway trains thundering through town, and by the clouds of smoke rising from the mill and by the streams of brilliantly colored waters that flowed from the mill's dye house and transformed local creeks to blood.

As a child I could see the young men and women from our end of town as they walked briskly millward in their clean overalls or dresses, and they carried lunch pails and chattered happily until they neared the huge gates that separated the mill from the civilized world.

That afternoon I often saw them again, now walking ghosts, as they trudged slowly homeward, as if every step was a burden too great to be borne. Their starched dresses and clean overalls were now covered with lint and they resembled eerie specters that had no place of peace in our world. The lint-covered ghosts carried the burdens of the world with them to their own hovels.

I watched and dreaded with unspeakable horror the day when I would quit school, as they had done, to make the mill my world. I looked desperately for an escape from a fate more deadly than any I could imagine, but there was none. I would belong to the mill, just as surely as I would belong forever to our part of town. I wanted to hop a freight car and disappear forever, but I knew I couldn't. Or wouldn't.

To the men and women and boys and girls who entered the mill in the morning and to the zombies who left it in the afternoon, it was not unusual that our part of town existed in a desperate and sullen world of lost hopes, and it was not unusual that a man would sell his shotgun in order to buy the groceries for that week, or that another man might buy the shotgun to kill a few rabbits or birds for food.

Alf, by everyone's estimation, however, was not a man to deal with. Often drunk, always belligerent, never smiling, he could shift rapidly between his only two moods: angry and vicious. Or he would snap from downtrodden to hopeless, from bitterness to fury.

The horse in this story was named Prince. The animal was a magnificent and enormous stallion owned by Alf. Several times each week Alf would saddle the horse, ride him up and down the street, stopping whenever he met someone unlucky enough to be in his way.

When he met a male pedestrian (it was a rare person in our part of town who had a car) he would dismount and confront the hapless man.

"You want to make fifty dollars real easy?" he would snarl. "All you need to do is ride Prince to the corner and back. You ride Prince and I'll give you fifty dollars in gold. But first I want to whisper something into Prince's ear. Now, you want fifty dollars or not?"

It was not a question. Everyone in our part of town wanted fifty dollars, but we never expected to see such a vast sum at one time in our lives. People on the south side were fortunate if they ever saw more than their weekly paycheck, which amounted to $10 or slightly more weekly at first, and then it climbed to thirty or even forty dollars a week for those who had been at the mill most of their lives. The pay rate at the time was thirty-five cents an hour and showed no signs of rising considerably. The only pay raise came in the form of overtime work and the time-and-a-half pay.

So, yes, everyone wanted fifty dollars. But Prince was another part of the equation. No one knew what Alf whispered into the ear of the horse, and we all could imagine that about the time the stallion reached the corner he would rear up on his back legs, toss the rider like a chip on the ocean, and then trample him into the dirt road until nothing remained but a bloodstained spot where once there had been a human being. Or maybe he whispered nothing at all. No one knew, and no one was brave enough to try to find out. Not if he had to ride Prince.

Alf continued to badger pedestrians, and by the time a crowd had gathered at a respectful distance, the local residents watched nervously and waited for the explosion that never came. Finally people just took the around-the-block routes to avoid Alf altogether. Some assumed that he was a harmless crank, but others knew that under the dirty white hat there was a brain that did not work like most people's do.

No one ever knew how Alf obtained his money, or, for that matter, if he had any or if the offer of fifty dollars was only part of the act. One thing that was certain was that somehow he had the money to buy Prince, or he stole him or terrorized someone into giving him away. Or maybe Prince was as much a renegade as Alf was and nobody wanted him around.

But he had to have the money to buy the gun and holster, as well as the shotgun and rifle he sometimes used for target practice in the back yard.

Between street challenges, the afternoon drama continued. For more than a week and a half I watched Alf as he sat on the street corner and leaned against the light pole and cradled the shotgun across his knees. Then one late afternoon he did not appear, and everyone on the street breathed a huge sigh of relief. Perhaps the imaginary buyer of the gun changed his mind. Or Alf changed his.

Or, I realized with an ominous chill, perhaps Alf had changed his mind about the man he planned to kill. The questions that no one dared to ask remained at the front of our minds and on the tips of our tongues.

The answer to the questions came only minutes before dark two days later, when my sickness had reached its worst. The air was still, the weather hot and insufferably muggy. Even the droning of insects in the August air seemed to have ceased in anticipation of the coming events. Already the thin metallic whine of mosquitos had begun, and the sound of slapping at the bloodsuckers came from porches up and down the street. No one spoke; they just slapped mosquitos and waited.

There was no warning, no preamble, no reason for anyone to be more frightened or worked than normal, which was an awesome level. It began like an explosion that was so loud it sounded as if it happened within a few feet of me. Then there were more explosions in rapid succession.

As I lay in my bed I heard the first gunshot, then the others, five or six of them. Then a woman screamed in hysteria and men began to yell. Minutes later we heard the sound of sirens filling the air.

My mother, nearly hysterical herself, came into my room, pulled down the windows (I never knew why but didn't ask how she thought the panes of glass might stop a bullet) and closed the homemade curtains.

Her face was drawn and pale, as if she had been sculpted from riverbank clay. As she looked at me I could see that she was trembling.

"Alf did it," she repeated. "He shot and killed Earn."

I needed to hear no more. Earn was a nickname for Ernest, one of our neighbors a street below us. "He killed him right there on his own porch," my mother continued. I didn't know how she knew, for she had not left the house. In fact, she seldom did. But she had it right. And the story about the shooting was made even more ominous by the fact that Alf emptied his revolver into the body of the man and then walked casually away into the woods.

The story that eventually came to us was that Alf had taken his six-year old daughter with him as he set out to murder the man who had somehow earned Alf's hatred. We never knew what it was, although adults spoke of motives in whispers we never comprehended. The daughter, we were told, went to the house, knocked on the door, and Ernest, seeing Alf, picked up his own revolver, ready to fight.

The two men opened fire, with the daughter standing in horror almost beside Ernest, who was apparently hit by Alf's first bullet and fell forward to the short flight of steps that led down to a walkway of dirt. As he fell, Ernest fired his own pistol and the slugs hit the post beside the steps. The police arrived and spent most of the night riding up and down the streets and stopping people to ask if they had seen Alf.

"No," one person told them, "and you ain't gonna see him either, not in that car. Alf's in the woods, not on the streets."

The police were guilty as charged. They had no desire to find Alf, who had already demonstrated that he was capable of killing another human being. Not as long as he had the provocation needed, and we did not know what that was.

For days afterwards Alf never reappeared. Rumors spread that he had moved to a distant city. Another story was that he was living with a friend nearby. Others said he was a wild man in the forest.

One day the milkman swore to us that he had met Alf on the street and that Alf had warned him that he was going to come after our family and slaughter us.

I never understood why he was angry with us, and then the rest of the story unfolded. He had engaged in an argument with various family members over a period of time, just as he had battled with nearly everyone in the neighborhood. He apparently planned to kill *everyone*.

We soon reached the point, however, that we could stay close to the house no longer. So we went to Black Canyon for a game of cowboys and Indians, then blackjack for stolen matches with a greasy deck of cards.

I now felt scared but fine. We played cards around a campfire until it began to grow late. That was when Froggy whispered that Alf was probably down in the cave and watching us. Juney began to blubber, which started Oopie to whining, and within seconds all of us were watching the mouth of the cave as if we expected Alf to show his face at any moment.

Then we were on our feet and running for our lives. No one had seen Alf, but we were certain he was there. We ran until we met Alf's son, who was pushing his bicycle along the forest path. He asked us what we were doing in the woods so late. Instantly, *we knew Alf was there!*

"Playing cowboy," we said calmly. "What are you doing here?"

I don't know what he said, because the aroma of fried chicken and hot biscuits escaped from the covered box in the basket of the bicycle and we took to our feet and ran furiously for home. *We knew.*

We stayed home for days. Then one Sunday morning the news came that Alf had been found in his barn. We ran there in time to see some men carrying the bloody body to the hearse. He had killed himself.

Why did he return to the barn? We never knew. Some said he had gone totally insane; others insisted that he wanted to die; still others said that he was tired of being a fugitive and living on the run.

Nobody asked us what we thought, but we were certain we knew why Alf came back. It was far deeper than guilt or madness.

He wanted to see Prince one more time, perhaps to make amends for mistreating the horse, whisper one last message into the ever-alert ears of the mysterious horse. Maybe he wanted to explain to Prince why he had committed his act and why he was now ready to kill himself. Maybe he simply wanted to be with his only friend in the world. And if I had to bet any money on it, I'd have bet that Prince understood every word Alf said.

One mile west of Dallas, just off the Cherryville highway, stands this huge oak tree, a reminder of the day in which a young mother became the last woman hanged in North Carolina. Miss Caroline Shipp, convicted of murdering her year-old son, began to give birth on the gallows as she was dying. Her body was stolen from the grave the first night and the skeletal remains were later found, reportedly, in the home of a prominent citizen.

Eighteen
The Last, Tragic Days of Caroline Shipp

On December 21, 1891, Miss Caroline Shipp faced death. The executioner came to the Dallas, North Carolina, jail early in the morning and checked in to see that all was proceeding according to the schedule.

The hangman had traveled from Cherryville, twelve miles to the west, the previous day, for in those days a trip to Cherryville was a two-day event. He had traveled by horse and wagon and had spent the night in Dallas so he would not have to rush the next morning in order to keep his appointment as Death.

Miss Caroline Shipp, presumed to be eighteen years old, although no one, including Miss Shipp, seemed to know for certain how old the young woman was, had been awake and waiting for hours.

At dawn she had received her last visitors from the world she had known all her life. The preacher of a small church outside town had come by, as had some of her former friends in her short and tragic life.

She had eaten her final meal: a breakfast of sardines and crackers, and she was ready to die. The officials took her from her cell and ushered her to a horse-drawn wagon. On the back of the wagon was the crude coffin in which she would be buried.

She climbed onto the flat bed of the wagon, and immediately a throng of neighborhood urchins and curiosity-seeking children also climbed onto the wagon. Miss Caroline Shipp sat on the coffin itself and talked to the boys as the wagon made its slow way through the sleet-covered roads of Gaston County. Dozens of other children on foot followed the horse and wagon on its journey to the gallows.

One of the bolder children on the wagon asked Miss Shipp why she killed her son. Miss Shipp denied ever harming her baby.

The hotels in Dallas had been filled to capacity during the final days before the hanging. It was estimated that three thousand people from around the nearby counties and some from across the state had traveled to Dallas to see Miss Shipp hanged. When the wagon and the coffin arrived, with Miss Shipp still sitting on the coffin, at the hanging tree, the field was full of spectators.

They had come prepared. Wagons circled the field, and the occupants delved into well-filled picnic baskets for the fried chicken, potato salad, and green beans. The three thousand diners, despite the sleet and freezing rain and the bitter wind that whipped across the field, enjoyed their meal while awaiting the feature attraction.

When the wagon arrived, finally, and all was ready, the center stage belonged to the executioner, who had Miss Shipp's hands tied behind her back. In her fingers he placed a handkerchief and gave her the instructions that when she was ready to die, she could drop the handkerchief.

Miss Caroline Shipp stood ready. Looking directly at the crowd, she lifted her voice and sang in a soft but pure voice the words to her favorite hymn, "Why Do We Mourn Departing Friends?"

The trembling fingers moved briefly, and the crowd surged forward for the best possible look as the woman prepared to let the white cloth flutter to the ground. Fathers lifted their sons to their shoulders so that they would have the best possible look at what would probably be one of the most memorable events of their lives.

The last notes of the hymn drifted across the field, borne by the wind that caused men and women to pull coats tighter to their bodies and to huddle together in an effort to escape the cold. At that moment, perhaps, Miss Caroline Shipp reflected for the last possible time on the series of events that brought her to this place and on this mission: to die for the murder of her son.

The young boy had died more than a year earlier. Miss Shipp reported to authorities that the child had become suddenly ill and had gone into convulsions that lasted several minutes before the pathetic child died.

Almost immediately the air had been filled with rumors that Miss Shipp had murdered her son. She had destroyed her only relative on earth. Caroline Shipp had no parents, brothers, or sisters.

Why had she killed her son? First, neighbors pointed out, she had no husband and had never been married. Her only real friends had been an older couple that had asked Caroline several times to give the child to them. She refused, saying, some said, that she loved her son and would not part with him.

Second, her boyfriend had reportedly told her that he would not continue seeing her as long as she had the child. He is said to have hinted that he would marry her, but only if the boy was not to be a part of their lives.

Someone in the community–that someone reported to be the couple who wanted the child–told authorities that Caroline Shipp had sent a messenger to nearby Lowesville to buy rat poison sold under the brand name Rough on Rats. The mailman admitted that he had bought the arsenic-based poison and that he had delivered it to Miss Caroline Shipp, who admitted only that there had been a large number of huge rats in and around her home and she wanted to be rid of them. She insisted that she had not in any way harmed her son.

A court order was obtained for the exhuming of the child's body, and on a bitterly cold night a group of men labored in frigid weather to unearth the tiny coffin and remove the body. The remains were taken to a local doctor's office where the postmortem examination would be conducted.

The results were unexpected. The doctor reported that there were no traces at all of arsenic in the child's stomach, liver, or other organs. Cause of death was undetermined.

Still the accusations arrived almost daily, and soon the local sheriff arrested Miss Caroline Shipp and charged her with murder. The trial date was set, and Miss Shipp was incarcerated while she waited to see what twelve men would decide about her fate.

The trial started at eight o'clock one morning, and shortly before noon the jury retired to deliberate. They were back almost instantly with a verdict of guilty. The presiding judge ordered that Miss Caroline Shipp on December 21, 1891, would hang by the neck until, as the judge said, she was dead, dead, dead.

By the time the execution date arrived, Miss Shipp had been behind bars for more than a year. She remained in her cell and had few visitors, some of whom came and went unseen.

The trial itself had been almost a mockery. Miss Shipp had no attorney to represent her. There were several "defense" witnesses who took the stand and used their allotted time to accuse and testify against the woman they had allegedly come to defend.

The same doctor who conducted the coroner's inquest and found no poison took the stand and testified that the organs of the young child had been laced with large amounts of arsenic: the deadly poison was in the child's stomach, liver, lungs, and virtually throughout his tiny body.

In an even more bizarre note, the state Department of Agriculture, according to published reports, had been asked to examine the organs, and the scientists there had found the arsenic. The problem here was that the doctor had not yet sent the organs when the state lab in Raleigh somehow found arsenic in organs they did not have in their possession.

It was also obvious that on several documents used by the prosecution that someone had clearly forged several names. It was clear that the trial was a mockery of justice in every sense. But the verdict was handed down, and the execution date had been set, and now Miss Caroline Shipp stood on the makeshift scaffold and held the white handkerchief in her slender fingers.

The bewildered and terrified woman, lacking family or loved ones or even casual friends, faced the world–and death– alone, as she had lived most of her life. Oh, she had known her boyfriends who used her for sex and had little if any regard for her otherwise. Her life had been spent as if she were a length of driftwood on the sea of life, and now she was ready to depart.

She completed the song and dropped the handkerchief. The executioner performed his duty. The body of Miss Caroline Shipp plunged downward and then jerked to an abrupt halt as she came to the end of the rope.

But everything had gone wrong, and it was to get worse. The noose had not been properly tied, or the slender woman's weight had not been sufficient, or the height had not been great enough.

She did not die! Her neck was not broken, and she swung from the rope in agony. People in the crowd screamed; men yelled for someone to do something. Mass hysteria would not have been far away if the crowd had possessed the human sympathy to ache from another's pains. Clearly, this was an event to remember.

A man separated himself from the crowd and ran to the struggling, suffocating woman. He clutched her feet and dropped his weight, tugging at the feet until the miserable woman's neck snapped and death mercifully ended her torture.

She died instantly, and the men gathered around to cut her down and lay the body on the ground. Someone checked her wrist for a pulse and found none. Then someone gasped, pointed, and stammered helplessly as he tried to verbalize what he had just witnessed.

There was a sudden, convulsive movement under the dress of Miss Caroline Shipp. The men stared in bewilderment; someone called for a doctor.

Caroline Shipp was giving birth! The dead woman's body was striving to leave a life on this earth, even after giving up her own earthly existence.

The men cut her down quickly and someone ripped away her clothing. Minutes later Miss Caroline Shipp gave birth to her second child.

From that moment no one can provide more than a guess at what happened. The child did not survive, and Miss Caroline Shipp was buried near the huge oak tree between the baseball field and the prison unit just west of Dallas. There was no one to pay for a grave stone, and Miss Shipp was interred in a pauper's grave.

But her ordeal had not ended. Not yet. That night her body was stolen from the grave!

Later the remains were located in the home of one of the county's most prestigious and influential citizens. The grave robbers were identified as members of the student body at the old Gaston College. It was assumed that the robbers had worked for hire for someone who wanted the skeletal remains for medical study. It was also reported that the man had been witnessed boiling some type of flesh and blood in a huge washpot in his back yard.

Miss Shipp's boyfriend, thought by many to have been the real killer, left the area quickly. His fate is not known. In recent years interested persons have discovered significant problems in the court proceedings and huge distortions of "facts" as presented earlier. The major problem, of course, was the testimony by the doctor who had earlier found no traces of arsenic and who suddenly recalled that the child's vital organs held large amounts of arsenic. We can only surmise why he changed his mind.

There is little left to say, other than to quote again a line or two from the pen of poet William Wordsworth:

"If this belief from Heaven be sent, if such be nature's holy Plan,
Have I not reason to lament what Man has made of man?"

Bill Bambach, football's losingest–and winningest–coach

Nineteen
Bambach's Bums: Losers Who Won Big

S ports, we all realize, have winners and losers, and there are inevitably more who lose than there are those who win. In a baseball game, we have one of each, as we do in football. But in a track meet there may be one winner in each event, and, strictly speaking, everyone else is a loser. The same is true of golf tournaments and Olympic Games competition and all other gatherings of gymnasts, skaters, or swimmers.

And in sports, the world loves a winner and hates a loser. Or, if hate is too strong a word, too often we lack real respect for those who ought to finish first (in our opinions) and don't. The Atlanta Braves touted themselves as the Team of the Decade, and in recent years they have lost eight consecutive World Series games. Supporters and fans of the Braves expected no less than a World Series title, and many feel cheated that they did not get one.

All I can say is, these people better be happy they did not play on one of the football teams of Bill Bambach, the all-time champion of losers. His teams not only lost games but lost them by scores that are beyond belief. The only games they ever won were by forfeit when the opposing team grew weary of scoring one touchdown after another, each time they had their hands on the ball.

"It's true," Bambach said. "We were the greatest losers of all time in any sport. But you want to know something? We were the champions year after year. You need to know the whole story before you decide whether we were lousy or great. Personally, I am confident that we were both. We were the greatest in both categories."

Bill, you must understand, taught classes to young men who had in one of several ways, often several of several ways, run afoul of the law and spent much of their time looking between bars. Because of the delicate nature of this story, no locations will be given except to say that the team played, and lost–and won!– in North Carolina.

"Here's the story," Coach Bambach said. "I taught kids who had found themselves in trouble early in life, and they gave up on themselves. Why? Because they were losers, and the world, as stupid as it seems, hates losers. Why should we? I mean, if a man runs for President and succeeds only in becoming Vice-President, he has failed and is therefore a loser. On the other hand, if he decides to become a garbage collector and reaches his goal, then he has succeeded. I don't get it. If a man aspires to win a Nobel Prize in literature and the best he can do is a Pulitzer or National Book Award, he has been a failure. But if he wants to write a porno book and does, he has won. It's absurd."

Bill taught not only sports but academic materials as well. He was the one-room school teacher all over again as he taught math, grammar and composition, history, art and music appreciation, civics, history, and whatever else the curriculum demanded.

"But I had trouble getting the kids to believe in themselves," he said. "And then I got the notion of teaching them what losing really is. So we formed a football team and we scheduled games with other units within our system. I coached my team well."

The strategy was simple: when Bam's Bums kicked off, they stood and watched with interest as the other team ran the ball back for a touchdown. When Bam's Bums had the ball, they made certain they fumbled on the first play from scrimmage, or they threw a pass that was certain to be intercepted.

"We never tackled a single ball carrier during the entire season," Bambach said. "We never gained a single yard by any means, method, or plan. Every time we had the ball, we fumbled it away or gave it up on an interception; when they had the ball, we stood and let them score. We lost games by hundreds of points with great regularity. And I think we won all of them."

How? How could anyone see himself as a winner when he never in any way approached a touchdown or any other kind of scoring? How could the players look themselves in the eye?

"It's simple," Bambach explained. "Most ball games have terminal points. In baseball, the team ahead in the score at the end of nine innings is the winner. In football and basketball, the team ahead when the clock runs out is the winner. In life there is no time clock. The game doesn't end when the buzzer sounds or the final inning is over. Even death doesn't end the game, because there is still more to prove, one way or another. And losing the game doesn't mean that you have lost in life. I wanted these young men to understand that they can lose a game and not be losers. At the same time I wanted them to know that they could make a stupid move in life and not be losers forever. I wanted them to understand that they are not losers until they themselves decide that they are."

How does the bizarre program work? Incredibly, according to the records. Bambach's charges left their temporary quarters at the end of their allotted time, and they have gone ahead with their lives. They own their own firms, some of them. Others work in high positions for important local, state, and national offices. They have in virtually every way redeemed themselves in society's eyes and, perhaps more important, in their own eyes. It would be difficult to find one single level of social advancement that Bam's Bums have not reached and where they do not perform well.

But, after all is said and done, how are the recidivism records?

"Recidivism?" Bambach asks. "What's that? These kids do not know what it is. We don't talk about it. We didn't include failing a second time in the master plan. These young men have gone back into the world, and they have married good wives and they have reared good kids. Oh, there have been divorces, and some have lost jobs. But they have never lost their sense of worth. They are living productive and happy lives, and if they can gain this much simply by losing a football game, then let's lose every game we ever play–as long as it is a game and as long as we are playing. But when we are living real life, let's be winners."

He fills his classroom lectures with stories of great people who failed miserably before achieving greatness. He advises losing on the football field and then be prepared to achieve success where it really counts. He tells his students of how Mahler, Edison, Lincoln, and myriads of other great men experienced one failure after another until they finally realized the way to their goals and to success. He tells the students that they, too, while perhaps not achieving to the level of genius, can carve out their success in the modern world. Any way you look at it, it makes more sense than building more prisons and wrecking more lives.

One of the few remaining pictures of Grat Springs

A beardless Abraham Lincoln, some say, resembles Grat Springs.

Twenty
It's a Wise Father Who Knows His Own Son

In Gaston County, just west of the Catawba River, there is a story that reaches to the mountains and then to Washington, DC, and from there to the history books of the nation. This story involves a United States President, an Uncivil War, a ghost, and a man buried standing up–and beside the first governor of Texas. Adam Springs is the hero of the story: he is a man who came into the Gaston County area and left an indelible mark there.

As a young man Adam Springs enrolled in the first class in the history of the University of North Carolina at Chapel Hill, and he finished his studies there with the first graduating class, a group of about thirty-five enterprising young men. Having completed his academic work, he returned to his home area. Springs lived for many years in the huge two-story white house that overlooks the South Fork of the Catawba River, a stream in which he loved to fish and enjoy other sports, when he wasn't building an empire from the cotton that grew all over much of the South.

Springs liked to set fish traps in the South Fork, and he looked the traps regularly and as regularly he enjoyed meals from the bass, catfish, perch, and other food fish from the stream. As he entered the business world, he needed help around his house, and he and his wife engaged the services of a young woman who lived not far away.

Her name was Nancy Hanks, and she was unimportant to American history but for one matter: she was the mother of Abraham Lincoln.

The question is whether Tom Hanks was the father of this nation's president who led us into and out of a Civil War that took more American lives than all other wars combined. There are those who insist that some-one in Gaston County was the biological father. And Springs is one of the names frequently mentioned.

They point out that Springs recorded in his journal words to the ef-fect that Miss Hanks came to the house regularly to perform cleaning and washing duties and other desirable services. This in no way proves or even suggests that Springs fathered Nancy Hanks' child.

What we do know is that Miss Hanks, still unmarried and, by com-mon consent, expecting, moved farther west to Rutherford County to the tiny community of Bostic, where she accepted employment in the home of Abraham Enloe. She continued to live there, the believers say, until her child was born, and some even contend that she named him Abraham out of respect to Mr. Enloe.

But that proves nothing, and nothing will be proven, ever, unless DNA testing is done, and this seems unlikely. The purely circumstantial evidence, however, is enough to excite many people who have followed the Lincoln legend.

Here are several examples frequently cited. Adam Springs had a son (another son?) named Grat, and Grat was remarkably similar in physical appearance, they say, to Abraham Lincoln. Once a doctor from Gastonia took his young son to Washington, DC, for the purpose of educating him through experiencing the nation's capital and by meeting some of the prominent people living there.

As doctor and young son sat on the street, the doctor noticed a tall, gangly man in a long coat and a tall hat approaching them. The doctor at once recognized President Abraham Lincoln and wanted to bring the man to his son's attention.

"Son," the doctor said, "look at the man coming toward us. Do you have any idea who he is?"

"Of course," the son replied. "That's Grat Springs from back in Gaston County."

There was no hesitation. The young man saw and recognized imme-diately one of the hometown favorites.

But that's not all. Many other people who came to Washington had much the same reaction. They all saw Grat Springs.

One such visitor was the person who was touring the famous hall of portraits. He stopped in front of the portrait of Abraham Lincoln and asked his companions, incredulously, "What in the world are they doing with a picture of Grat Springs here in Washington?"

Some time ago I came upon a newspaper photo of Grat Springs, and about the same time I found a picture of Lincoln when he did not sport a beard. For my own interest, I placed the two photos side by side to see if I could detect any family resemblance.

In a word, the similarities were striking.

But the legend of Adam Springs continued beyond the Lincoln possibilities. When Springs died, according to local legend, he wanted to be buried across the South Fork River from his house so that he could watch over his fish traps. One local legend, repeated many times, is that the ghost of Adam Springs even today walks the banks of the river and, carrying a lantern, looks for the vandals who made a nasty habit of robbing Adam Springs' fish traps. There are even people who worked in the Springs house who insisted that they saw the ghost of Adam Springs on the stairway of the mansion which, incidentally, holds the first bathtub west of the Catawba River.

The land holdings of the man were astonishing. The story is that Adam Springs could mount a horse in McAdenville and ride all the way to Salisbury, North Carolina, without ever leaving his property.

Another popular story insists that Grat Springs, who inherited the land from his father, rode over into Mecklenburg County to the site of a new and luxurious hotel that had been completed in recent months. He asked to see the manager.

"Is something wrong, sir?" the manager asked.

"Well," Grat Springs replied, "it seems that you folks have built your hotel on my land."

And they had. But, gracious gentleman that he was, Grat Springs told the owners that he had no real need for the land but that he at times needed a place to get away from home and everyone he knew, and he agreed to let the hotel management keep the building on the land as long as they always had a room and hot meals for Grat Springs when he needed accommodations.

Was Adam Springs the father of Lincoln? It's a good story, and that's what this book is about: passing on the good stories. Nothing can be known for a fact, and nothing is assumed as a fact. It's just a popular local story, folks.

Robert Eng demonstrates his martial arts skills.

Twenty-One
He Gave Up the Ring for the Cross

When I first met Robert Eng, he walked into my community college class of freshman grammar and composition. At first glance, I thought of the old joke about where does an 800-pound gorilla sit. The answer is, "Anywhere he likes."

Eng was not an 800-pounder, but he was without doubt a healthy young man. He was also a serious and highly agreeable student who took everything in stride. Nothing seemed to ruffle him in the least. He came to class, did his work, and left.

Then one day in my office we struck up a conversation, and he informed me that he would soon be fighting the reigning kick-boxing champion, an undefeated giant who had never been knocked off his feet. I expressed not only shock that one of my students would have attempted such a reckless act but also fear that Eng would be badly hurt in the encounter.

"He's never been knocked down," Eng said again, "but, then, he's never fought me. He'll not only go down, but he'll go out as well."

The fight, I believe, was held on a Saturday night, and during the weekend I wondered whether Eng had been badly hurt or if he managed to survive the fight with only minor injuries. When I saw him on Monday morning he was grinning from ear to ear.

It seems that Eng knocked out the champion in something like one minute or less of the first round.

One day he invited my entire class to come to his gym where he would put on a karate demonstration for us. We went, I to take photos for magazine articles and the class to see what made him tick.

We weren't long in seeing. For a few minutes Eng punched and kicked the heavy bag, and then he got down to business. He began with the obligatory breaking of cement blocks, a feat which, if common, is still astonishing. He broke them with his hands, his feet, and his head.

Now, if you have ever worked with cement blocks, you know that they are rather fragile. You can drop one and break it into several pieces, but they are not soft, and they do not crumble like crackers when they are hit.

Still, I was not totally awed. But Eng was just warming up.

Next, he had a series of boards stacked between two stacks of cement blocks, and an assistant poured lighter fluid all over the boards and then lit them. When the flames were leaping three feet into the air and spreading at least two or more feet wide, Eng thrust his head into the flames and broke the boards.

Again, I know that wide pine boards are not particularly tough. Even I might be able to break one without undue difficulty. But Eng broke half a dozen of them, which is hard enough, but he also had the problem of the flames.

Still, we all know that we can pass our hands rapidly through high flames and not be burned badly, if at all. But Eng did not pass his hands through the tips of the flames: he shoved his head, hair, eyes, and all, into the center of the flames and cracked the boards and let them fall into a heap on the floor.

For his next demonstration, Eng lay flat on the floor and let his assistants place a long and wide board across his chest. Then four full-grown men, all fully developed and healthy, stepped upon the board, two at each end. And Eng's chest supported the weight, which had to be at least six hundred pounds.

The show became more and more fantastic. At one point the aides placed a noose around Eng's neck and then looped the other end of the rope over a rafter and pulled him off the floor several feet.

Eng, his neck muscles tensed to the incredible point, hung there and lifted his feet straight out in front of him and the assistants broke 2-x-4s across his knees.

Eng then took off his shirt and lay down on a bed of very sharp nails, then lifted hands and feet into the air so that only his back was exposed to the nails. Then I did the same thing.

This trick was not difficult. We all know that a full-size United States Army tank exerts less ground pressure per square inch than does an automobile, even a compact car. The explanation is that the tank, although it weighs about 100,000 pounds, has the weight distributed evenly over several long feet of wide track, while the car has all the weight on a small portion of four tires.

From another point of view, three hundred nails in a board can distribute the person's weight so that only a few pounds of pressure will be exerted against each nail. The more nails, the less the pain when you lie on the nails. If you want to see a real trick, watch someone lie down on only *one* nail, or two, three, or four.

But Eng wasn't cheating. He was simply showing some of the physics involved in what he was doing. His next demonstration further exemplified the laws of physics.

Here, Eng lay with his head in one chair and his feet in another, with the entire length of his body suspended between the two chairs. Then his aides placed about one hundred pounds of cement blocks, the four-inch solid types, and Eng supported the weight of his own body plus that of the blocks. Then one of the assistants used a sledge hammer to break the cement blocks.

What Eng was demonstrating here was that when the blocks are hit with the weight and power of a sledge hammer, the force of the blow takes the path of least resistance; that is, it spreads outward, rather than down. But with all the explanations in the world, you still have the matter of the immense strength needed to support the dead weight as well as the force from the blow.

Weight, as you will see, is not a real problem with Eng. Years ago, when I first met him, when he went jogging he, believe it or not, strapped the engine of a full-size car onto his back and jogged while carrying the car engine. If you have ever tried to remove a car engine from the compartment in a car, you know that no human being is likely to be able to lift such weight. But Eng not only lifted it; he ran with it.

At one point he stood perfectly still and let people hit or kick him in any part of his body. He wore no protection of any sort, and he asked only that the blows stay away from his eyes. The invitation included hitting or kicking him in the testicles, abdomen, or any other part of his body. He seemed to be totally impervious to the pain.

In another demonstration, he stood stock-still and let people, two on a side, run toward him while they held two-by-fours, two-by-sixes, or other dimensions of lumber. Eng braced himself and the approaching assistants crashed into him so that the lumber caught him solidly across the chest. The lumber fragmented, but Eng apparently felt nothing.

One of his crowd-pleasing stunts was to lie flat on the pavement and let people place "runners" made of two-by-ten lumber spaced the exact width of the wheels on a full-size automobile. Then the car, or truck, approaches at a modest speed, the wheels climb the runners, and the vehicle runs across Eng's chest and legs. When the car passes, he leaps to his feet, ready for the next stunt.

But if the karate and superhuman aspect of his character is all you see, you are woefully misjudging Robert Eng. He is a good cook, an artist, and a decorator. He even sews well.

But the greatest challenge ever to come his way struck Eng back in the mid-nineties. He admits that his life was a shambles.

"I felt tired, listless, sullen, and immensely unhappy," he says, "and I had no idea what was wrong. I had lived carelessly, and it had to occur to me that I had some sort of incurable disease. So I went to the doctor, who could not find anything wrong.

"Then one day my tiny (at the time) daughter asked me if she could go to Bible School at a nearby church. I didn't especially want her to go; the church had never in my adult life been central to me. But I took her anyhow, and I let her out on the corner because I did not want to walk into the church.

"That evening she came home bursting with happiness. She asked if I'd like to hear a song she had learned, and naturally I said I did. I wanted to hear anything she had to say. As incredible as it now seems, she sang 'Jesus Loves Me.' I don't think I had ever heard the song. Then that little girl asked me if I would pray with her, and I had to tell her I didn't know how. Her response was, 'That's all right; I'll teach you.' And she did.

"And suddenly the Big Tough Guy was in tears. I had won all sorts of Toughest Man in the World titles, and now a little girl had me on my knees and in tears. She defeated the man who couldn't be whipped. Or she and the Lord together did. And that was the beginning of the end of my problems.

"Not long afterwards, I attended a church meeting, and I sat there wondering how in the world I could ask God to forgive me of all of my sins and accept me as one of His own. The service ended, and I had not found the courage to go to the altar and accept Jesus as my Savior.

"The next night the same thing started to happen, and when the church was empty, I made up my mind to go to that altar and kneel and wait until the preacher came back into the church. I was prepared to stay there all night and all week if necessary. But that wasn't necessary. The preacher returned soon, and he prayed with me, and a miracle happened. All of my illnesses disappeared. For the first time in months and months I was happy, free of worry and pain, and I felt wonderful for the first time in ages."

Not long afterwards Eng returned to college, this time to study religion. He graduated, completed his seminary work, and became an ordained minister.

Almost immediately he was giving church programs in which he demonstrated his physical toughness and his new-found spiritual strength. As an athlete, Eng could relate well to the young people at the meetings, and he found that he could incorporate physical conditioning, clean living, morality, and Christianity into his work.

At this time he envisioned building his own church. That is, not his church but His church. That dream has now become a reality. The new church in the Kings Mountain-Shelby area is moving ahead at gratifying speed, and Eng's wife and friends are all working with Eng to help to finish the physical work and to extend the spiritual part of the program into nearby communities.

"It's taken a long time," Eng said, "and for a while the road was rocky and rough. That was my training period. I learned that whatever happens to me is God's will, and I celebrate events that in an earlier life would have been devastating to me. My entire life is for the first time together and harmonious. It's like a dream come true, but not in a dream in which I am rewarded. My reward comes from serving God and from being able to help others."

He adds, "When the Bible said that a little child would lead them, I had no idea how literal that passage could be. The greatest part of my life has been to understand what it means by becoming reborn and learning that my strength, though a gift, is no match for God's."

Eng was for years active nationally and internationally in martial arts competition. But now, while he remains active in martial arts and sponsors local contests, he devotes more and more time to his ministry. His journey to this point has been remarkable, and it promises a fantastic future.

    The gravestone of Little Cherry in Cherryville is one of the most tragic symbols in this part of the state. The child lived part of one day but was apparently born healthy and could probably have enjoyed a full and happy life. The people of Cherryville demonstrated their sympathy and goodness as they raised money for a funeral and the gravestone. The killer of Little Cherry has never been identified, and the mother of the child has never been located. If you visit Cherryville, you will find one of the nicest and cleanest cities in the South, a place where great athletes and students thrive and where the people are constantly ready to lend assistance when it is most needed. The story of Little Cherry is only one of the narratives you will find there, of good people coming to the aid of others. And when all is said and done, helping others may be the highest calling the human being can have.

Twenty-Two
A Tiny Life That Mattered

L ittle Cherry never drove a car, wrote a book, or even read a book; she never wrote her name, spoke a word, or set foot in the town of her birth. To our knowledge, she never enjoyed the taste of mother's milk or even milk of any sort. She never knew the warmth of love or the reward that comes from bringing warmth into the life of a family.

Little Cherry, you see, lived less than one day; for all we know, she may have lived less than one hour. No one knows who her father was. Her mother's identity is similarly a mystery.

All that is known is that on the hot afternoon of July 29, 1957, some children were playing in a wide pool in a creek that runs though the neat and attractive town of Cherryville, a few miles west of Dallas and Gastonia. If you think of Shelby, Gastonia, and Lincolnton as a huge triangle, Cherryville would be somewhere in the center of it.

Cherryville itself is noted for several interesting and important reasons: for years it was the world office for Carolina Freight. The nationally-known Cherryville New Year's shooters bring people from all over the area to witness the rare celebration. And Cherryville is known for the fine amateur baseball teams it fields year after year.

There is also the C. Grier Beam Trucking Museum and the downtown Cherryville Historical Museum, both worth a stop. But don't go through Cherryville without visiting the Cherryville Cemetery located on NC 150, across the street from the Cherryville United Methodist Church. In the cemetery there is a tiny grave with a simple stone that bears a brief and cryptic message.

The message reads: July 29, 1957 Little Cherry Found Dead in Creek Near Here. That's the entire story of Little Cherry's life.

The children who went to the creek to play on a muggy, hot July day had waded in the small stream for several minutes before they came to a huge pool near one of the city streets. The pool is perhaps twenty feet wide and twenty feet long, and at its deepest point it is perhaps two feet. It would have been a superb place for the children to cool off and play in the water if it had not been for their horrible discovery.

At first they thought they had seen a doll floating in the water, and they waded over to get a closer look and even to take the doll from the water, dry it out, and keep it as a toy.

But as soon as they touched the object, they knew it was not a doll but a human being. They ran home to tell their parents, and soon the parents and police arrived.

Little Cherry, the medical examiner ruled, had definitely been born alive and was alive when her tiny and pathetic body had been thrown into the creek. The cause of death was drowning.

There were no physical problems or abnormalities; Little Cherry would have been a sound, healthy, happy, loving child, had she been permitted to live more than an hour or two.

But the child's mother, her father, or even a stranger had decided that the child would not live. The theories were that an unwed mother, perhaps little more than a child herself, had delivered the baby in the back seat of a car or in a dingy room someplace. It is guessed that the mother felt or knew that she could not keep the child, and she could not, in fact, allow anyone to know that she had ever given birth.

Speculation is pointless. What matters are facts, because there are no known motives, and the most likely ones provide us only with grief that such conditions prevail and affect people in such a tragic manner. One death resulted from what may have been a momentary pleasure that led to months of anxiety and possible pain.

The facts are that a child died, other children were scarred by the horrible discovery, and adults in town had their serenity shattered by the tragedy. But another fact is that human beings, no matter how they differ in looks, occupations, philosophies, and motivations, often respond as a unit when there is an emergency or a common cause. Little Cherry, never having the slightest inkling that she was doing so, gave the people a common cause, and they responded magnificently.

Such motivations add to the nobility of the human race, and they make a dent in the baseness of character that allows or causes such events to become part of our lives. Little Cherry's death is not significantly better or worse than many such occurrences, but her death created a benevolent human bond, which makes the world a much better place.

There are no clues to the mother's identity; no one seems to know whether she lived in Cherryville or perhaps had come from a nearby town for the express purpose of murdering her infant child.

But the people of Cherryville decided that if the child could not have a family and a life, she would at least have a funeral and a proper burial. They collected money for a grave plot, a tiny casket, and a gravestone, which is all that remains of Little Cherry today.

The only strange part of the story today is that each Christmas, Thanksgiving, and Easter, a mysterious woman in a car with out-of-state plates, appears, places a decoration on the grave, and drives away.

The child's mother? It would be nice to think that somehow she developed a conscience and found a way to grieve over her loss. Perhaps her child would rest easier, knowing that now someone loves her.

I must add quickly that there is no way to know that the woman is the mother of Little Cherry. For all anyone knows, the mother herself may be dead, perhaps a murder victim even as the child was.

It is difficult to state that there are no clues whatsoever in any major crime, but the police have drawn a blank at every turn, and the odds are overwhelmingly great that no further progress will be made in the police investigation.

Today it is difficult to find many people in Cherryville who recall the tragic event clearly. There are many who were living at the time who still reside in Cherryville, but most of them, presumably, can know only what was in the newspapers at the time.

Cherryville, however, has moved past the tragic death of the tiny child; however, they have not grown callous. Time, whether we approve or not, mercifully has a way of erasing the stark reality of many events that would otherwise prove to be too great a burden for us to endure. If you visit the grave of the slain child, though, you will find that the universal suffering pains are never far beneath the surface. Perhaps that, too, is good. We can never afford to forget such unspeakable events.

Twenty-Three
A Modern-Day Methuselah?

If you drive down US 321 south of Gastonia, you will soon arrive at Olney Presbyterian Church, a beautiful and historic place of worship that abounds in history and antiquity. Some of the earliest European inhabitants of the area lived near Olney church.

And if you want proof of the age of some of the graves, walk to the back of the church to the cemetery and look at some of the dates, which range from the modern to the period of the American Revolution and even earlier. Now search for the grave of William Barnes, a modern-day Methuselah if there ever was one.

According to his gravestone, William Barnes was buried on September 7, 1823, age 218 years!

If the age of William Barnes at his death could possibly be accurate, then Barnes himself would have been a contemporary of Shakespeare, Milton, Jefferson, and Lincoln. He would have been born in 1605, even before the King James Version of the Holy Bible had been printed. In his lifetime he would have spanned some of the most memorable events in modern history.

His life would have included the Gunpowder Plot, the paintings of Rubens and El Greco, Shakespeare's *Winter's Tale* and *The Tempest*, the Bard's farewell to the stage, and the major works of Galileo–before Barnes was old enough to go to school.

By the time he was ten years old he could have learned about, as the events occurred, the publication of the Kings James Version of the Holy Bible, the imprisonment in the Tower of London of Sir Walter Raleigh, and the dramatic saving of the life of Captain John Smith by the Indian princess Pocohontas.

When he reached age fifteen, the *Mayflower* had set sail for America, and Raleigh had been beheaded. By the time he reached his twentieth birthday, Harvey would have issued his thesis on the circulation of the blood and Galileo had improved the microscope significantly.

In his early adulthood he could have been a part of the Pilgrims' settlement at Plymouth or, a little later, at the Massachusetts Bay settlement and, not long afterward, in terms of the time span of Barnes, the Salem Witch Trials.

He could have kept up with the Thirty Years War, witnessed the formation of Harvard College, later University, the first in the New World. He could even have recited the best-known work of Englishman Thomas Mouffet, who wrote a famous treatise entomology, known as *Theatrum insectorum*. No, that's not the work everyone knows. Mouffet also wrote a tiny poem about his young daughter, Little Miss Muffet.

Barnes could have also been on hand when the American Revolution was fought, and again in 1812 when this new nation again took on the Mother Country in battle.

As indicated elsewhere, not many people give any real consideration to the possibility that William Barnes lived to be the oldest person in the history of the United States. I'm sceptical myself, but the many foolish things I've done do not include arguing with a tombstone. That doesn't mean I believe the information carved there.

What I believe is of no consequence. What may matter most is that the story is simply a fascinating one. It is a link in that eternal mystery of how the Past affects the Present and the Future. It may matter that back in the dim and dusty past someone in a stonecutter's shop made a mistake, and that mistake intrigues us today.

Just as our mistakes will intrigue future generations.

Some people argue that Barnes lived to be 21 years old, not 218. Others say he was only 18 when he died; still others adhere to the notion that he was 28. Nearly all guesswork is based on the idea that an extra digit was placed in the death age, but no one has explained how someone made a typographical error in granite.

It doesn't matter, because we'll never know the answer. So perhaps the best plan is to visit the church, appreciate its beauty and history, and visit the grave of William Barnes and make your own guess. Or just engage in speculation if Barnes is the oldest man in our history.

Twenty-Four
Carrying His House Down The Mountain

When Webby Williams of Lake Lure went to work for the first time in his life, he was not yet five years old. When he was sixteen he received his first payment for his work: thirty-five cents.

To say that Webby grew up in poverty would be like saying that the weather gets nippy at the South Pole. He recalls that everyone in his family worked every day but Sunday, which was their church day.

His first jobs included feeding hogs for another family, hauling in firewood, shucking or husking corn, gathering nuts for winter's use, and chopping kindling. But he was never paid. Not in money, at least.

"We had a big family," he says, "and we all had to pitch in. Whatever we could bring home helped us out. So when I finished my work, I could take home the scraps left over from the table in the house where I worked. Now, you might not think that you'd want to gnaw a pork chop bone or a piece of fat left on a piece of beef. But we were hungry."

He did not find it embarrassing or humiliating to eat other people's leavings. His family was delighted to get the bits of meat left on the pork-chop bone or the chunk of fat off the beef roast. The few grains of corn left on the discarded ear of corn would mean the difference between going to bed hungry or well fed.

As well-fed, that is, as Webby's family ever was. During this time in the South being well-fed was a luxury for many people.

Webby was almost a grown man when he received his first cash payment. Prior to that time, he carried hundreds of pounds of food scraps to his home and family. When he reached adulthood, Webby went to work for a man who paid him a few cents a day.

Webby also found a pretty young woman and fell in love. When he and his wife were married, Webby promised her that one day she could have a house of her own in which to nurture their children.

So when he received his few cents pay at the end of the week he bought one piece of lumber and carried it on his shoulders down the mountain where he worked. Labor is what we're talking about, not some of the sit-and-push-buttons kind of responsibilities. Webby worked hard, and he treasured every piece of lumber he could afford to buy with his tiny salary.

He bought the materials for the entire house, so he could start building the house: first, the footings, then the foundation walls, then the subflooring and the wall framing. It took him more months than he likes to remember, but he completed the house, and there he and his wife reared their own family and reveled in the love they shared for each other.

Happily, they were able to enjoy the house for many years; unhappily, Webby's wife died, and he was left with grown children and no one with whom to share his need for spousal love. Then he became a missionary, preached in Haiti, and found his new love. He says that it was love at first sight for both of them.

They were married, and disaster struck again. This time one of his neighbors was burning some grass and leaves, and the fire spread to Webby's house, his pride and joy. Webby was down at the lake when he realized that his house was blazing, but by the time he ran home, the fire was completely out of control. All he could do was sit and watch the flames destroy all of the work, all of the happiness, all of the love that he had invested into the house that he had carried down the mountain.

By this time Webby was up in years, too old and too frail in health to carry another house down the mountain. He and his new wife had been blessed by the addition of several children of their own, and now they were homeless.

At that point the people of Bill's Creek community and neighbors around Lake Lure decided it was time that they return a little to a man who had given so much of his life to others. They set up a benefit campaign and sold barbecue plates to raise money.

I was standing on the porch of the building where the meal was served, and Webby stood beside me as the well-dressed couple arrived and approached us. The man asked which of us was Webby. My friend identified himself and the couple than asked who I was.

"I'm Robert Williams," I said. "Webby's brother."

Suddenly an arm like a flesh-and-blood log wrapped around my shoulders and practically broke my ribs.

"I've waited all my life for a white man to stand beside me and say we are brothers," he said, tears in his eyes.

Then I heard a voice behind me, one deep enough to have come from a grizzly bear in a huge barrel, and other powerful arms grabbed me.

"Then you must be my uncle," Webby's son said.

As the benefit ended, there was not enough money to get Webby his new home. At least thousands more were needed. Then a huge car arrived and a man stepped to the porch and asked how much was needed. We told him, and he pulled out a checkbook and wrote a check for the needed cash.

"Webby is the best worker and finest man I have ever known," the man said, and then he drove away. There were very few dry eyes in the crowd when the benefactor departed. Everyone wanted to see a long-deferred payment made. The check cleared the bank, by the way.

What does Webby's story say to the rest of us? First, it's an unusual person who gets through life without a personal tragedy of some sort. At one time or another we will all likely face the challenge of fighting back or enduring the agony of loss. It is a magnificent trait of the human being that the individual will continue to carry on his work simply because he believes in it, whether the work is building a house for a bride whom you want to have the best you can provide. Or it may be carrying the Gospel to distant parts of the world. It could be the mere fact of caring for your loved ones and dedicating your life to them.

Or it might be that there is a brotherhood, almost invisible at times, at work in our lives. It may be that we care much more than we like to admit. Under our veneer of selfishness and status symbols, there is in most people a heart that still pumps warm blood and reaches out to people in need. There are still people, countless good individuals, who cannot see the suffering of others without suffering themselves.

The poet John Donne once wrote, "Any man's death diminishes me, because I am involved in mankind." He could as easily have written, "Any man's pain hurts me, because I care about others. I care because, as corny as it may sound, there is, after all, a brotherhood of man that includes a great many people whose lives are forever intertwined. The human race is, happily, one giant set of twins joined at the heart and indivisible."

Ponder demonstrates the strength of his teeth and muscles.

Twenty-Five
His Bite Is Better Than His Bark

About a dozen miles north of Statesville, just off NC 115 toward North Wilkesboro, you will find the home of Joe Ponder, who lives in a community known far and wide as Love Valley. This town will be featured in a later book. But for now Joe Ponder is plenty of story in himself.

The first time I met Ponder, I found him to be a quiet, mannerly, kind, considerate, and gentlemanly sort of person. Although we arrived without calling ahead (a tactic I deplore but was guilty of on this occasion), he invited us into his workshop and into his mind. He even insisted that we take small gifts from his shop as we left.

Later that same day we watched him perform. Joe Ponder does not sing, dance, do magic, crack jokes in a stand-up routine, or emote his way through some of the heavier passages from the works of William Shakespeare. He just bites things.

And there is a reason that his bite is much better than his bark: Joe Ponder has what must be the strongest teeth in the history of the world. He does things with his teeth that most people cannot do with a block and tackle or farm tractor.

For starters Ponder, dressed in a tasteful sweat suit, addressed his audience by telling them that he wanted to dedicate this performance, as he does with all of his performances, to God, who gave him the strength and determination to develop his act and to try to demonstrate to audiences that Man's Power is increased many times when coupled with God's Power. That said, he launched into an act that shattered any previous belief I had held concerning the man's teeth. He certainly put teeth into his act. Just looking at the props he had assembled before our arrival was awesomely intimidating.

Everyone in the audience looked around and pondered (horribly atrocious pun fully intended) what on earth the man planned to do with all of the equipment standing or parked nearby. There was, to our right, an eight-foot stainless steel cage about seven feet high, and in the cage there was a scantily clad and immensely attractive woman. With the woman there was a full-grown cat that looked like a jaguar or leopard.

Adjacent to the leopard, cage, and bikini-dressed woman, there stood a steel framework with steps leading to a small platform on each side. No sign of life was present there.

Behind the steel framework stood a mule of the sort that we once used to plow our fields back when escaping from the farm was our major concern in life. To the left of the mule was a target range with a rifle (without a stock) propped safely in a wooden frame. I noticed that the missing stock had been replaced by a contraption that reminded me of double hooks on the wrist of a man who had lost his hand, except that the "hooks" were rounded and connected.

To our extreme left stood a parked full-size tractor and trailer rig, one of the eighteen-wheelers we encounter on every highway we travel. A stand, which looked like a speaker's platform, stood directly in front of us.

What did they all have in common: firing range, stockless rifle, mule, leopard and woman, semi-truck, platforms, and all the rest? Joe Ponder did not waste any time; he went straight into his act.

From the speaker's platform he explained briefly that he had once been a professional boxer who fought on the fight cards of some of the greatest pro boxers of this century. But Ponder had never hit the big time in the sense that he never won a championship or, to the best of my memory, had never fought for the championship. He also explained that human teeth are extremely strong and durable but at the same time they are somewhat fragile and easily cracked.

"For this reason," he said, "I will wear a mouthpiece. You know that fighters and even basketball players wear them in order to keep from having their teeth broken or knocked out. The mouthpiece in no way makes what I do any easier. If you think it does, I welcome you to use all the mouthpieces you can find and repeat what you see me do."

He then went to work. When he had finished none of us had any desire to try to equal his performance.

Ponder started with what he described as solid rolled steel bars that were, to the best of my judgment, half an inch thick or possibly slightly larger. The bars were about three feet long, perhaps longer.

He placed one of the bars in his open mouth, grasped the ends of the bar in each hand, and pulled down with a sudden burst of power and speed. The bar was instantly twisted into a pretzel.

He removed the bar from his mouth and tossed it at the feet of the people nearest the platform.

"Three or four of you might try to straighten the bar," he said, "just to satisfy yourselves that it's real."

I watched as four men, two on each end, vainly and ineffectually tugged at the bar. They made no progress at all.

Ponder then moved to the stainless-steel cage, mounted the platform erected there, and grasped the two bars that looked like handrails running over the top of the cage. With his feet planted firmly on the platform beside the cage, he bent forward until he could grasp what looked like a steel ring in his teeth.

He began to push up powerfully with his shoulders and arms and with his neck as rigid as a steel beam. As his head and upper body rose, so did the huge stainless steel cage, the leopard or jaguar, and the trainer inside. The cage cleared the ground by several inches before Ponder ran out of arm room.

By this time I was astonished, and not just by the incredible durability of Ponder's teeth. It was obvious to anyone watching that teeth, while a vital part of the act, were not *the* act itself. If two or three of us had placed the steel bar in the forks of a tree, for example, and if good and strong men pulled on the ends of the bar, we never could have bent it the way Ponder did.

The man's strength was prodigious! I wrote earlier about Robert Eng and how he jogged with a full-size automobile engine strapped to his back, and here was another human being with more strength than I could imagine.

While Ponder lifted the cage and its contents, I could not help noticing how his neck muscles bulged like immense ropes. After all, the teeth were holding the weight, but Ponder's shoulders, arms, and neck were lifting it. Old Ironjaw of the ancient comics might have had astonishing teeth, but he couldn't have done what Ponder did.

Next came the platform and the mule standing peacefully nearby. Ponder repeated the basic stunt we had seen earlier, but this time there was a steel ring attached to a harness-like assembly that circled the belly of the mule. Ponder bent over, took the ring in his teeth, and again the powerful arms, shoulders, and neck exerted their immense force, and the hooves of the mule left the ground and rose into the air several inches.

What struck me about the entire stunt was that the mule did not change expression as Ponder lifted it. To the mule, which may have been used regularly, this was just matter-of-course. And, again, the strength of the man's massive muscles was more astonishing than the teeth.

I did some quick calculating. The trainer in the cage had to weigh at least 110 pounds, which would have been enough for Ponder to amaze me, if he had lifted only her. The big cat weighed at least 150 pounds. Then the cage would have weighed 200 pounds at least and probably much more. That's 460 pounds, at the lowest figure.

The mule weighed several hundred pounds, but that's the best I can guess. According to the *Encyclopedia Britannica,* the largest mules weigh from 1200 to 1600 pounds, while the smallest mules weigh 600 pounds or more.

In another stunt Ponder had bathing beauties sit on each side of a rig, and he lifted both of them with ease. Again, he was lifting well over 200 pounds with his teeth, neck, and shoulders, in this case, because he did not use his arms except to help balance the load.

Next we moved to the firing range where Ponder placed the odd stock of the rifle into his mouth, and while he held the entire rifle straight out from his body and sighted down the barrel, he used a squeeze bulb to pull the trigger. He scored ten out of ten bullseyes by firing in this bizarre manner.

Then he went to the tractor-trailer truck and, using a special ring for a tooth-hold, he backed up and pulled the rig along with him. Then, to prove that the truck wasn't rolling downhill, he pushed it back to its original location. You can't have it both ways: the truck did not move downhill in both directions.

Joe Ponder may not have made it to the top in the boxing world, but there is no doubt that he has the world's strongest teeth.

Joe Ponder pulls a full-size tractor-trailer rig with his teeth.

Ponder bends a steel bar that four men could not straighten.

Lou and Cecil Barrier

Twenty-Six
The Gifts from the Magi

Yes, I know that the title of O. Henry's famous short story is "The Gift *of* the Magi," but that's not what this story is about. This one is about a man and his wife who did not give their gifts foolishly but very wisely. Like the famed Magi of the New Testament, they came bearing gifts, but theirs was not as impractical as frankincense, gold, or myrrh. These people brought material goods, of course, but they brought more valuable commodities as well.

They brought hope, faith, and courage to face the future and the world. They also brought a lot of themselves, too.

I had known Cecil and Lou Barrier for years, but as is so often the case, I did not know the people behind the public persona. It took a call from a magazine editor to start me to probing, and what I learned was nothing short of remarkable, and some of it bordered on the incredible. The story of this doctor, a genuine country doctor from the past who endured into the present, and his wife, a former nurse and then everybody's guardian angel, moved me as few have.

When the editor called, for several minutes I could not think of anyone who fit the description the editor wanted. Then it hit me with an almost blinding flash that the Barriers were and always had been, as long as any of the area residents could remember, exactly the people who personified the spirit of Christmas giving.

Why did it take me so long to think of these people? The answer is simple: they were always working, giving, helping others, and they gave their help so completely and without demands to such an extent that they were a fixture in people's minds. It was almost as if we were geared to wonder who else, other than the obvious choice of the Barriers, could we select as models of Christian giving.

The editor who called said he wanted a story for a Christmas issue of the magazine, a story that would reflect the spirit of giving and the love inspired by Christmas, but he wanted the article to be about people who presented Christmas everywhere they went every day of the year. Following is the story I wrote. I prefer to leave it in the original form so that you, the reader, can see what I learned and how I felt as I progressed in this story from only a basic familiarity into the genuine understanding of these two people.

Sadly, what started as a tribute became a memorial for Lou Barrier, who became suddenly ill just as the story was going to press, and she lingered for several days before losing her fight against death.

Here is the story as it unfolded.

When the Magi carried their gifts to Bethlehem, they started a tradition that has existed for 2,000 years. For many people in northern Cleveland County, one couple has come to embody that spirit of selfless giving: Dr. Cecil and Mary Lou Barrier.

For 30 years the Barriers comforted, cared and gave to people in need throughout the county. Their Earthly partnership ended on Nov. 7, when Mary Lou died at Carolinas Medical Center in Charlotte following a month-long illness.

Their legacy of loving and giving will continue to live as long as people care about each other, their friends say. "They loved each other with a devotion that is both rare and beautiful," says longtime friend Dawn Taylor, "and they loved their friends and neighbors and their church, their community and their God. I have never in my life seen anything to equal their concern and caring for others."

The husband-wife team began when Dr. Barrier, then an intern at the Medical College of Virginia in Richmond, met a young nurse named Mary Lou Lamm.

Friendship blossomed into love and the couple were married on November 26, 1960. Shortly afterwards they came to the Belwood community in Cleveland County to set up a medical practice.

People soon discovered that the Barriers had much more to give than medical help.

"They both have hearts as big as a tin tub," said friend Azalene Hoyle shortly before Mary Lou Barrier's death.

Recalled her husband, Edwin, "When there was sickness in the community, Lou Barrier was the first one there. She would leave her own work to bring food and to help in any way she could."

The stories of the Barriers' generosity permeate the community: free medical care and love for those in need; generous gifts and support for their church, St. Peter's United Methodist; free medical exams for the Burns High athletic teams; food, money and shelter to victims of the 1989 tornadoes.

"We lost everything," said a tornado victim who asked not to be identified. "In the wake of the storm came Cecil and Lou Barrier, bearing unflagging good cheer, encouragement and support from every angle. They didn't bring covered dishes; they brought meals. They brought whatever they thought we needed."

"In our entire lives our family has never witnessed such enormous acts of love and kindness."

Many people tell stories of similar selfless, second-mile giving by the Barriers.

Gerald Willis of Belwood was operating farm equipment when he plowed up a nest of yellow jackets. He barely made it back to the house.

"I remember that everything suddenly went black, and that was all I remembered until I regained consciousness," he said.

Then he added, "When I opened my eyes, Dr. Barrier was there. He had left his office, given me the shot that saved my life and saw that I could travel by ambulance safely to the hospital.

"I owe my life to that man, and to this day, years later, he has never sent me a bill."

Dawn Taylor was associate director of bands at Burns High from 1978 to 1984. The Barriers provided strong financial support for the band, but their love extended far beyond the music room, she said.

"Cecil and Lou exemplified Christian love and unselfishness in all areas of life," Taylor said.

She recalls accompanying the Barriers on Christmas Eves as they drove throughout upper Cleveland County and delivered groceries and other articles to families in need.

"We went into one home that had only a dirt floor," Taylor says. "In another there were people totally helpless to secure food and shelter. In one area someone had broken into the house and had stolen all the Christmas gifts. When the Barriers left, they had left Christmas in its deepest meaning behind them."

The Barriers seemed to view their generosity as just a normal part of living, like breathing. Once, after Cecil Barrier had helped two South American visitors pay a hospital bill, this writer asked Barrier why he had done it.

"Well, they needed help and I was in a position to help them, so why not?" he replied.

Lou's attitude was much the same.

"It's just hard for us to rest easily when we know of people we could help and who need our help," she once told this reporter. "We can rest after the help is given."

Christmas 1991 will be different from past Christmases in upper Cleveland County.

Lou Barrier will not be spreading her love, concern and other gifts. That job will fall, it is hoped, to the scores of men and women who have been touched by the Barriers' love.

And perhaps some folks will see a second change: an extra star, brighter and more glorious than the rest, in the Christmas heavens.

As O. Henry pointed out in his classic Christmas story, people who love the most and devote themselves to others are the real Magi.

The people who knew and loved the Barriers will say that O Henry must have been writing about Lou and Cecil.

That was the first story, and it was intended to be all of it. Then, five weeks from the time Lou Barrier died, Cecil Barrier was visiting his son in Raleigh and during the night he suffered a fatal heart attack.

The same editor called and asked if I could do a sort of eulogy for the magazine, since we had introduced the Barriers to the public. Or to that tiny part of the public that did not already know them.

I asked how long I had, and the editor, who called fairly late one evening, asked if I could get the material in the mail to him early in the morning. There were only two possible options, and one of them was no option at all. I could somehow find a way to write about the death of Dr. Cecil Barrier, despite my own despondency that came from losing two superb friends. Or I could decline and let the magazine go to press without the story.

That, as I said, was no option. I had to write the tribute.

I made my way to the office and sat down to write. What follows is the first draft of the article, word for word. I did not change one syllable, and neither did the editor. The story said what I wanted it to say at the time, and we left it as it was. Here is that story.

I attended funeral services for a friend Wednesday, Dec. 18. In reality, however, the service was for two friends: Dr. Cecil Barrier and his wife, Mary Lou, who had died five weeks before her husband's death.

After the services I met a man and asked if he was a friend of the Barriers.

"No," he said. "They were not friends of mine. I never met them."

What an incredible statement! How fantastically true!

What the man said, regardless of what he meant, was that the only reason they were not friends is that he had never met them.

If he had known them, of course they would have been friends!

And when I went to the computer to begin this note, I realized for the first time the significance of the Barrier file, which is, because the computer that I used at the time would not accept long file names, CECILOU.

How fitting! Her funeral service was not only for her, just as his service was not only for him. The services were for CECILOU and for everyone who knew and loved them. They were man and wife, friends, partners in every way; they were the embodiment of Plato's wonderful notion that no man can find happiness until he discovers the other half of his being.

Earlier I wrote a tribute that became a memorial to two people whose lives mattered to all of us, and I quoted a number of people. This note is not theirs. They have had their say. This is what *I* think and what I feel.

CECILOU, you were more fortunate than most. You found your completion in each other's presence, and there was too much love for one union to contain, and you shared it with your family and with your church and friends and everyone you met who needed it and there is still an excess. It overflows each of us even now as we think of you.

A neighbor said that it is hard to believe that you are gone. I had no comment for him. How could I tell him how wrong he was, that you are not gone and never will be gone from us?

Gone? Your friends included doctors, nurses, farmers, teachers, mechanics, factory workers, school kids, elderly widows, the helpless, the rich, the educated, the illiterate. While they live, the memory of you is alive and well!

Gone? While everyone who passes your house-- your home! – and recalls visits there, smells the wonderful aroma of the miracle kitchen of the Barriers, and experiences again a handful of the many memories and gifts of your love and caring?

Not with us? While I sit in the chair that was once your office chair, and while my computer sits on your old office desk, a desk where every scratch, every mark, is a symbol of a sick one healed, a hopeless one given hope, a needy one given help?

You will be here among us every time we see from our front porch headlights knifing through the midnight darkness and for the briefest of moments you are again returning home from a late house call in some remote part of the county.

Gone, while we live in a house we could not have built without you to fight for us and encourage us? We see you and sense your presence in everything you touched, and you touched all of us in myriads of unforgettable ways.

Lost to us? While the church you worshipped in bears the mark of your love and dedication at every point, from door to altar to organ to chimes to flowers, and while the eyes of your friends glisten with tears whenever they unwillingly glance at the church cemetery?

The CECILOU file will remain in the computer, but even if it is somehow erased, the heart is not subject to power glitches and the memory of mankind exceeds that of any electronic device– in matters of genuine importance.

And everyone has a special memory compartment where the best and warmest elements of human life are memorialized. Your place is permanent.

If all physical evidences of your lives among us are obliterated, we will nevertheless be surprised by a glimpse of a stranger who looks disturbingly familiar, an inflection of a voice, the peal of delighted laughter, the weight of a warm hand on our shoulders, and for a fleeting moment you will be beside us again. Or we will meet a mutual friend who, if not for your care and professionalism, would indeed be gone.

Gone? You will be gone when moonlight over silky water brings no joy and when the first flowers of spring gladden no hearts. Gone? You will be gone when–and only when– spring fails to delight, autumn fails to thrill, the rose refuses to bloom, lovers refuse to share their innermost thoughts and hopes and dreams, when glowing fires on bitterly cold nights give no comfort, and God relinquishes the world to darkness, for memory and eternity are but varying points on the same continuum.

Until then, you are with us. We know you are there because we are surrounded by your testaments of love. We were privileged to be your friend, and we are honored that you were ours.

That was it. It was all I could think of to say about a man and woman who cared infinitely for others–and found a way to make that caring real and lasting.

If the Barriers happened to be riding around the Upper Cleveland County area and happened to see an old woman laboriously scrubbing clothes in an old washtub, odds were great that the next day a brand-new washing machine would be delivered to the woman's house. And if she did not happen to have electrical power to her residence, that would come, too, and the Barriers would pay the bills.

If they saw an old man trying to start a lawnmower, a new lawn mower arrived within hours. If they learned about a family in need, they provided medical aid, groceries, clothing, blankets, a new heating system, or whatever else was needed.

Once Cecil Barrier, out late one night on a house call, drove the new

Cadillac he had just bought down a rutted country road. A friend with Barrier asked him why in the world he drove a new car into such terrain.

Barrier's answer was to the point: "Who do you think bought this car?" he asked.

After the tornado destroyed our home and our insurance company did not remember our names and after FEMA informed us that we were not eligible for any help, we realized that we had lost everything we owned, and we had no way, at the time, of fighting back.

Remember that tornado victim mentioned earlier? I was that person, of course, and Dr. Barrier one day handed me a Christmas card. In it were four hundred dollar bills. That money helped me to reestablish my office so that I could continue writing, and it helped me and my family to progress from victims to victors!

It has now been many years since Cecil Barrier left the Jonas Ridge community and several years more since the Barriers left Belwood. But their legacy remains as if they had departed yesterday.

This isn't to say that two people make a community. What it really is intended to say is that no community, no matter how large or small, can really afford to lose two people like Cecil and Lou Barrier. But this is also meant to say more. It says that Belwood has continued to prosper and grow in its ever-so-slow graceful manner. And it will continue to grow and prosper for many years to come.

It will continue to thrive because people like the Barriers set their examples and these ideals are being continued and cherished. That's what earthly immortality is all about. Shakespeare is more revered now than he ever was in real life. Van Gogh, Michelangelo, Rembrandt, Verdi, Brahms, Beethoven, Bach, and the rest of the truly great artists and composers and authors will continue to live in our minds and hearts for one simple set of reasons: they understood their lives as well as anyone ever has, and they have taught us part of their secret. They felt an inner beauty and they struggled desperately to bring it to the surface, to put it down on paper or to offer it through the piano or violin or cello or carve it in stone.

They could not express it all to all of us, because only the classical mind can understand the classics fully. But they presented us the gift or as much of it as we can comprehend. It is now our duty and responsibility to build on that gift. That's what people like the Barriers do for us. They give us the head start, and we can perpetuate their values and then add our own.

Twenty-Seven
Men–and Women–to Match Mountains

You can reach Doughton Park easily from I-40 by exiting at Statesville onto I-77 north. Leave I-77 in Elkin and take US 21 north toward Sparta. Shortly before you reach Sparta you will intersect with the Blue Ridge Parkway. Drive south for 15 minutes to Doughton Park. And you can reach the home of one of the hardiest families in the history of the South by hiking–not driving–about ten miles through a wilderness. Or you can take the easy way out and enjoy the experience by reading the following pages.

The park is open seven days a week, 24 hours a day every day of the year, unless the Parkway is closed because of bad weather. Don't even think about going there when there is snow on the ground, and don't consider hiking into the forest unless you are experienced and in reasonably good shape. Face it: most of us can't begin to compete with the Caudills.

Doughton Park is a 6,000 acre expanse of wilderness with only one highway, the Blue Ridge Parkway, reaching it. Named after Congressman Robert Lee Doughton, the park has 36 miles of hiking trails, superb overlooks, the historic cabin of Martin Caudill and his wife and children, and the Little Glade Mill Pond, a beautiful place to stop for quiet and serene nature study.

To prepare yourself for the trip through the woods, stop at the Brinegar Cabin just on the border of Doughton Park. At the Cabin you can make a visit into the past to enjoy the way the pioneers in the area lived. The cabin is highly authentic, as are the skills and crafts practiced by the persons at the cabin. If you are lucky you might see the actual weaving or spinning process on the earliest equipment.

Drive (or walk) to Wildcat Rock (the picnic tables are located near the parking area) and park in the paved area. Climb the short flight of steps and the narrow trail to the Wildcat Rock Overlook from which you can see, almost one mile below, the cabin and small clearing where the Martin Caudill family lived.

There is a makeshift trail leading down the slope of the hill straight to the cabin. I do not suggest that you take this trail, although you may see others attempting it. This is a route both strenuous and dangerous.

If you want to see the cabin close-up, you can drive a few miles and try the Basin Creek Trail, which is 10.9 miles round trip. Drive south on the Parkway to the exit for NC 18 to the town of Wilkesboro. Follow this highway south for six miles to Longbottom Road (State Road 1728). Turn left and drive for four miles to State Road 1730. Take SR 1730 for three miles to a bridge over a trout stream. Here you will see a place to park and the entrance to Grassy Gap Fire Road.

If you hike this trail, you will ford the creek several times, so be prepared to carry along dry socks, to wade barefoot, or hike in soggy socks. As you hike you will past a series of old chimneys, a millstone lying in the creek, and other evidence of a once-vital village. The houses in this area were washed away by the tragic flood of 1916. The Caudill Cabin is one of the few that survived one of the most devastating floods in the history of North Carolina.

Martin Caudill's cabin is at the end of the trail. When you reach the cabin you will see that the residence, where Caudill and his wife reared their 17 children, is little more than a hut. There are cracks in the walls and in the floor, and there is very little room inside the cabin.

You can imagine the family huddled around the tiny fireplace as the high winds and subzero temperatures chilled the valley and clearing where deer, bear, foxes, and other animals once roamed the forests. Or imagine the family sleeping in the tiny loft or in the family part of the structure. Far more dramatic, in a sense, is to imagine the family as they made the trek you just completed whenever they wanted to buy or trade for flour, coffee, or other staples. Any time any member of the family wanted to visit "civilization," that person had to make the 10.9 mile hike and cross the same creek you crossed about a dozen times on your trip in. The Caudills were doubtless men and women of honor.

What is their message? It takes life to love life, as poet Edgar Lee Masters told us long ago. That truth has not faded in the least.

Twenty-Eight
The Year without Nights

During the first months of World War II, North Carolinians living in the coastal area were closer to the war than were most of the United States soldiers on active duty overseas. Not only were there German submarines operating nearby, but German soldiers actually walked up and down the coast of Ocracoke Island.

Many Tar Heel residents know little, if anything, about the terribly devastating months during which German submarines sank as many as five ships in one night, many of them so close to the coast of Hatteras Island and Ocracoke Island that islanders later said that it was possible to read a newspaper on the beach at midnight, by the light of the burning vessels.

During the first six months of World War II, more than 400 ships were sunk off America's coastlines, many of them virtually in the harbors. And North Carolina was not spared the carnage. In fact, the area off the coast of Hatteras Island has been labeled "Torpedo Junction" because of the enormous numbers of ships sunk by the U-boats.

The Germans themselves referred to the helpless vessels in the shipping lanes as a "turkey shoot" or as *Paukenschlag,* or drum beat. But whatever the name, the secret war of Hatteras and surrounding territory will go down in American history as one of the costliest conflicts in the nation's history.

It will also be remembered by scholars as one of the most inept battles this country has ever fought, a mini-war in which a handful of U-boats massacred ships leaving American ports while top military advisors in colossal acts of misjudgments flatly refused to accept the much-needed and often-offered assistance from Great Britain.

Admiral Ernest J. King, commander-in-chief of the U. S. Fleet, proved to be a man not only inept and stubborn but often totally ignorant of the needs of the nation and of the U. S. Navy in particular. A high-ranking member of the staff of Sir Winston Churchill described Admiral King as "blunt and stand-offish, almost to the point of rudeness." The same staffer added that King was intolerant and suspicious, especially of all things British. It took months of strategy to undo the horrible losses of lives and war materials.

Perhaps the most brutal assessment of King's performance came from General Dwight David Eisenhower, who reportedly said, "He is an arbitrary stubborn type, with not too much brains and a tendency toward bullying his juniors. One thing that might help win this war is to shoot King."

The slaughter of the innocents began on the night of January 18, 1942, as the tanker *Allan Jackson* sailed northward sixty miles off Cape Hatteras. This 4,038 ton ship loaded with more than 70,000 barrels of crude oil was detected by the sub U-66. The ship was running with all lights ablaze as U-66 commander Richard Zapp stalked the ship for four hours before he felt that he was in the ideal position. He gave the command to fire the first torpedo.

The second mate aboard the ship saw the torpedo coming, but it was too late to maneuver away from a direct hit. Within seconds a second torpedo hit, and the *Alan Jackson* broke in half and sank quickly.

Zapp's next conquest was a Canadian passenger liner, the *Lady Hawkins,* carrying 300 passengers. More than 200 of these men and women perished when the ship sank. By the end of that month, eight more ships had gone to the bottom, and three remarkable conditions accompanied the sinkings. First, Admiral King made no significant tactical changes in the feeble efforts of the United States government to mount a defense against the subs. Second, there were no important changes in the shipping patterns. Third, the United States government refused to acknowledge that there were German U-boats in North Carolina waters or that there had been any damage sustained as a result of enemy attacks.

Admiral King brought in only a handful of boats that had neither the size, the speed, the maneuverability, nor the fire power to fight against an unseen foe whose very existence was staunchly denied by the government. Even if the boats had the luck to spot a submarine, the sub's speed could easily outdistance the fastest vessels in the area. Few if any planes were available for use as spotters, and even if there had been planes, the pilots could not have seen the subs, which submerged to the bottom of the Atlantic during daytime hours, only to rise after dark and again engage in the "turkey shoot" that was costing the United States and her allies millions and millions of dollars in critical war supplies and inestimable losses in manpower.

Cities along the coast did not enforce blackouts at night, and the German subs could easily spot tankers and other vessels silhouetted against the coastline lights. Even the beacons from the Cape Hatteras lighthouse and other lighthouses were not extinguished. The German commanders of the U-boats wrote in their logs of the glee and disbelief in their unexpected good fortunes as they sank ship after ship and the United States made no changes to prevent even further attacks.

The British government urged the United States to take at least two minimal steps: to accept the British offer of armed trawlers to help in the sub patrols and to send out ships in convoys rather than singly. During March the Germans sank ships at almost the incredible rate of one per day, and in one single tragic day the U-boats sank a total of five ships during the twenty-four hour period.

And yet neither the President of the United States nor the commander-in-chief of the American Fleet admitted that there were any losses. At first the German commanders laughed in disbelief as sub attacks were blamed on ships hitting mines.

One of the most dramatic losses made it impossible, however, for the government to continue its denial of shipping losses and hundreds of deaths of passengers, crew, and service men. The ship that unfortunately forced an open admission was the *Caribsea.*

One of the engineers aboard the *Caribsea* was James Gaskins, an Ocracoke Island resident. When the ship left port, his family did not hear from him afterward, and in such cases it was usually accepted that the war prevented communications.

Then one day the name plate of the *Caribsea* washed up on the shore of the island, and prominently visible was the name of the unfortunate James Gaskins. There was no way the government could deny the loss of the ship, and more and more admissions were issued in coming months.

One of the most touching stories of the secret war was that of the sinking of the *HMS Bedfordshire*, a British armed trawler on loan from

England. The *Bedfordshire* was sunk in May 1942 off the coast of Cape Lookout. The exact date of the sinking is unknown, but one day the bodies of four British seamen washed up on the shore of Ocracoke.

Local residents appropriated a burial ground for them at the end of a narrow street on the island. The street was then renamed British Cemetery Street, and the Union Jack was hoisted to the top of the flagpole there. No other flag flies over the graves, and the location is one of the few places in the United States where a foreign flag flies alone.

At the entrance to the cemetery are the words of Rupert Brooke inscribed upon an information sign: "If I should die, think only this of me: That there's some corner of a foreign field that is forever England."

The lines from Brooke's poem "The Soldier" seldom fail to touch anyone who pauses to read the story of the *Bedfordshire* that appears on a nearby plaque. But just across the island there is another tiny graveyard with a story that is equally touching.

At the Ocracoke United Methodist Church there is a beautifully carved wooden cross mounted on the wall behind the altar. The wood used for making the cross is from the name plate section of the ship *Caribsea* on which James Gaskins died.

A short distance away is the Ocracoke Lighthouse, and behind the lighthouse there are several graves of family members who were important to the island. One of the gravestones marks the symbolic resting place of James Gaskins. His epitaph says simply, "Lost at Sea." Accompanying the brief inscription is an appropriate quote from Tennyson's "Crossing the Bar": "But such a tide as moving seems asleep, too deep for sound and foam, when that which drew from out the boundless deep turns again home."

The stone and the wooden cross pay a far greater tribute than mere words can to a man who gave his life in a secret war, but his death helped to make the war public information. Like the British sailors aboard the *Bedfordshire,* Gaskins earned his small slot in American history, and a permanent place in the hearts and minds of those who visit the Outer Banks and who value courage and honor and sacrifice and heroism.

Lighthouses became one of the greatest assets to the German U-Boats because the strong light silhouetted ships and made them easy targets.

Inside the United Methodist Church on Ocracoke Island you can see the cross made from the wood on the name plate of the Caribsea.

Toccoa Falls in North Georgia

Twenty-Nine
The Dream That Would Not Die

Toccoa is a Cherokee word meaning "beautiful," and a delightful place it is, with a waterfall flowing through the college campus. A few years ago the campus and the waterfall figured prominently in one of the greatest tragedies ever experienced by a college campus, and the courage shown as the campus and the college family put their lives back together is nothing less than inspiring. The waterfall is a physical symbol of the eternal struggle of mankind against incredible odds and the devastating power of Nature.

Many people are not aware that the college that figured so prominently in the tragedy was once a North Carolina school located not far from South Mountains State Park but on the opposite side of the mountain. How that transfer from the hills of the Tar Heel State to the mountains of north Georgia occurred will be explained later. But for now think about going to Georgia, at least in your imagination.

Half an hour from I-85 will bring you into the beautiful Georgia town of Toccoa. To get to the college campus and the waterfall, follow Georgia State Highway 17-A through Toccoa. Just outside town the campus lies on the left side of the highway. You will pass an entrance hut. When the road forks, stay to the left and proceed to the back side of the campus. Enter to the waterfall and park via the bookstore.

In the early morning hours of November 6, 1977, after torrential rains had filled the Kelly Barnes Lake just above Toccoa Falls College, the earthen dam, built in 1877, gave way. As the dam broke, 176,000,000 gallons of water roared down the tiny gorge just above the campus. The 55-acre lake was emptied in approximately eighteen minutes.

Then the flood roared over Toccoa Falls and filled the streambed with a huge wall of water moving at a reported speed of 180 miles per hour. The torrent washed away virtually everything in its path.

The wall of water was 35 feet high, and the high water mark was six inches from the upstairs ceiling of buildings beside the usually gentle Toccoa Creek. Visit the creek under normal conditions and you will see little more than a strong brook, but on the night of this tragedy the wall of water was a force of incomprehensible strength and unmitigated fury as it crushed everything in its way.

Within a span of about eight minutes, buildings were crushed like matchboxes, cars were smashed against one another, and, worst of all, 39 persons perished in the flood as the estimated 700,000 tons of water and hydraulic force demolished man-made structures.

Today, visitors to the scene can find little evidence that a flood ever occurred on the campus. The memorial stones bear their mute testimony to the tragedy, and a somber attitude permeates virtually everyone who visits the scene.

But Toccoa Falls is not a place of sadness, the people of the area insist. They point out that the college had a glorious beginning, has enjoyed an impeccable reputation through the years, and its future seems to hold even greater potential.

Ironically, Toccoa Falls College had its origin in North Carolina, rather than in Georgia. In fact, the original campus was located only a short drive from several major highways and within a short drive from several towns of considerable size, but if you are in the Golden Valley community at the present time, you will be fortunate indeed if you can find anyone who can show you where the original South Mountain Institute was located. In fact, it would be unusual for you to find anyone who ever heard of the school. When I was there everyone wanted to send me to the Baptist camp or similar locations rather than to the school that once dominated the area.

In 1907 Dr. Richard A. Forrest established Golden Valley Institute in the tiny community of Golden in Rutherford County. The names "Golden" and "Golden Valley" were interchangeably used. Four years after the institute was organized, its founder decided to move the campus to Georgia.

The story of how the college found a home is a remarkable one in that Dr. Forrest, when he approached the banker who owned the land where the college is now located, had only $10 to his name, and he offered to buy the land if the banker would accept the $10 and the promise to pay the rest when he could.

"I will owe you the other $24,990," Forrest told the banker, "if you will trust the Lord and us."

"I can trust the Lord," the banker said, accepting the cash and arranging the transfer of property.

It took far more than trust, however; in fact, it took months of gruelling work, more money than anyone thought it possible to raise under the conditions, and a great deal of faith on the parts of all those who wanted the college to succeed in Toccoa.

But succeed it did. At the present time the school seems to be going strong; it boasts a modest-sized student body, a Christian radio station, and a great deal more than should be (but often isn't) associated with getting a college education.

Today visitors (and visitors are welcomed to the campus and to the park where the waterfall is located) can see the campus that emerged from the flood. Toccoa Falls College is a beautiful place, with tasteful buildings, a dedicated faculty and student body, 1,100 acres of beautiful land.

The 186-foot waterfall is only one of the attractions. Nearby are shopping and sight-seeing opportunities as well as restaurants and overnight accommodations. And visitors need not worry about another flood. The dam was never rebuilt.

Don't think that people there will ever forget the horrors of that fateful night. That memory, as unpleasant as it is, will never fade from the forefront of people's minds. Even those who weren't around or even born at the time of the flood will hear about the tragedy year after year.

There is a slight admission charge ($1) for each visitor, and at the book store there is a gift shop. One of the items on sale is a book entitled "Dam Break in Georgia," which tells the story of the flood that claimed 39 lives but did not damage the faith or the future of Toccoa Falls College.

While this is not a travel trip but instead a story of the death and rebirth of a college and a way of life, while you are in the area you can visit many other scenic and inspirational points. I strongly recommend trips to Dahlonega, Helen, Cleveland, and Gainesville, among other fine Georgia locations that will inspire and inform you on important topics.

Waterfalls are plentiful in the mountains along the borders of North Carolina, and the peaks are among the most impressive in the East.

Thirty
A Baker's Dozen of Peak Performances

This special chapter is not people worth meeting, nor, in the strictest sense, is it stories worth repeating. It is, however, your opportunity to encounter your own stories and to savor them and repeat them as you relate them to others. This is a visit to thirteen mountain peaks that are either in North Carolina or are on the border of one of this state's splendid neighbors. So read on, and prepare to start your travels and story-gathering.

"Spring is the mischief in me," Robert Lee Frost once wrote about an attitude, a state of mind, a perspective, a viewpoint. The Poet Laureate of the gentle aphorism was writing about why we insist on building walls, but if the bard ever visited the mountains of Western North Carolina, he could see—and approve of—some of the finest walls every constructed.

And they were built by Nature, not by laborers or by human nature. These are the walls that separate clan from clan, state from state, and culture from heritage, and while doing so they create peak experiences equal to those anywhere east of the Big Muddy.

It is impossible to drive or walk these peaks without encountering beauty around every curve, under every footstep. Each autumn it is a tradition for the family to take the fall leaves trip, but it must be noted that in the spring there is a stark beauty unseen at any other time of the year, and in the summer there is such a proliferation of loveliness that only blindness of the soul could find lacking.

For those who wish to create their own peak experiences, there are countless peaks and valleys waiting, and while it is virtually impossible to limit the attractions, I have tried to keep the best—each for a different reason—peaks down to a baker's dozen.

You can make the complete loop or use I-40 as a dividing line and do either the peaks above or below the interstate. No matter which way you travel, each trip is of a different length and each journey explores a different part of the mountains of Western North Carolina (the first word is capitalized here for a simple reason: once you leave the Piedmont and Foothills, you are in a totally different state), Northern South Carolina, Eastern Tennessee, and, if you opt for the below-I-40 version, the northeast tip of Georgia.

For the whole nine yards and thirteen peaks, drive down I-85 until you reach Exit 92 in Gaffney, the beginning of the Cherokee Foothills Scenic Highway. At the first intersection follow SC 11 west and continue until you reach the Cowpens Battlefield where you can stop for a picnic lunch, a walk, or a history lesson.

Remain on SC 11 through Chesnee and Cleveland until you reach River Falls Road. Turn here and drive to Jones Gap State Park for some rewarding scenery as you watch the trout stream as it weaves its way through the park, or you can hike any of the 46 miles of trails in the 4,000 acres of the park.

Peak No. 1

For your first genuine peak experience, you can travel in one of two ways. First, you can drive on SC 11 until you reach the junction of US 276. Follow this highway to Caesar's Head where you can park, enjoy the panoramic views, and try to find the head of Julius Caesar (Or was it Octavius or Augustus or Sid?) on the cliffside. If your imagination runs a little to the free side, you can even see Caesar sticking out his tongue at some unseen entity, presumably Pompey.

The second way to reach the 3,266-foot elevation of Caesar's Head is the old-fashioned way: by walking. At the Jones Gap State Park you can buy $2 contour maps with all the hiking trails clearly marked, and you can select your own trail and hike to Caesar's Head, as long as you have someone to drive the car and wait for you. You can also camp at the park if you wish.

Leaving the Mountain Bridge Wilderness and Recreation Area (which includes both Caesar's Head and Jones Gap) drive north into North Carolina and into Brevard on US 276. While there is much to do in Brevard— shopping, dining, camping, waterfall viewing, etc.—you can intersect with US 64, the famous waterfall highway, and head west through Rosman,

Toxaway, and Sapphire. You can leave the peak adventure briefly by taking NC 281 south to Whitewater Falls, said to be the highest waterfall east of the Mississippi. Follow signs to the parking lot and walk 200 feet to the overlook. If time and energy permit, you can hike to the very bottom of the falls, but be forewarned: the trip down is at times dangerous, but the trek back up is strenuous and time-consuming.

You can also hike upward from the overlook to the rim of the falls. Again, be careful. You will see signs informing you that a number of people have fallen to their deaths over the falls, and you are well advised to stay behind the barriers and to exert uncommon care when hiking near the ledges.

Return to US 64 and continue west through Cashiers and toward Highlands. Before you reach the city limits of this quaint and beautiful mountain town, you will see signs directing you to the Whiteside Mountain area.

Peak No. 2.

At Whiteside Mountain you can park at the base (after driving on SR 1600, also known as the Whiteside Mountain Road, a little more than a mile on a dead end road) and take the hiking trail to the top of the 5,000-plus foot peak. There are no roads, so if you want to see the top, you must walk.

There are adventurous persons who wish to scale the 450-700-foot rock cliffs from August to January, but in other times of the year climbing is prohibited because of the nesting peregrine falcons. These birds are on the endangered list and their propagation is a primary consideration. But you can still hike the trail, which is roughly two miles long and at times arduous and difficult.

From the peak of Whiteside Mountain you can see for miles and miles into North and South Carolina and huge parts of northern Georgia. Even if you don't climb the mountain, you can enjoy the panoramic views from the overlooks alongside US 64.

Peak No. 3

If food and overnight accommodations are a concern, you can leave US 64 in Highlands and follow NC 106 into Dillard, Georgia. There you will find antique and souvenir stores and some of the most beautiful terrain anywhere east of the Mississippi. You will also find some of the best food in the South.

Stop at the Dillard House for a banquet at moderate prices. For $12.95

per person we were served on an all-you-can-eat basis barbecued chicken, fried chicken, country ham, filet of flounder, shrimp, prime rib, seven vegetables, and almost a dozen wonderful desserts. You can eat all you want of everything, and more food will be brought to your table as long as you wish to eat. There is also a salad bar.

In Dillard you are perched on a mountainside that offers more of the incredible scenery of the area. You are three miles from Clayton, where some of the Olympic kayaking activities were held, and one mile from Mountain City. Here you can trout fish, ride horseback, canoe, hike, and enjoy motoring through the area. From Dillard drive two miles south to Mountain City where you will find the entrance to the Black Rock Mountain State Park, which is the highest state park in Georgia. You are at an altitude of 3,640 feet above sea level and from the top of the mountain you can enjoy scenic overlooks which provide spectacular views of the most outstanding terrain in the Georgia Blue Ridge Mountains.

As you return to Highlands (the drive to Dillard is only 11 miles and well worth the time and effort) look for a fantastic waterfall on the mountainside just outside town. The waterfall is inaccessible from the highway but you get a fine view of it from your car, particularly later in the day when the sunlight strikes it head-on. The poorest view is early morning. In drought conditions the waterfall is diminished terribly.

Back in Highlands continue west on US 64. Just outside town you will see Bridal Veil Falls on the right side of the highway. The volume of water is not great, but the falls are attractive and unique in that you can drive your car under the falls if you wish.

For another unique waterfall stop at Dry Falls, which requires a five-minute and very easy walk on a paved path to the base of the falls where you can walk behind the falls and stay dry despite the enormous volume of the Cullasaja River.

As you drive through the Cullasaja Gorge you will see a series of waterfalls, some of them majestic and all of them beautiful. Drive through Franklin (better yet, stop at the two museums there, both of which are excellent) and as you drive toward Hayesville look for signs directing you to Standing Indian recreation area.

Peak No. 4

About 14 miles west of Franklin you will see the sign that directs you to Standing Indian Mountain. This is State Road 1448, which leads to the

5,499-foot peak that is so-named because of the resemblance of the peak formation to a standing Indian. The legend is that the Indian betrayed the code of his tribe and was, like Lot's wife, turned into a pillar but of stone rather than salt.

At Standing Indian you will find space for tent camping, trailer camping, hiking trails, fishing opportunities on Kimsey Creek, showers, drinking water, and beautiful scenery. There is a small fee charged for using the area.

From Hayesville move on to Murphy and to Robbinsville via US 129. In Robbinsville, where famed Indian Chief Junaluska and his wife Nicie are buried and where, in the nearby Santeelah Lake where the movie *Nell* was filmed, you can reach the newest and in many respects the finest of the scenic drives in the South.

Peak No. 5

Follow NC 143 north of Murphy and intersect with the superb Cherohala Skyway, which opened only a few years ago and is still one of the best-kept secrets among North Carolina highways. This road is astonishing. You climb from 3,000 feet to 5,240 within only a few minutes, and at the crest of the mountains you have a view that is unparalleled except on the Blue Ridge Parkway.

The peak here is not one but a series of crests that greet the tourist with one scenic expanse after another. In honesty there is not one place on the Cherohala Skyway that is not scenic and beautiful. For 51 miles you can enjoy a drive that is almost one of solitude. On our trip I doubt that we met more than a dozen cars during the entire drive.

Near the end of the Skyway you are in Tennessee, and before the Skyway ends you will note that the highway has become Tennessee Highway 165. Also near the end of the drive you will see a road sign directing you to Bald River Falls. This drive is incredibly beautiful as it leads for six miles along the Tellico and Bald River. At the end of the six-mile trip you will see on the right side of the road an incredible waterfall that can be seen from the car. You can park on the opposite side of the bridge and walk back for a better view.

Half a mile upstream you will see Tellico Baby Falls where the kayakers love to practice their waterfall maneuvers. On a warm day you may see dozens of kayakers guide their crafts over the falls and into the 12-foot deep plunge pool.

Drive into Tellico Plains and follow Tennessee Highway 69 northwest to Madisonville, where you are within a few miles of the Lost Sea, Fort Loudoun, and the Sequoyah Birthplace Museum, all worthy of your visit. The latter two charge no admission and are great for the history buffs and the younger people on the trip.

Peak No. 6

Tennessee Highway 411 is, unless the weather is bad, an extremely pleasant drive. In winter months there is a great deal of fog in the area. Remain on this highway until you reach Maryville, home of Maryville College and one of the prettiest towns you are likely to locate in east Tennessee. The majestic courthouse and gorgeous churches of all denominations mark nearly every block of downtown Maryville. When you leave town, follow US 321 east to Gatlinburg and then change to US 441 and drive to the North Carolina border.

As you enter North Carolina within a few miles you will see the turnoff to Clingman's Dome, which has an elevation of 6,642 feet. You are in the Great Smoky Mountains National Park, a wilderness area that includes 520,000 acres, 275,000 of which are in North Carolina.

Expect crowds. The park has more visitors annually than any other park in the United States, with more than 10 million visitors each year. At Clingman's Dome you can find hiking trails that lead for miles into valleys and from peak to peak.

But the most popular hike is the short .5-mile walk up a paved incline to the observation tower. The tower offers a great look at nearby peaks, valleys, lakes, and streams. The tower has a circular overlook affording a 360-degree view. Plaques on the observatory walls identify prominent landmarks and tell a brief history of the area.

Remember that even on warm days the temperatures at the mile-high–plus– peaks can be chilly. In spring ice remains on the shaded side of the peaks for weeks after sunny areas have thawed. You can walk from the oven to the refrigerator in a matter of seconds.

Peak No. 7.

From the Great Smoky Mountain National Park you can leave by driving to Cherokee and then taking US 19 back to I-40 and to Asheville. If time permits and you want a loop drive, head south on US 19 to intersect with the Blue Ridge Parkway.

Notice the mile markers as you enter the Blue Ridge Parkway. When you reach Milepost 422 you will turn off into a small parking lot and you are at Devil's Courthouse. You can view the peak from the parking lot, or you can walk north along the side of the Parkway for 100 yards and then take the half-mile trail to the top of the mountain where the Cherokee god Judaculla, the one-eyed Satanic creature, sat in judgment of the courage and morality of the Cherokees.

The trail is short but strenuous, and you may be grateful for the benches placed strategically along the trail for the relaxation of hikers. At the top you are rewarded by another of the incredible panoramic views of major peaks in the area and the mountains of three states, perhaps four, if the weather is clear.

Peak No. 8

Continue north on the Parkway for fifteen minutes until you pass the Mount Pisgah Inn on the right. Immediately afterward you will see the parking area for Mount Pisgah, which, like Devil's Courthouse, rises to almost 6,000 feet. Again, the trail to the top requires hiking, and the total trek is three miles, round trip. The trail is wide but strenuous on the way up.

At the top you will see the incredible estate once owned by the Vanderbilts, who once possessed 125,000 acres of forest and farm lands in the area. The family, whose wealth in 1877 was estimated to be more than $100 million, had trails blazed from the family mansion to the Mount Pisgah area so that hunting trips could be made easier.

Peak No. 9

Leaving Mount Pisgah, drive northward past Asheville to Milepost 364 and you will find yourself at Craggy Gardens, which in early summer is ablaze with blossoms from rhododendron and laurel. The glorious flower display is 5,220 feet above sea level, while nearby Craggy pinnacle is 5,892.

On this peak you will find 700 acres of hiking trails and scenic beauty. There is a picnic shelter for protection from the summer storms which occur almost daily in the hot months. The hiking trail is a round trip of 4.9 miles, much of it through flower displays never seen by those who remain in the area near the parking lot.

The trail to the top of Craggy Pinnacle is steep but wide, and you will hike among rhododendron all the way to the top, where you will again have a 360-degree view of surrounding mountains and valleys.

Peak No. 10

No peak experience would be complete without a visit to the highest point east of the Mississippi. To get to Mount Mitchell, with an altitude of 6,684 feet, continue northward on the Parkway until you reach the exit for NC 128. Follow signs to Mount Mitchell State Park, where you will find an observatory tower and the burial site of Dr. Elisha Mitchell, the man who accurately calculated the height of the mountain and proved it to be higher than Mount Washington in New Hampshire.

In the terrain surrounding Mount Mitchell you will see 40 peaks that are more than 6,000 feet high and 80 peaks that are 5,000 feet or higher. Ironically, the mountain killed Dr. Mitchell, or at least a nearby waterfall did. When Mitchell did not return from a hike, a search party including Zeb Vance, future governor of North Carolina, combed the mountains and found the body of Dr. Mitchell at the foot of a 40-foot waterfall.

Mitchell was buried in Asheville, near the graves of Zeb Vance, novelist Thomas Wolfe, and short story writer O. Henry (William Sidney Porter), but later the remains of Dr. Mitchell were transported to the mountain he had made famous. Later, Gov. Locke Craig campaigned to have the mountain preserved for public use as a state park, and in 1917 the area became the very first state park in North Carolina history.

Peak No. 11

It's downhill the rest of the way, but not noticeably so. Even though you have been to the top of the highest peak in the state, there are others almost as high and others, though much lower, with unsurpassed beauty.

The next stop is Roan Mountain, near Bakersville. If you wish to remain on the Parkway as far as possible, drive until you reach the exit to US 226 near Little Switzerland. Follow US 226 north to Bakersville, where you will intersect with NC 261 which leads to State Road 1348 (Roan Mountain Road) which leads to the Roan Mountain parking area.

At Roan Mountain (6,285 feet above sea level) you are at one of the true beauty spots in the world. The highway cuts through a narrow valley, and on one side of the highway you have hiking trails, profusion of rhododendron, and mountain balds that are spectacular in themselves and more beautiful in that they offer great views of surrounding mountains and even towns below.

The Appalachian Trail crosses Roan Mountain, which is on the North Carolina-Tennessee border. You can follow it across several peaks before backtracking to the highway.

Peak No. 12

Next stop is Mount Jefferson, which you can reach and stay in the loop by continuing north from Roan Mountain until you intersect with US 19E in Tennessee. When you have driven east until you reach the NC 184 intersection, continue driving north and east until you reach NC 194, which will lead you through Boone and on to West Jefferson.

Near West Jefferson you will drive alongside the second oldest river in the world: the New River, which is younger than the Nile only. Near Jefferson you will find New River State Park, which is on the Mount Jefferson Road just off US 221.

Mount Jefferson was named in 1975 as a Natural National Landmark because of the history, plant life, and geological importance of the mountain. When Dr. Mitchell of Mount Mitchell fame climbed to the top of Mount Jefferson, he wrote that he had never seen anything more beautiful.

Atop the mountain there are educational displays that point out that Africa and North America were once one land mass, and when the two land areas moved, the sediment became the black rocks that still mark the mountain.

Peak No. 13

The final stop on this mountain peak loop is Stone Mountain. When you leave Mount Jefferson, drive over to NC 16 and follow it south until it crosses the Blue Ridge Parkway. Take the Parkway north through Doughton Park (one of the most delightful spots on the Parkway and in the state) and continue to the exit to US 21.

Stay on US 21 south to Roaring Gap. Four miles before you reach Roaring Gap you will see State Road 1002 that leads off to your right, or to the west. Stay on SR 1002 until you intersect with SR 1739, which leads into Stone Mountain State Park. Along the way you'll see Widow's Creek Falls.

Drive past the Park office on the John P. Frank Parkway to the picnic area. A trail from the picnic grounds leads through a small meadow and to the Stone Mountain trail. You can climb the mountain from either end, but most people like to go up the steps— all 289 of them—up the mountain. The steps parallel Stone Mountain Falls, which are almost 400 feet high from top to bottom, although they are more cascade than true waterfall.

You can hike along the crest of the 300-million-year old mountain to the other end and descend via a fairly easy trail back to the parking lot. Or you can watch rock climbers as they work their way up the sheer rock.

When you leave, retrace your route into the park. Drive south when you reach US 21 through Elkin. On the south side of Elkin you will intersect with I-77, which will take you back to Charlotte.

At the end of the trip you will have traveled a near-perfect loop that led you through parts of four states, past a dozen super waterfalls, among majestic mountains and beautifully tranquil valleys, and along the main streets and lanes of the small towns that dot the mountains of the four states. You have, in essence, followed the borders of the states, and along the way you have witnessed the finest scenery and historical terrains you could expect to find.

There are many other peaks along the borders of the four states, and you can find information on them in a number of books. One book I can recommend (because I wrote it) is *100 Practically Perfect Places in the North Carolina Mountains*. This book has 456 pages and more than 100 photos of the best sites to visit: mountain peaks, waterfalls, scenic towns and cities, historic or beautiful churches, antiquated churchyards, best educational spots, hiking trips, driving tours, and much more, because North Carolina has an immense amount to offer.

You have sampled a baker's dozen of superior trips. But there are a dozen baker's dozens to go before you have made a good start. It would, in truth, take several lifetimes to see all that this spectacular state has to offer. So, when you have finished reading this book, take off!

As I said at the beginning of this chapter, this is not exactly a story about people worth meeting or tales worth repeating; however, the stories and the people are there. Think about Dr. Elisha Mitchell, for example. Think about Chief Junaluska and the many other outstanding characters who made the history of the borders around North Carolina.

Make certain to visit the grave of Junaluska at Robbinsville. Learn about the cattle drives that once took place in this part of the state. Or when you are in the northwestern part of the state, learn about the Linvilles and Daniel Boone. The stories are everywhere, and you'll have plenty that are well worth repeating.

Esmeralda Inn in Hickory Nut Gorge

Thirty-One
The Inn That Rose from the Ashes

If you want to pay a visit to one of the most delightful and charming places in North Carolina, follow I-85 from Charlotte, if you are in that vicinity, to Kings Mountain, then take US 74 bypass around Kings Mountain and through Shelby and into Rutherford County. For some of the best scenery, drive through Chimney Rock and west toward Gerton and Bat Cave and toward Edneyville. From Asheville take US 25, and from South Carolina take I-26 north.

Once you arrive, you will find, in season, trout fishing (all state licensing regulations are in force), and shopping at dozens of gift shops, and eating in some of the finest restaurants between Charlotte and Hendersonville and Brevard. There are beautiful country roads and excellent sight-seeing and photography opportunities. Many local campgrounds (private fee camping) and picnic areas are nearby.

One superb historical site to visit is the Esmeralda Inn, privately owned, on US 74 two miles west of Chimney Rock. Built in 1891, the Inn was so-named because a noted writer, Frances Hodgson Burnett, lived nearby and she had written a book entitled *Esmeralda,* which was widely read and which later was adapted for the stage and enjoyed a year-long run on Broadway.

Miss Burnett at the time was best-known for such works as *Little Lord Fauntleroy, The White People,* a book about the world of superstition, *A Fair Barbarian,* and the most recently famous *The Secret Garden.* She collaborated with world-famous actor William Gillette, who was the outstanding stage interpreter of Sherlock Holmes, on the stage version of *Esmeralda.*

The tiny community once known as Esmeralda is on the banks of the Rocky Broad River. The highway leading past (and through) the community was once a Pony Express and Stagecoach line stop, and among the celebrities who lived at the Inn was General Lew Wallace, the Civil War officer who rose to literary fame through his novel *Ben-Hur.* Wallace lived at the Esmeralda Inn while he completed the stage version of the work. He resided in Esmeralda for weeks, staying in Room 9 of the Inn, while he wrote. The completed drama ran for 194 performances on Broadway, debuting on November 29, 1899.

The Inn itself was destroyed by fire in 1917, and the owners rebuilt it on the same site. It has been in operation almost continuously since that time. Among the latter-day celebrities who have stayed there are Clark Gable, Mary Pickford, William S. Hart, Gloria Swanson, and Douglas Fairbanks. In fact, the famous people who have stayed in the Hickory Nut Gorge are an all-star team of talent.

Before reaching Esmeralda, visitors will pass through the towns of Rutherfordton, Lake Lure, and Chimney Rock. After leaving the area the next towns are Gerton, Bat Cave, and Asheville, in one direction, and Hendersonville and Brevard in another direction.

The drive from Rutherfordton is a delight, with curving roads, frequent and beautiful expanses of the Rocky Broad River, and glens and mountains on both sides of the river. Beyond the Inn there are more delightful mountains and streams, with fishing, canoeing, and other activities available.

The Esmeralda Inn is closed during the early winter. For details on schedules, call (828) 625-9105. The dining room opens, as does the rest of the Inn, on March 15. Dining hours for the rest of the winter are 5:30 until 8:30 PM and will be open for lunch later in the spring. There are 13 rooms available for overnight guests. Many of the gift shops and restaurants in the area are open year-round, but it is wise to call during winter months to be certain that desired destinations are open.

Note: In recent months the Esmeralda Inn once again fell victim to fire and burned to the ground. But, like the mythical Phoenix, this inn keeps rising from its own ashes. The owners made a public statement that the inn was not relegated to history. They insisted that they could and would raise the money to help to rebuild the inn and to restore it to its original grandeur and historic interest.

In late 1999 the Esmeralda once again opened its doors to the public. And once again residents of Hickory Nut Gorge could see the lights of the landmark inn blazing at night, and once again people from all around the area could drive to Chimney Rock and Bat Cave for a lunch or dinner.

The Esmeralda Inn, old and new, has been an institution for many years and for many people. When you visit, you are in history as you make your way from one historic or beauty spot to another.

Lucas Mansion in Hiddenite and the giant crystal there

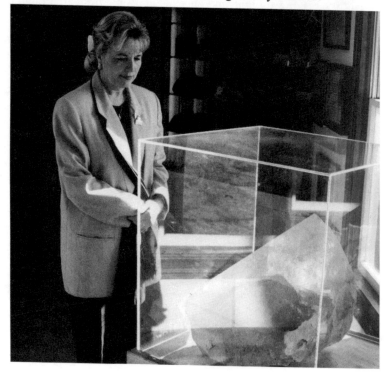

Thirty-Two
Big Treasures from a Tiny Town

Many years ago I discovered Hiddenite as a place to play baseball. Sandwiched among a series of small towns, including Taylorsville, Stony Point, Loray, and Scotts, Hiddenite turned out a surprising number of excellent baseball players, some of whom went on to play professional baseball.

While I was playing there, usually as a member of the visiting team, I heard constant references to people's finding small gem stones known as Hiddenite. Being curious, I asked what the stone is and how it can be detected.

They informed me that hiddenite is one of the rarest gems in the world and that it is found, almost one hundred per cent, there in the hills surrounding the little town. One man at a ball game had a tiny piece of the stone in his pocket, and he proudly displayed it, telling us that he had been plowing just before coming to the ball park, and he saw the stone in a new furrow.

Already, he told us, he had been offered $700 for the stone. Keep in mind that this was back in the early fifties, and $700 was a small fortune. I could not imagine having that much money in my pocket. In fact, the most money I ever possessed at one time in my life, at that time, was eight dollars and change.

More to the point, some of the locals informed me that the discovery of hiddenite was not the big story. The kicker was that wherever hiddenite is found, they insisted, you are also likely to find emeralds and other precious stones. They had my interest now, but I was more interested in baseball than in precious stones, so I relegated the story to the back burner. But it didn't stay there too long.

Years later I was teaching in a small college, and one Monday morning two of my students rushed in to tell me the good news. They had been digging at Hiddenite in one of the places where you buy a bucket of dirt and sift through it, or you can pay a fee and dig to your heart's content in the earth itself.

The big news is that the couple had unearthed an emerald so large that the proprietor immediately made them an offer of $1000 for the stone, they said. I have only their version of the story, so I cannot declare that it is the unvarnished truth, because other figures have been at odds with some of the other reported versions.

They reportedly sold the emerald for a thousand dollars, then they learned to their dismay that the buyer had in turn sold it to a large gem dealer in New York for many times the price of the original sale. Then the story got out of hand, because the dealer in New York reportedly had the stone cut and mounted and several years ago it was evaluated at a small fortune–or a large one.

But you can see why people like to go to Hiddenite to dig for the precious stones that are occasionally found there.

Hiddenite is the scene of the discovery of some of the finest gem stones in North Carolina. In addition to the stone Hiddenite itself, there have been major finds, such as emeralds, amethysts, smoky quartz, tourmaline, rutile, garnets, sapphires, sillimanite, aquamarine, monazite, and many other precious and semiprecious stones.

To get there, from Charlotte take I-77 to Statesville; take I-40 through Statesville and just on the other side of town leave I-40 and take NC 90 from Statesville to Hiddenite, a tiny town between Stony Point and Taylorsville. To dig or pan for precious stones, once in Hiddenite, turn right onto the Sulphur Springs Road (State Road 1001) and look for signs directing you to Hiddenite Gems, Inc.

In a scenic area of this type, the most enjoyable activities are panning for precious stones, picnicking, camping, and enjoying guided tours, enjoying the birds and the other wild life visible during daylight hours, and waiting eagerly for The Big One to appear in the panning and washing process. In Hiddenite itself there is a museum that features a huge doll collection, a local gem collection that features a 294-pound quartz crystal, the largest in the United States, a changing art gallery with ten different displays each year, and home furnishings and decor that recreates the life style in previous decades.

Start the tour with the Lucas Mansion and the Hiddenite Center. The museum is open every day all year. Hours are nine each morning until 4:30 in the afternoon. Monday through Friday. Saturday and Sunday hours are 2:00 P.M. until 4:30 P.M.. Admission fees for the guided tour of the mansion are $2.50 for adults and $1.50 for students and senior citizens.

During the holiday season each winter there are seasonal programs staged for visitors. Prices of admission vary, and you are urged to call to determine the works to be staged and the admission prices. There is so much to do in this small town, in truth, that you can easily spend the entire day or a weekend while you enjoy the offerings. Be advised that this is not a tourist trap, so you can expect genuine fun.

Hiddenite Gems, Inc., is within five minutes of the Lucas Mansion. Here you can engage in digging, sluicing, rock-hounding, and bird-watching and animal-study of the wild life in the area. There are many deer, foxes, quail, herons, and other forms of wild life.

If you choose to dig for gems, you pay a small fee (which varies, depending upon the type of digging you wish to do) and you can carry your own pick and shovel into the forest or fields and dig on your own, or you can use tools provided by the company. If you wish, you can actually stake out your own claim and rent it by the month or year. During this time no one will be permitted to enter your claim area or to dig there.

You can also buy buckets of vein material and use the nearby flume for sluicing. Some of the buckets are native soil, and you take your chances on finding valuable stones. You may, if you wish, buy buckets of "enhanced" materials in which you are guaranteed to find interesting and beautiful stones.

In the office you can make arrangements to have stones you find cut, polished, and mounted. The findings are so promising that diggers from as far away as Canada lease areas and come down twice a year to explore and dig.

For those who wish to spend the night, there is the Hidden Crystal Inn, also within five minutes of the mines. The inn is open year round and offers bed-and-breakfast accommodations. There are twelve rooms and one suite. There are some good places to eat nearby, and most of the time you will find the prices quite reasonable and the servings plentiful.

And for the doubting Thomas who refuses to believe that there are still precious stones waiting to be found, keep in mind that the fabled Carolina Emerald or Tiffany Emerald was found only a few short years ago at the Hiddenite Gems fields.

For an updated version of what is being found at Hiddenite, look at the story of Jamie Hill. Hill, who lives in Alexander County where Hiddenite is located, was digging in 1998 in a claim he had dealt for and he found an immense emerald, a whopping big 88-carat crystal from which the Carolina Queen was cut.

The Carolina Queen, after cutting, is an incredible 18.8 carat stone that has been described by professional jewelers as the finest emerald ever discovered in North America. At this time there has been no appraised value published, but it is assumed that the emerald will be worth perhaps what you could win on a Regis Philbin show!

A second stone cut from the original crystal is the Carolina Prince, which weighed in as 7.8 carats. It, too, will bring in lots of loot if the owner decides to sell it.

Was the immense emerald crystal the last of the precious stones to be found in Hiddenite? Of course not. It is entirely possible that the greatest emerald ever discovered will be found while you are reading this chapter.

Better still, it may be found by you after you read this chapter and drive to Hiddenite, just outside Taylorsville, and make your deal and start to dig. Best yet, it may be found by me while you are still reading this chapter and trying to decide whether to try your hand at digging.

But don't quit the daytime job and go up there and start digging by moonlight. In the first place, check in as you enter and learn what the rules are. Claim-jumping in the old West would get you a bad case of lead poisoning. A gentle hint: it isn't looked upon favorably at Hiddenite, either.

Don't think that you have to dig to have a good time. You can spend hours in the Lucas Mansion and other nearby attractions. You will also find that Hiddenite, like many small towns, is a superb place to visit over and over.

Fontana Dam and surrounding mountains

Thirty-Three
Best Place by a Dam Site

No matter what the weather reports and travel brochures tell you, the real attractions of the Fontana Dam and Fontana Village area are the mountains. In the fall the peaks and valleys are one vast artist's easel of colors and designs, and in winter the stark beauty is, if possible, even greater. In October the leaves are still magnificent, and the springtime beauty is unparalleled. And summer and winter both have their own special attractions. If the colors have faded, the mountains have not, and their eternal beauty will last until you get there. If you need a specific attraction, it would have to be the impressive Fontana Dam

Learning about the magnificent engineering feat alone is worth the drive to the mountains. And the mountains are always worth a trip.

From Charlotte, the distance is 216 miles, depending upon your route. There are two good ways of getting to Fontana and these are detailed below. Driving time is four hours, also one way. If you are traveling from other parts of the state or South, you can take I-40 to Asheville and then take the Great Smoky Mountains Expressway, or if you are coming from South Carolina you can take I-26 out of Greenville or Spartanburg.

From Charlotte take I-85 south to the US 74 exit south of Gastonia and near Kings Mountain. Follow US 74 west until you intersect with I-26. Follow I-26 northwest for 32.5 miles to I-40 and then take I-40 west for 19.2 miles to US 19 west of Asheville. Take US 19 west for 45 miles to State Road 28 and follow it for 28 miles to Fontana Dam. Don't let the state road label dismay you. The highway is excellent all the way to the dam.

Best of all, the entire route is beautiful no matter what your point of origin. You drive past sparkling rivers, energetic creeks, mountains and valleys, quaint stores, antique shops, and great places to eat. If you are lucky you will see an array of animals and birds as you drive. In warmer weather the woodchucks and bears are out and about, as are deer. At night there are numerous raccoons in the area, and there are countless hawks, owls, and even an occasional eagle.

Keep in mind that you are not just driving through mountains and valleys; you are touring history. There are wonderful folk tales and stranger-than-fiction stories told about some of the legendary characters that once lived in the mountains and created their own histories. Don't neglect or fail to pay respect to the Native American history and culture of this part of North Carolina.

At the Fontana Dam itself you have two immediate options. You can drive across the bridge and take an immediate left out to a pair of over-looks. From these vantage points you can enjoy a superior view of the lake above the dam and the dam itself. This is a special spot to watch the Incline Tram that transports visitors from the welcome center above to the power-house below. And back, of course.

If you wish to stop at the visitors center first, you can find persons on duty who can tell you about the history of the dam and area. You will learn, if you ask the right people, that at 480 feet the Fontana Dam is the highest concrete dam east of the Rocky Mountains. The dam is 2,365 feet long and has three generating units with a total capacity of 225,000 kilowatts.

Construction started on the dam on New Years Day 1942 and the first electricity was generated on January 20, 1945. Total cost of the project was $74.7 million. Through use of a huge illumination plan, the workers could toil night and day in their haste to ready the dam and prepare for the much-needed delivery of electricity and power.

The lake has a shoreline of 240 miles and the reservoir with its 11,685 acres has a drainage area of 1,571 square miles. The construction of the dam provided 6,340 jobs and the project required 34.5 million man-hours.

One interesting aspect of the dam is that the Appalachian Trail crosses the top of the dam, which required 2.8 million cubic yards of concrete to complete.

One of the major purposes behind the construction of the dam was flood control. The area receives 75 to 80 inches of rain each year, and in the past the Little Tennessee River flooded to such an extent that nearby towns (and even faraway towns) were in danger. Cities as far away as Chattanooga were flooded.

Before the dam could be built there had to be a railroad constructed into the area, and near the construction site a village for the workers and their families was constructed. The workers toiled in three shifts 24 hours a day and the hills were brilliantly lighted by spotlights all night long. Because of the importance of the dam and its hydroelectric power, workers were urged to work faster and faster in order to complete the massive project in record time.

Visitors to the area can find dozens of good places to eat and a wide variety of outdoor activities ranging from hiking and fishing to shopping and touring the mountains. What had once been a construction village is now a tourist resort, and fishermen can try their luck at landing rainbow, brook, and brown trout, large and smallmouth bass, walleye, pike, perch, sunfish, and crappie.

Nearby are campgrounds, interpretive trails, swimming in warmer months, picnic facilities, hot showers for hikers who have dubbed the visitors center and its comfort station the Fontana Hilton, tennis, and other outdoor activities.

Details: there is no fee for using the visitors center, but there is a small charge for the half-hour round trip down the Incline Tram. Tickets were $2 for the ride at this writing. Prices may have increased since then.

The Thomas Wolfe House in miniature at Maggie

A street scene at the miniature village from the turn of the century

Thirty-Four
A Visit to Lilliputia

In Maggie Valley the real question is not what is the attraction but what isn't attractive. Few small towns in the state or in the South can offer so much in such a small space. But if we must list only a few attractions, the Lindsey Miniature Village is a delight, and there is the Ghost Town in the Sky as well as the Soco Gardens Zoo, which, though small, contains a surprising number of animals one would not expect to find in the North Carolina mountains.

Keep in mind that some of the attractions are closed in the dead of winter, while others stay open only until after the end of the fall tourist season. An attraction or two will stay open until Christmas.

From Charlotte, one way, the distance is 163 miles. Driving time is four hours, also one way. However, in peak tourist seasons the drive may take longer. The highways tend to become more congested in late afternoon when everyone decides to return home at the same time.

From Charlotte (I keep using Charlotte, because everyone in the state knows where it is, and it is difficult to list best ways from every imaginable part of the state) there are two fairly easy routes. The first one is to take I-85 south through Gastonia to the US 74 exit, which you will follow through Shelby. Remain on US 74 bypass through Forest City, Spindale, and around Rutherfordton until you reach the I-26 intersection. Take I-26 until it intersects with I-40 at Asheville. From this point remain on I-40 until you reach the exit for US 19. Remain on US 19 until you reach the US 19 Alternate, which will lead you into Maggie.

As you drive, you will quickly see that the highway is almost as good as an interstate, and the scenery is terrific. Plan to stop to enjoy the views.

The story about the town's name is that Uncle Jack, as he was known by his friends, wanted to have a post office, but he couldn't talk the United States government into cooperation. So he decided to keep a meticulous count of all the mail he picked up when he drove to the big city on business. After several weeks he presented his findings, and the government agreed that there was a sufficient volume of mail to justify a post office.

But the post office had to have a name, and Uncle Jack offered Jonathan (for the creek running past his home), and Cora, Mettie, and Maggie, after his three daughters. He hated to make the decision himself for fear of having his choice seem to be preferential. The post office chose to make it easy on Uncle Jack and decided upon Maggie, and the post office was established.

Maggie Mae herself worked in the post office from 1904 when it was founded to 1907, when she married Ira Pylant and the two moved first to Tennessee, then to California, and finally to Texas where she died in 1979 at age 88.

When you enter Maggie, you will see the Lindsey Miniature Village on the right, shortly before you reach the major business area. The address is 250 Soco Road. The Miniature Village features, as the name suggests, a complete village on a Lilliputian scale. There are the homes of Billy Graham, Carl Sandburg, Thomas Wolfe, and other notables. The Waynesville courthouse is there, as is the main street in Asheville at the turn of the century. The Biltmore train station as it appeared in the 1890s is a delight, as is the miniature train that traverses the village and outlying territory. The truth is that the little town is a delight from one end to the other. However, during holidays and particularly during the autumn when the leaves are turning, the traffic in Maggie can be horrendous. Vacationers in summer, when schools are out for holiday, also congest the town.

At the Soco Gardens Zoo, which is the only privately owned zoo in Western North Carolina, you will find bears, snow leopards, wallabies and their families, llamas, emus, alligators, coatimundi, and other mammals, plus cobras, a fer-de-lance, pythons, and dozens of huge rattlesnakes.

Just on the other side of town (there are only two sides to Maggie) you will see the entrance to the Ghost Town in the Sky where you can enjoy more than 30 rides and shows, as well as the traditional gunfights, authentic Cherokee native dances, country music, a dance hall and saloon, and the roller coaster.

Thirty-Five

An Emerald as Big as the Ritz

Earlier you read the story of the gigantic emerald discovered at the Hiddenite digging fields, but so far the story of the Gargantuan, the mammoth, the King Kong of emeralds has not been told. And there are several reasons for the silence.

From the outset I must tell you that I saw the emerald; other than that, I have only the word of the people involved for the truth of the story.

Let me give you a couple of stories before I launch into the story of the emerald (with apologies to F. Scott Fitzgerald for the title allusion) as big as the Ritz. Let's talk first about Knobby, the Bigfoot.

As told before, I named Knobby. This is not a claim or a boast (or an apology): it is a fact. But after I had written several stories about Knobby, there came an avalanche of people, among them writers, local historians (too often hysterians), and film makers of sorts who laid claim to the name. To this day, I am confident, these people have convinced themselves, in their efforts to convince others, of the legitimacy of their claims.

Second point: while I was writing about Knobby for one of the largest morning papers in the South, a writer from another paper wrote her own stories that bore an astonishing similarity to mine. It did not matter whom I interviewed; the other writer found a way to interview the same people on the same day that I did, and the people being interviewed all said exactly the same things to her that they said to me.

Think about it. How many people can make the same statement in exactly the same way, time after time, unless the statement has been carefully thought out and even rehearsed? We invariably change at least a phrase or two or the order of the presentation.

Not my interviewees. They told the other writer exactly the same material they told me, and they did not vary in the least. It was obvious that she was simply reading my stories and putting her byline on them. I was slogging around in swamps at three o'clock in the morning or freezing on some mountaintop while gathering my data for my stories, while my imitator slept soundly under her electric blanket and then "wrote" her stories in the comfort of a warm office.

So (and I have told this story in another context, so you may know how it ends) I interviewed a man named, for purposes here, Danny Poole. He gave me some great quotes, and, as expected, I read them again when the rival paper came out that evening. So, to vary the cornball buzz phrase, my man called her man to find out just how she managed to get the same material that I unearthed. That is, my editor called her editor, who called her in.

She interviewed the same man I did, she told them, by doing just what I had done. She called him.

Nope, we said. He doesn't have a phone.

Then he called me, she said. We asked what time he called, then told her that Danny was out of the house and was actually in the forest where Knobby reportedly lived, and this was in a day before cell phones invaded us.

Then she remembered that she had actually driven to his house. Not a good response, we told her, because when pressed for details she could not recall whether the house was in Cleveland or Burke County and whether it was one-story or two-story, a mobile home, a log cabin, or a tent. She could not recall whether he lived in the city or in the rural area or whether he lived on a mountaintop or on the bank of the river.

When she finally bowed her neck and told us that she wasn't worried about plagiarism because she could prove that she had talked to Danny on a number of occasions and we wouldn't ever be able to prove that she hadn't, we informed her that we had made up the man, name, address, and quotes and that she had been quoting a man who had never existed.

So what happened? She was promoted to a larger paper, one of the largest in the nation and in one of the most important cities in the world.

That said, here's how I learned about the emerald as big as the Ritz, and here is that story.

One morning my phone rang, and the caller identified himself as the man who had found the emerald. He said that he had read some of my previous works and wanted me to write his story, in exchange for a deal on some writing arrangements. And here is that story, with very minor changes to protect people who shouldn't be involved in this story at all.

The man, who we shall call Ananias simply because there is not likely anyone by that name living in this country at this time. There is another reason that the more perceptive readers have already divined.

Ananias, it seems, had done a great deal of extensive and highly expensive work for a second party, who had used a legal loophole to avoid payment. Ananias was destroyed emotionally, financially, and spiritually. He was crushed. Instead of receiving payment of well over one hundred thousand dollars, he was left with a stack of bills he could not pay. His business, bank account, credit rating, and reputation were all ruined by the one soured deal.

In desperation he packed his gear, drove to the mountains, set up a camp, and began to dig. He spent a week sitting on a huge rock and breaking open smaller rocks. For six days he found nothing. At night he prayed that he would find the greatest emerald of them all, but all he found was worthless. So he packed up and left.

He drove halfway home, changed his mind, and returned to the place where he had sat on the huge rock while he worked. This time he broke open the former seat, and to his awe, shock, and disbelief out tumbled the Emerald as big as the Ritz.

For several ecstatic minutes he stood and gaped at the immense stone, the largest of the sort he had ever seen. The emerald was not just big; it was huge, gigantic.

He packed again and this time he drove home in a frenzy. In his pocket he carried the emerald. When traffic permitted he drove with one hand clutching the stone through his trousers, lest somehow the emerald should slip out and be lost.

His troubles were over! thought Ananias, who had never read Steinbeck's classic novelette, *The Pearl.* Ananias could pay off his creditors, make good the checks he had written, restart his business, and regain his place in his world. The emerald had saved him.

Or so he thought. He consulted with a gemologist, who weighed the emerald, tested it, and did all the abracadabra that gemologists do to evaluate a stone. The emerald, he told Ananias, dwarfed the famed Carolina emerald, which weighed in as 13.5 carats. The new stone weighed more than 100 carats!

Even better, the Cockatrice (my name for the emerald), was virtually flawless. I talked with the gemologist, who explained to me that all emeralds have flaws, some more so than others, but there was no such thing as a perfect emerald. The Cockatrice (read the book of Isaiah if you want to know why the stone was so-named; read, also, my novel *The Eye of the Cockatrice* for more insights into the name and potency of the creature and the stone) was as close to perfection as stones can get.

The imperfections, it should be noted, often take form as gas bubbles, and when the stone is cut, the superheated drill bit touches one of the gas pockets and the stone explodes into fragments.

As good as the luck of Ananias was holding, it was not as perfect as his stone. The lucky man found that his stone could not be appraised until it was cut, and it couldn't be sold for anything like its real value until it was appraised. However, the gemologist said, a conservative figure for the emerald would be in the hundreds of thousands of dollars. But the gemologist wasn't able to cut the stone for the market.

So what was he to do? He had several million dollars in his hands, or pockets, or safe box, and he was still broke. Not only that, there were creditors who wanted their money, and they reasoned, logically enough, that if Ananias had all that money, then he should be making an effort to pay what he owed them.

Finally, the world's unluckiest lucky man took the bull by the horns and borrowed enough money to buy gas for a trip to New York. He knew he wouldn't be able to pay for food along the way, so he had his wife prepare him gallon jugs of iced tea and water, and he bought loaves of bread and some sandwich materials.

He reasoned that he would be able to drive straight through–a motel room was out of the question–and he could stay nourished by the water, tea, and rather ordinary sandwiches. He left early one morning and did not stop until he was in New York City.

When he drove down the crowded street where the prestigious jewelry store was located, he searched in vain for a parking place, not understanding that the last parking place in New York disappeared about the same time the last passenger pigeon in the world died in a Cincinnati zoo.

Frustrated, he found a fire lane, nosed the front wheels of his truck across the curb, and drove down the sidewalk until he was parked in front of Tiffany's. There was no way he could bring himself to walk the streets of the World's Meanest City, in the eyes of many, with the World's Biggest Emerald protected only by his hand and the cloth of his trousers.

He entered the jewelry, asked to see the chief gemologist, and laid the emerald on the table. The gem man's eyes virtually popped from his head. The emerald was nearly eight times as large as the one the jeweler proudly called the Tiffany Emerald.

Ananias asked what the stone was worth, and the reply was, "It's value is incomprehensible! The sky's the limit!"

"What will you give me for it?" Ananias asked.

"We wouldn't give you ten bucks for it," the gemologist deadpanned.

"Why not?" the distraught man asked in frustration. "It's the best and biggest emerald in the world."

"It's uncut, and until it's cut, it has no real value," the man replied. "Why should we buy it, when we already have the best?"

It was a perfect Catch-22 puzzle. It's like losing out on a job because you have no experience, and yet no one will give you a job so that you can get experience.

"What can I do?" he asked, hopelessly. All of his dreams and wild fantasies of wealth were rapidly going down the pipes.

"You have two real choices. You can hire someone to cut the stone for you. We'll be happy to do so for $100,000. Or you can get someone to cut it for you for a percentage of the worth of the cut stone."

"I don't have the $100,000," Ananias said. "And there's no way I can borrow the money. I have no collateral."

"Then make a percentage deal with someone else," the gemologist advised. "But a word of warning: there are unscrupulous people in this business, and they will ask you to sign a waiver for damages in case the emerald explodes during the cutting."

"How bad can that be?" the richest poor man asked.

"As bad as this: the cutter leaves you in an office while he takes the stone back to the cutting room. He will sit back there and read a magazine for two or three hours, then he'll come back out and show you a handful of emerald fragments and tell you that the stone blew up when his drill bit struck an air pocket. And your emerald will be safely stored in the safe in the back office. And you drive home both empty-handed and empty-pocketed."

Defeated, the man drove back to his home where he found court papers waiting for him. It seems that the people who wanted their money had hired an attorney to haul Ananias over the coals of the courtroom. When the old argument that you can't get blood from a turnip surfaced, the reply was, "But we sure as hell can get the turnip. Or, in this case, we can get the emerald."

So there it was! The distraught man would lose the courtroom battle, because the judge could not reasonably rule that the creditors, including at least one elderly person, could not get their money while the owner of the priceless emerald lived large.

There was one more ingredient to the Disaster Pie that has not been revealed at this point. You've probably guessed it: the people taking Ananias to court were the same ones who cheated him out of his fee and put him into bankruptcy in the first place!

They were going to get the blood *and* the turnip.

Weeks after I wrote my stories, I had a phone call from a relative of the emerald finder. She informed me that her husband had been ordered by the judge to turn the emerald over to the court. The husband told the judge that it was impossible to do so, that he had attempted to cut the emerald himself and it had exploded. He pulverized what was left of the once priceless stone.

The judge did not believe him, and the legal battles were just getting underway. It was a no-win situation for Ananias and no-lose for the people behind the lawsuit. It was also win-win for the attorney. I asked a friend of mine, an attorney, if he could possibly go to that part of the state and perhaps help the unfortunate man.

The lawyer returned several days later. "There's no helping him," he said. "That judge has made up his mind and I don't see that anything we can do will change it."

At that point, then, the matter rested.

Many months later I was in the mountains at one of the mines where you pay five bucks or so for a bucket of dirt and then wash the ore to see if there are any precious stones in it. The owner had told me earlier that the buckets were "salted," with low-grade and once in a while some high grade stones. These were used to keep the customers coming.

While we were talking, a third party joined us, and eventually the conversation veered to the Emerald as Big as the Ritz. I was somewhat reluctant to share my viewpoints, and they didn't ask. All I wanted to know was what happened.

"I don't know if this is the right case," the new man said, "or if there are several of this sort. But I can tell you one side of story that I had some personal relationship with. One man, possibly not the one you speak of, found a huge stone nearby but the discovery was kept rather quiet, and for good reason. It seems that this one man did not obtain the emerald in exactly the manner that you have described. I can't elaborate, because the particular case I speak of has not been fully resolved. There might be a dozen such cases, and this is only one of them. People tend to get overly enthusiastic when it comes to digging for and finding precious stones. "

I don't know, either. All I know is that one man found a huge stone, and I held that stone in my hands and marveled that such a tiny thing, relatively speaking, could mean so much to so many people.

Or that it could create such hopes and produce such heartbreak!

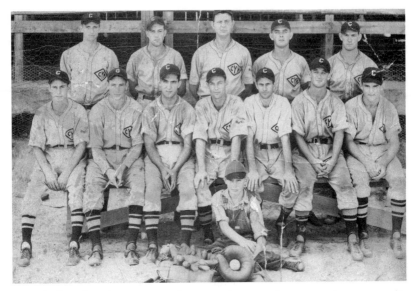

A few decades ago, nearly every town and crossroads community had a baseball team. Many of the athletes from these small towns were highly gifted, and some went on to play major league baseball. Shown above is one of the old teams. The Rocks are not shown because they want very badly for people to forget about them.

Thirty-Six
The World's Worst Baseball Team

E veryone who hasn't been under a rock or in a cave for the past several decades is familiar with the lovable characters created by Charles Shulz in the wonderful comic strip *Peanuts*. In this strip, one of the most pathetic losers of all time is Charlie Brown, the butt of Lucy's insults and practical jokes as well as the laughing stock of the neighborhood. To Charlie Brown a good day is one in which he does not suffer an extreme number of humiliations.

When Good Old Charlie Brown's team plays baseball, he has a dog

(Snoopy) often at shortstop, a grouchy curmudgeon in right field, and another player who likes to play the piano while playing the ball game. To my knowledge, Charlie Brown's team has never won a ball game. That makes him the world's worst loser, right?

Wrong, unless you want to get really literal about it. The worst team ever assembled, at least in the professional ranks, took the field in 1951, and when the season was over, they had ruined the town for baseball, possibly forever.

The team was the Granite Falls Rocks, and never was a team so aptly named. They made one rock-headed play after another, time and again snatching defeat from the jaws of victory. This was also perhaps the best-balanced baseball team ever assembled, and that includes the New York Yankees of 1927 and, unless you are a purist, of 1999.

You see, the Rocks had atrocious fielding. They could turn an easy ground ball into a three-run error without breaking a sweat. And if the fielding was bad, the pitching was equally awful. This was a staff that could lose to a team of grandmothers–by nine or ten runs.

Most teams hope for a twenty-game winner, or at least a hurler who can rack up fifteen games. Not the Rocks. They'd have traded their grandstand for a two-game winner.

If pitching and fielding were less than admirable, the hitting was a joke; however, there is no truth to the rumor that some of their players did not even bother taking a bat to the plate with them. They carried a bat, but they just did not know what to do with it. It was told by many in the streak that one night the Rocks managed to get a batter as far as first base (no one was quite certain how) and the manager put in a pinch hitter, a left-handed batter to face the left-handed pitcher.

Did I mention that the managing was at least as bad as the hitting and pitching and fielding? At any rate, so the apocryphal story goes, the pitcher delivered the first pitch about two feet outside, and the hitter took a hefty swing at it and missed badly. The second pitch was inside, and the hitter swung again as the ball nearly cleaned out his rib cage. On the third pitch, the pitcher tried to pick off the runner at first and the batter took another huge swing, flung his bat against the dugout, and muttered, "I never could hit a blankety-blank left-handed pitcher."

That was perhaps the only one of the stories about the team that was not true. (For all I know, it *might* have been true; I just don't have it from a good source.) I didn't get to see the Rocks play often, because I was attempting to play for another team that was marginally better and might have even been a good team if several of our players had been able to find the park on game days.

Bad hitting, terrible pitching; abysmal fielding, unthinkable managing. What's left?

For one thing, base-running. The Rocks were one of the few teams capable of stretching a triple into a single, and they had the unique facility of having two or more runners on the same base now and then. Admittedly, the occurrences were rare, because the Rocks just did not get that many men on base.

All things considered, the team was a fiasco at best; at worst, it was a tragedy. It was also a disaster, from every standpoint, except that very few fans were injured during the playing of the games. But if the physical injuries were absent, humiliation wasn't. Nor were embarrassment, chagrin, shame, ridicule, insult, mortification, and despair.

The players did not even look good in hotel lobbies.

But I have been far too hard on the Rocks. There were some high points of the season. For instance, on the first day of the season they were tied for the league lead–until they played their first game.

And the team had fourteen winning streaks during the 1951 season in the Western Carolina League. That's the good news. The bad news is that each of the winning streaks lasted for one game only.

The most charitable thing that could be said about the Rocks is that they played consistently: they were consistently bad, awful, horrid, and inept. It is questionable whether they would have recognized ept if it had bitten them on the ankle.

The sad news is that before the season started, the fans in the small town near Hickory were truly excited about the prospects of having their very own pro baseball team. Now they would not have to go to Hickory, Marion, Lenoir, or Morganton to see a pro ball game. They didn't have to stay home to watch "I Love Lucy" episodes: they could see slapstick comedy right there in their own ball park.

On the morning of the second day of the season, the Rocks were tied with three other teams for the last place in the league. That was the highest the team would soar for the rest of the year. It was, to be blunt, dangerous when this team soared at all: they were likely to crack into the basement walls.

After that first night, the Rocks had the cellar of the league all to themselves as they lost one game after another. They became the first team in baseball history to be mathematically eliminated from the pennant race by July 4.

By July 10 the Rocks had a record of 13 wins and 50 defeats, for a won-lost average of .206. That, too, was their high point of the season. For those of you who don't keep up with sports, a .500 record is a good one; anything higher is terrific. By the same token, a .400 won-lost percentage is woeful, and anything below that mark is catastrophic.

On July 19, the Rocks' record was 13-57 for a .186 won-lost percentage. By July 26, the record had dipped to 13-62 and the won-lost percentage had dropped even further to .173.

Then, wonder of wonders, the Rocks won a game, and at the end of July, their 14-64 record pulled them up to .179 percentage. But that, as the Jack Nicholson movie says, is as good as it gets. For the rest of the season, the Rocks just tried not to get hurt.

August in the Carolina foothills can be a brutal month in terms of heat, humidity, and depression. In Granite Falls, which is, by the way, a delightful town filled with wonderful people, thriving businesses, good schools, fine teachers, and in general a superlative and wholesome air about the place, you can still find people who talk about the Rocks.

August is also the month in which baseball teams that have not played up to their potential during the early season, whether from injuries, bad luck, poor managing, or mediocre players, must make their pennant drives. The Rocks were not thinking about pennants.

They'd have been delighted if they could elevate their team to the level of mediocrity. But such giddy heights were not in the cards for the Rocks.

Their record in August is the worst won-lost record in the history of baseball for one month. It is a record, unenviable as it may seem, that can never be broken.

The Rocks lost their final 39 games of the season, including a few at the end of July and the others during August. They did not win a single game in the entire month. Their won-lost percentage for the month was, of course, .000. For the entire season, their record-setting won-lost percentage was .127.

Their final record was 14-96, making them one of the few teams in history to approach losing one hundred games.

Ironically, on the last day of the season the Rocks came close to breaking their 39-game losing streak. They lost the final contest by a score of 5-4 in fourteen innings.

Long before this final month, however, the owners of the team had begun to deal their players to anyone who would take them. The management had to release several players simply because they could not afford to pay them, and the replacement players had to be willing to play for nearly nothing.

The released players hooked up with other teams in order to finish out the season. The team I was on signed several of them, and, to no one's surprise, many of the athletes turned into reasonably good players as soon as they escaped the Rocks.

Am I poking fun? Not really. The Rocks laughed at themselves, and I didn't have the right to point the accusing finger at anyone. Ask me sometime about my game in Concord. It tops the Rocks.

In fact, I must deliver a disclaimer of sorts here. While the Granite Falls Rocks were, indeed, a very bad team, there were many other teams that were almost as bad. In fact, if they had been in the same league with the Rocks, the other teams' records might not have been much better than that of the Rocks.

It stands to reason, as indicated earlier, that for every baseball winner there must be a loser. It also stands to reason that in every league, there must be a team finishing in the cellar. In a league operating at the same time as the Western Carolina League, a young man who pitched earlier in the North Carolina State League one night struck out all twenty-seven batters who faced him. We have to ask what caliber of player he faced, for he never had a record even remotely that good while he played in our league. Another player who lost sixteen straight games went to a team in another league and promptly won sixteen in a row.

Say this for the Rocks: they were good sports. They played the game with all their heart, and they gave the fans a treat each time they took the field. My hat is off to them for hanging in there rather than folding and slinking off into the sunset. It take guts to lose night after night, and it takes courage to keep going back out there to try again.

Ask Charlie Brown if you don't believe me! My hat's off to him, too.

Thomas Dixon

Thirty-Seven

The Thirty-Day Storm

When the poet Thomas Gray wrote his "Elegy Written in a Country Churchyard," he pointed out that in the quiet and secluded cemetery there might rest some "mute, inglorious Milton" or "some Cromwell guiltless of his country's blood." Gray advises us that some men and women simply do not care for the limelight, and it is always somewhat shocking to realize that from tiny towns sometimes giant books force their way through an author's mind.

On January 11, 1864, Montgomery Blair, a member of the Civil War cabinet of Abraham Lincoln, sneaked into the beleaguered city of Richmond, Virginia, for the purpose of negotiating a peace that might end the Civil War, the bloodiest conflict in this country's history.

On the night Blair arrived in Richmond, there was a significant arrival in Cleveland County, North Carolina. Near Buffalo Creek, which in turn is near Fallston and Shelby, Amanda Dixon gave birth to a son who would do everything in his intellectual power to keep the flames of the South's pride at fever pitch.

Thomas Dixon, son of Amanda and Thomas Dixon, Sr., would grow into manhood and at the same time into one of the best-known writers in American history. Ironically, if he were writing today, he would have to modify his message considerably or fail miserably.

Thomas Dixon, the Younger, grew up in a family that was devoutly Baptist. Tom's father was not only a Baptist preacher but also a powerful evangelist. It has been said that the reason there are no many Baptists in Cleveland County is that Thomas Dixon the Elder preached so persuasively and memorably.

One claim is that Dixon the Elder converted and baptized more than 5,000 believers at revivals during his ministry in Cleveland County. That figure does not include those that were baptized during the minister's regular sermons outside the area.

The entire Dixon family was, in many ways, memorable. A. C. Dixon was said (by no less an authority than his father) to be the best preacher in the family. Frank Dixon, a brother to Tom, was one of the famed lecturers and orators in the South. Tom's sister Delia (a name favored in the Renaissance because the letters, unscrambled, spell *ideal*, the highest level on man's search for perfection) was also brilliant.

Delia Dixon was a rarity among women during this time period: she became a medical doctor in an age when women's place was thought to be in the home. Not only did she complete medical school, but she also had the highest score on the comprehensive examination.

After she left Cleveland County to apply for a position as doctor at Meredith College, the interviewers asked her to list her major qualifications for the job. "My greatest qualification is that I am my brother's sister," she said.

Thomas Dixon the Younger grew up in a family that had once been slaveholders. When Thomas Dixon the Elder married Amanda McAfee, the bride's father gave Dixon a wedding present of thirty-two slaves.

As Thomas the Younger grew up, he quickly won a reputation for being a captivating speaker and preacher. While A. C. Dixon was said to be the best preacher in the family, Tom attended Wake Forest College and became known as a near-perfect orator, his speeches convincing many people that Tom was even better than his brother.

The story is told that Thomas Dixon became a state legislator before he was old enough to vote. He retired after one year, then studied law before eventually returning to the ministry. As a preacher he pastored churches in Boston and New York, and wherever he went he preached the gospel of white supremacy.

The racism that marked many of Dixon's novels came to him easily. The brother of Amanda, Tom's mother, was Colonel LeRoy McAfee, a leader of the Ku Klux Klan, and Uncle LeRoy regaled Tom with stories of the Klan's activities in the area.

After young Thomas Dixon completed his studies and spent several years preaching and lecturing, he turned to writing. He was thirty-eight years old (the same age as Thomas Wolfe when he died) when he wrote and published his first major work, *The Leopard's Spots*. The book was an instant success, attracting readers (and enemies) from all over the country.

Five million people heard Dixon lecture, and millions more read his twenty-two novels. Only two of his books, *The Leopard's Spots* and *The Clansman,* are recognizable today.

But those two books set the country on its ear. The latter book, *The Clansman,* reminded the readers of the problems besetting the nation after the Civil War. So powerful was the novel that one of the foremost film-makers in the world, D. W. Griffith, engaged Dixon to write the screen-play for his novel. The movie that resulted has been called the greatest motion picture ever made.

The film was, of course, *Birth of a Nation*. When the movie was released, millions of people paid two dollars for a ticket to see the film. Two dollars was, at that time, an incredibly high price for a ticket to see virtually any motion picture or stage presentation.

President Woodrow Wilson urged his entire cabinet to see the film and asked them to bring their families with them as well. Critics praised and blasted Dixon for his books as well as for his screenplay, and today the standard studies of American fiction, such as Alexander Cowie's *The American Novel*, do not even mention Dixon's name. They don't need to; Dixon's name will endure in Cleveland County and in Shelby, where he lived. In fact, Dixon Boulevard is named after the town's greatest writer.

The story behind the writing of *The Clansman* is that Dixon threw himself into the writing with such fury that he at times wrote seventeen hours in one day. The result was that he completed the entire novel in one month: a month-long storm of passion, anger, and frustration that left us bewildered, confused, anxious, and somehow richer.

Dixon's fate has been like that of many other writers who have somehow offended the nation's conscience. He is virtually unread today, and in recent times even D. W. Griffith, who directed *Birth of a Nation,* considered by many to be the greatest motion picture of all time, has been stripped of some of honors earlier bestowed upon him by Hollywood.

While this is in no way an effort to defend Dixon's social views, it is interesting to note that members of the communist party, which had as its final goal the overthrowing of the American government, had not in any way been similarly disparaged. The dramas of communist playwrights are still being staged, even more than before, and the producers, writers, directors, and actors win top awards regularly. The producers, actors, directors, and writers of pro-German works after World War I remain securely in their places of honor in Hollywood and on Broadway. Books have been written to salvage the honor and reputation of traitors to this country.

But there are no voices lifted in defense of Thomas Dixon, whose only literary crime was that he did not share a social view that would later become popular. Even Mark Twain has fallen into disrepute in many circles, and there are efforts to have his writings removed from public school books.

End of tirade. Except to say that writers, like truth, seem to be constantly in and out of favor. Hemingway, probably the purest and truest writer this nation has ever produced, is being taught and read less and less, while less talented and dedicated writers soar to popularity and remain there. The same can be said of Herman Melville, Nathaniel Hawthorne, James Fenimore Cooper, Henry James, Theodore Dreiser, Jack London, and a host of other outstanding writers headed toward oblivion.

Final expostulation: it is not necessary that we agree with all that a writer says and thinks. If he says it well and if there is a reasonable motive behind his message, it deserves, in the name of freedom, to be heard.

Thirty-Eight
North Carolina's Super Celebrity Murder

L et's start the investigation of this murder mystery with a look at the status of the crime: it is still unsolved, after more than half a century. The crime was committed in broad daylight with perhaps a thousand or more people standing within a few feet of the killer.

Yet, somehow, the killer stabbed a man in the back and the man fell to the pavement, lurched to his feet, and ran into a house where he bled to death as several people tried to help the dying man.

One more comment: I know who killed the man. At least, I have had witnesses come to me and tell me that they saw the killer and the victim and they saw the stabbing. Everything they have told me holds up well; it is not a cock-and-bull story. The informers have nothing to gain or lose. They simply knew that I was in the market, always, for good stories, and they came to me with this one.

My own investigation tells me that the killer was in the same area as the victim; that is, he was within a few inches of him. We know that the victim provoked the killer, perhaps unreasonably. The killer became angry. This much can be verified. I do not have a video tape of the bayonet ripping through the man's flesh, but that's all that is lacking.

Next item: I will not reveal the name of the killer in this brief chapter. Nor will I reveal it at any other time, unless circumstances change and also change my mind.

Why not identify the killer? Because he was a well-known leader in American society for a period of years, and he had an immense following. The man also died of natural causes, so there is no reason to report the name of the killer to authorities.

Let's set the scene. The location is Belmont, halfway between Charlotte and Gastonia. The year is 1934. The social setting is yet another labor strike in Gaston County, only months after the Loray Strike had been settled, or as settled as such a conflict can ever be. The scene is a public street near one of the largest mills in the town that was once known as Garibaldi and was later changed to Beautiful Mountain, or Belmont.

At this point I'm going to let Colonel Don Scott of the 12th Infantry tell his side of the story. Colonel Scott was speaking out in response to a pamphlet entitled "Can Guns Settle Strikes?" This brochure was signed by six North Carolina persons in rather high places, one of whom was Dr. Frank P. Graham, president of the University of North Carolina in Chapel Hill.

"I am going to give you the facts," Colonel Scott wrote, "just exactly as they were, no hearsay, or otherwise gathered. I was present at the time of this trouble in Belmont, under orders of the Adjutant General's office. I was called to duty a very short time after troops were sent to the various localities within the state. I was the direct representative of the Adjutant General. I visited practically every unit on duty, and I am in a position to give the facts just as they were."

Scott goes on to explain that the National Guard troops were on the scene for several purposes: to protect the people in the towns and cities from harm, to see that people who wanted to go to work could do so without being put in danger, to provide protection for the mill owners and the workers.

When Scott arrived in Belmont, he proceeded to the Hatch Hosiery Mill where there was a mob of several thousand people assembled: men, women, and children, "all in a very ugly mood." More trouble began at the Knit Product Plant, and again thousands of people gathered, and the ugly mood remained.

"All through the day the soldiers, including myself, were subjected to the most vile treatment at the hands of this mob," Scott continued. "There is no profane word written that we were not called, not only by the men, but the women and young girls were the worst and the most vile. The soldiers were ordered not to say a word back, and I will take an oath that not a soldier answered back."

Throughout the day and night threats continued.

"Wait until night," the protesters called out to the National Guard troops. "We will get you then." All day long the mob stayed across the street from the National Guard headquarters, and as darkness fell, the crowd grew ominously larger. When it was nearly fully dark, there was a sound of gunfire and the noise of breaking glass.

Colonel Scott rushed to the window and found a rock the size of a man's fist. The rock had barely missed the head of a soldier. After the rock struck the window, the mob advanced threateningly. The crowd surged toward a Guardsman, and a man tried to take the rifle and bayonet from the National Guardsman.

The soldier wrested the gun free of the man's grip and then stabbed the man with the bayonet that was fixed on the end of the rifle barrel. The man turned and ran across the street and into a house. He collapsed in the kitchen of the home, and there he bled to death.

The mob leaders contacted Colonel Scott and told them that they were coming to get the soldier, who used unnecessary deadly force. They demanded justice.

Scott replied that if the mob came, the National Guard troops would defend themselves. Apparently Scott's veiled threat made sense to the mob, and they did not appear.

The man's death was investigated, but no one was ever identified to authorities. There was an uneasy peace following the murder, and for weeks the tension was so great that there might have been an all-out war if someone had acted irresponsibly.

Now, who killed the man? I said earlier that I am not going to reveal the man's identify, but I did not say that I wouldn't provide clues. First, the man's first public appearance of note came not because he aspired to office but because a friend died. His second major leap upward in society came because a second man died, also of natural causes. He was moved up on the ladder of success by another death and by being in the right place at the right time. After that he was a fixture and an authority in his field. He died not long after his retirement, but before his death he became one of the most recognizable figures in American or at least Southern heritage.

He is still regarded today as one of the finest elected officials the state of North Carolina has ever produced, and his name is still respected throughout the United States. It's up to you from here on in.

Lash LaRue, one of the most popular of all the western "B" movie stars, teamed with Al "Fuzzy" St. John of the old Keystone Kops.

Thirty-Nine
The Law of the Lash

When I was growing up in the mountains and foothills of North Carolina, one of the few delights to be found indoors was the once-a-week (if we were indeed fortunate) chance to go to the local theater and watch a cowboy movie. Even now, I still tune in one of the "B" westerns that featured such cowboy heroes as John Wayne, John "Dusty" King, Ray "Crash" Corrigan, Hoot Gibson, Wild Bill Elliott, Bob Livingstone, Ken Maynard, Buster Crabbe, Tex Ritter, Charles Starrett, and Bob Steele.

We never cared much for William Boyd, better known as Hopalong Cassidy. He was too old, too obviously fragile, and his movies were lacking singularly in the violence we enjoyed so much. Neither did we flock to see Gene Autry or Roy Rogers, both of whom seemed too sissy for our tastes. It was a little too much for us to see thin, short, and unmanly Leonard Slye from Cincinnati show up as Roy Rogers and whale the tar out of the huge outlaws. And Roy seldom lost his hat in a fight and never seemed to lose any blood. We liked the huge, brawny men like George O'Brien, who had been a fleet boxing champion in the United States Navy.

Late in the evolution of the oaters came Whip Wilson and Lash LaRue, both of whom, as their nicknames suggested, used a bullwhip. Both were okay, but Lash LaRue, complete with his black hat, black shirt, and black pants, seemed more realistic. Not only that, Al "Fuzzy" St. John, formerly of the Keystone Kops comedy series, added greatly to our thrill when we saw the two together. One of my fantasies as a child was that one day I'd be able to meet some of my heroes.

You have to understand what a thrill it was to go see these movie heroes. First, we had no television sets. We listened to the radio, but it wasn't the same as seeing the movies. We'd work all day in order to earn twenty-five cents. With the quarter in our pocket, we could see the movie for nine cents, and that included the feature, a chapter in a serial, the Eyes and Ears of the World news, previews of coming attractions, and a two-reel comedy featuring the Three Stooges, Leon Errol, Edgar Kennedy, and some kid named Bob Hope, who once was a professional boxer under the name Packy East. Wonder whatever happened to him?

After the movie we'd stop at a beer joint and order through a tiny window, because we were not allowed inside the place. We could get a hot dog for a nickel, a hamburger for another nickel, and a twelve-ounce Pepsi for five cents. That left us with one cent out of the quarter we started with, and for that penny we could buy a package of Kits, small caramel squares in a neat thin cardboard box that we could use as a make-believe boat when we headed for the creek later.

Pretty heady living for an eight-year old!

One day Wild Bill Elliott came to the theater where we saw so many movies, and we had a chance to speak to him as he whisked past us. Another time Sunset Carson came to town. On another day Don "Red" Barry came along.

But we simply saw these people or waved at them. We never got to see them up close, or sit and talk with them. Not until I knew that Lash LaRue was living–not just passing through but actually living!–not far from us.

By this time I was much older, of course, and so was he. But I called and asked if I could visit with him. To my shock, he agreed, and when I told him the visit would also result in a couple or three stories in newspapers or magazines, he was delighted.

I had followed Lash LaRue's career since the days of the old westerns had slipped away and most of the heroes were either dying or dead. Ken Maynard died, I think, in a rest home. Jack Randall died either from a fall from a horse or from a heart attack. Buck Jones perished a hero in the Coconut Grove night club fire in Boston. Don "Red" Barry reportedly committed suicide. We were losing all of them. I knew that if I ever expected to meet a hero, I had to act fast.

Lash was living just south of Shelby when I went to meet him. He drove an ancient Cadillac with longhorn cattle emblems mounted on the inside of the doors. On the back seat lay a trio of whips neatly coiled and ready for use. Lash himself, gray-headed by now and moving with less than the grace that characterized his movie action, greeted me as cordially as if we had been longtime friends.

And he opened the door for any and all questions, some of which, he promised me, he would disregard if he did not want to answer them. He told me in delightful detail how he had come to star as a whip-carrying hero in western movies.

"I had done some community theater in the Los Angeles area," he said, "and I saw a notice that a small company was casting for a western movie. I decided to try out for the role, although I knew little or nothing about the West or its heroes."

The director liked Al (his real name) and his reading. Then he asked if he could use a bullwhip. LaRue didn't hesitate.

"I told him I'd used one all my life," he said. The truth was that he had never held one in his hand in his life and, for that matter, he wasn't even sure what one looked like or how it differed from any other type of whip.

"The director told me we'd start shooting in two days. They fitted me in the all-black outfit I was to wear in the movie," he said. "And as soon as I left I rushed to a prop store and bought the whip and took it home so that I could start working on using it. I mean, how complicated could it be?"

He laughed. "I found out very quickly how hard it could be. In fact, I nearly beat myself to death with the damn thing before I finally reached the point that I could crack it without taking chunks of flesh out of my hide. I was scared to death that I'd remove one of my eyes with the whip. The movie was popular, and the director and the producer said we'd do a series of them, so I kept on practicing with it and finally reached the point that I was reasonably good with it. We set up most of the scenes so I couldn't accidentally mar someone's face for life. It took weeks for the holes in my own arms, shoulders, and back to heal. A bullwhip, I admit, is a terrible weapon in the hands of an amateur. The thing that saved me was that I worked with some fine and highly talented people. Fuzzy was one of them; he was the best."

Lash had nothing but compliments for his comic sidekick. He said repeatedly that Fuzzy was the best of them all. "You know that Charles Starrett had Smiley Burnette, who also acted with other stars. The Range Busters had Max "Alibi" Terhune, and other stars had their own pals."

He continued, "We had Dub Taylor, Andy Clyde, and a dozen others in the comic sidekick roles," he said. "But I never met anyone who could handle any scene the way Fuzzy could. He was almost a contortionist, and he could turn anything into a prop that produced a scene that was hilarious. The director simply handed us a script that had our scenes blocked out. But for Fuzzy's scenes, there would be only a note that said, 'Fuzzy Business.' That would be good for five minutes of sidesplitting humor."

Among the topics LaRue would not discuss was how old he was. "Too old," was all he would say. "There's no room anymore for people like me."

How many times was he married? "Too many," he said. "I never found the woman who was right for me, or I was never right for them. I didn't use my head much in my earlier days. Or later days, either."

He talked candidly about how after the western movies he went to more complicated and more expensive movie roles, but always in a bit part that, as he said, he could have mailed in. He had walk-on roles in some fairly big-budget films, and in some of his rare meatier roles he received good reviews from the critics.

But, as Bob Steele and a few other western stars made the transition to television (Bob Steele appeared as a regular in *F Troop,* which had a long run on the tube), LaRue never seemed to make the transition. He gravitated downward, and eventually he wound up in life's seamy side."

Like a true hero, however, he refused to stay down where too much booze and powders had landed him. He found Christianity and became a preacher to the fallen. Little by little he worked his way back up, and he began to receive personal appearance requests, and his films were sold in video cassette format.

"I'll be all right," he told me as we parted. "I wish my story had turned out better, but I can thank God it didn't turn out any worse. You'll be hearing from me soon." I did. I picked up the paper one day and read that onetime cowboy star Lash LaRue had died in Los Angeles.

With him died a huge part of the legend of the western movies that gave opportunities to such future stars as Lee J. Cobb, John Wayne, Rita Hayworth, Robert Mitchum, and a host of others. Television has lately filled the gap left by the departing old-timers, but not in my mind. I still live in the thirties and forties where the music had tunes you could sing or whistle and the movies had stars you could admire.

Steve and Dotty Leatherwood

Forty
Bluegrass Is Live at Leatherwood's

The North Carolina mountains are not just stone and soil; they are living organisms that strive and strain to give birth to the forces that will continue the species, to provide living proof of the mighty power that invests itself in everything it touches. It was this power that created the waterfalls and the once-mighty chestnut tree and the black bear and the white-tailed deer. This was the power that springs to life with the cougar and the pheasant, the field mouse and the elk that once inhabited this surreal stretch of granite that somehow engendered the oaks and the hickories and the field daisies.

This was the power that erupted in novelist Thomas Wolfe and compelled the fertile imagination and titanic intellect that bequeathed *Look Homeward, Angel* and *You Can't Go Home Again*. This force pitted Wolfe's heritage against his own uncontrollable force of creative energy, and it was this same power that sharpened the mind and pen of William Sidney Porter, better known as O. Henry.

The written word and the painting and the drama did not stand alone as the offspring of the Mountains. Bluegrass, too, erupted, and created people like Earl Scruggs. Correct that: there is no one like Earl Scruggs. He is as unique as a Shakespearean drama or a Pavorotti aria or a Frost poem. And if you want Bluegrass today, spend Saturday night in Shelby.

Visit the Courtsquare Opry on any Saturday night and you will see in a flash what's going on in bluegrass music. The Saturday night show runs year-round. First, it's family entertainment, with no rough or unseemly behavior. Admission at this writing is $6 for adults and $5 for senior citizens. Here's what you get for your money, after you pass through the commercial part of the store and enter the huge back room, where there is a stage as well as rows of seats of all sorts and people of all persuasions who come for one reason: to celebrate the joys of bluegrass music.

As the show begins, there is an open-mike session during which time anyone and everyone who plays bluegrass music has his place in the sun, or at least in the spotlight, and his fifteen minutes of fame. Then the headline acts take over, with outstanding bluegrass bands from all over the Carolinas performing. There are some great acts, like the Hudson Family, with every member of the family down to the kindergarten age singing and playing. The Dollar Brothers from Lenoir are among the best you'll find anywhere. You will see such bands as the Catawba River Boys, Stoney Gap, Southern BG Partners, Out of the Blue, Maple Ridge, Daren Aldridge Band, Radio Dispatch, Powder Creek with Dewey Farmer, None of the Above, Inside Track, Right Track (Burgess Family), Al Wood and Smoky Ridge Boys, Northern Border, Strings of Fire, Lee Ward & Southern Express, and New River.

During intermission there are jam sessions all over the building. You will find individuals who want to pick and sing or fiddle with people who share a love for the music. Sometimes the strangers have only heard of Leatherwood's and want to see what it's like. Part of the wonderful fascination of the show is simply watching the timid young people who enter, pay their admission, and then stand on the fringe of the crowd and shift their weight from one foot to another while they are also weighing their options. After a long internal debate they may slip to the door and disappear, only to emerge from the darkness later with their guitar or fiddle tuned and ready to go. Minutes later the stranger is an old friend of the musicians who are fixtures there.

It's a good idea to arrive before show time. You'll want time to peruse the racks of comic books and other attractions you've forgotten.

If you grew up on Batman, Superman, and Captain Marvel comic books, you're in for a shock as you see who has replaced the Green Lantern, the Little Atom, Blue Beetle, Spy Smasher, the Torch, Hawk-Man, Captain America, Wonder Woman, the Hulk, Spider Man and the Flash. Some of the heroes are still very much alive but perhaps more than a little changed. Replacing some of the "retired" heroes of the past are Cat Woman, Darkman, and the other members of the new breed of comics. This New Breed, by the way, has been here for much longer than you would believe.

You can shop or just look through collections of records, tapes, and CDs as well as memorabilia and relics from bygone days. It's truly a step back in history.

Or, if you wish, you can come several hours early and take part in the Swap Meet & Jam Session every Saturday from 10 AM until 1 PM. There is no admission price, and you can meet fellow enthusiasts (or old heads) who will introduce you to the thrills of buying, selling, and trading what the Leatherwoods call "Bluegrass Stuff."

But who are these people who spend every Saturday night of their lives immersed in bluegrass music? You will find that the family that promotes the music is at least as interesting as are the performers on the stage.

First, Steve Leatherwood came by his love of bluegrass music naturally. Born in Waynesville, he grew up in Clyde, not far from Asheville. He spent his early years as an admirer of the music style and also as a lover of the performance. He plays the trombone, piano, bass guitar, fiddle, guitar, and mandolin, He takes the stage along with some of the visiting groups and plays and sings along. When he is not on the stage, he works professionally as a middle-school counselor in the local school system and occasionally teaches psychology on the university campus. In addition, Steve finds time to write and publish a number of periodical articles and newspaper columns, conduct a series of workshops in Humor, Health, and Healing, and work on a series of books he plans to publish in the near future. He has written widely about antiques and the art of buying and preserving them.

Steve's wife Dotty (the two have been married for more than three decades, after having been high school sweethearts as they were growing up in Clyde) plays the clarinet and sings like an angel.

She works as a hospital administrator and has written and published articles on her career work. When she is standing in the audience and singing along with the people on stage, make it a point to stand near her. It's an unforgettable treat.

The sons of the Leatherwoods, Jeremy and Jeff, devote much of their time to the store and to their own music and writing. Jeff plays the trombone, tuba, and cello, while Jeremy is a percussionist and history buff.

Why do they spend so much time with bluegrass music? "For the fun of it," Steve replies at once. "All of this is to have a good time and help others to enjoy the music and have a great evening's entertainment at a relatively low cost. We have lots of games here, and we know that if a kid is in here, he's not going to get in trouble, and he's not on the street and exposed to the problems found there."

One of the rewards of the bluegrass involvement is that of seeing some of the performers who showed up to play a tentative tune or two go on to play in bands and, like one of the recent groups, go on to record a popular CD and tapes.

All in all, not a bad way to have fun.

The Dollar Brothers are frequent guests at Leatherwood's.

Vance House in Weaverville

Forty-One
A Quick Man with a Quip

Zeb Vance of just outside Weaverville was without doubt one of the most intriguing men in North Carolina history. He served as an officer in the Confederate army and as senator from the Tar Heel state.

But it is Zeb Vance the man that commands our greatest interest. It is Zeb Vance the wit, the humorist, the observer and evaluator of human life, the human spirit that flamed in his breast that made him one of the best stories to emerge from the mountains of this state.

This is not an attempt to chronologize Zeb Vance's achievements. It is not an effort at biography. It is instead simply a glimpse of who the man was, what he was like, and why it would be of interest to you to drive to Weaverville, just off the Blue Ridge Parkway, to see Zeb's home and to relive, if only for the moment, some of the vitality that surrounded the man. The house is comfortable but not luxurious.

Vance was an orator. That's a good place to start, because oratory is a lost art. It has been replaced by yelling, shouting, name-calling, whining and bleating, selfish and unintended parodies of ourselves, and, above all, the whimpering and righteous indignation that we can summon at the precise moment the television camera sweeps across the crowd.

Zeb Vance was an orator in the style of Daniel Webster, Henry Clay, Ralph Waldo Emerson, and a short list of other Americans who had something worthwhile to say and said it in a dramatic and effective manner.

Zeb was often described as the finest orator in the country. He was equally at home in private or club conversations.

When Zeb Vance spoke, people paid attention. He, like many other noted public speakers, could come up with half a dozen down-home anecdotes or stories that could simultaneously be hilariously funny and at the same time cut to the heart of the matter being discussed.

Once he sat in Washington and heard a constant droning over the need to spend federal money on flood control along a river in Rhode Island. Zeb listened to all he could endure, then stood and shook his fist and declared that he was against spending all that money for flood control in a state that was so small he could urinate halfway across it.

"The gentleman from North Carolina is out of order," the man with the gavel insisted. Zeb wasn't through. Not yet.

"Damn right I'm out of order," he thundered. "Otherwise I could urinate all the way across the state."

The story is told that when Vance was in Yankee land after the Civil War some of the smug company secretly hung a picture of Jefferson Davis in the privy and waited to see Vance's reaction when he entered the toilet and saw his former leader being desecrated, in a sense. Nature finally demanded, and Zeb left for the toilet. When he returned he did not say a word.

Finally, one of the company asked Vance how he liked the new decorations in the outhouse. Zeb replied that the portrait was highly suited for the toilet. He added that if there was ever a man who could scare the dung out of a Yankee, it was Jeff Davis.

During the Civil War, Vance was taken into custody and sent to Salisbury. As he and his escorts finally arrived at their destination, Vance was ordered to report to the headquarters of the commanding officer. Almost as soon as Vance arrived, the commander asked if the rumors he had heard were true: that Vance, as a way of humiliating a brave soldier, had been forced to ride a mule rather than a handsome horse, during the trip.

Vance looked shocked at the suggestion. "No, sir," he said in the greatest sincerity. "I rode no mule. In fact, I never even saw a jackass until I walked into this office, just now."

But Zeb Vance was more than simply a fast man with a quip, although his reputation as a wit reached far and wide. He was also a man with an intense loyalty to his soldiers, and he demonstrated that loyalty, even when he was mistaken about his men.

After the war, Vance received the news that one of his former soldiers had been charged with murdering a woman, and the man needed an attorney desperately. Vance, who recalled the man as being a fine soldier and also a man whose energy could be used to entertain the other troops during times of great stress, sent word that he would arrive as soon as possible to take the man's case.

He even offered to represent the former comrade in arms at no fee. Such was his loyalty that he would forego the money he would have earned as the man's attorney and even pay his own living expenses while he was away from home.

When he arrived at the jailhouse, he entered the cell and took one look at his client–and realized that he had never seen the man before in his life. The client's name was Tom Dula (pronounced Dooley in the mountains surrounding Wilkesboro), and the man Vance had known was also named Dula, but the two bore no other similarities.

But Vance took the case anyhow, and he defended the man with energy and determination, but the evidence was too great against Dula, and the jury found him guilty of murder and sentenced him to hang. Still Vance refused to give up, but in the end he was not able to save the man he had defended, and Tom Dula prepared to die.

The story is that Dula played the fiddle and entertained the crowd that had gathered for the purpose of seeing a man die. When it was time for the noose, Dula held out his hand, extending it toward the crowd.

"Look at this hand," he told the crowd. "It does not tremble in fear. I never harmed one hair on that girl's head."

He touched the noose lightly. "You have such a nice new rope," he said, "I should have washed my neck."

Moments later Tom Dula was dead, but, for the record, he never hung down his head. Soon the mountain people were singing the sad ballad about Tom Dooley, and decades later the Kingston Trio recorded the song and it became one of their greatest hits.

It is doubtful that Zeb Vance found the song entertaining. It represented too much that was wrong when an innocent man, as Vance said about his client, must die because a rather worthless woman had died and another had accused Dula of murder.

It would be wrong of me to suggest Zeb Vance was a wit without a semblance of seriousness in his attitude. Like most real wits, he was at his most serious while he was joking. As Bernard Shaw once observed, his way of joking was to tell the truth, which is the funniest joke of all.

When Vance was engaged in warfare, he managed to keep his wits and at the same time share his wit with those around him. The man loved to laugh, and he loved the South and North Carolina, particularly the North Carolina mountains.

The Civil War gave him a great deal to joke about, because it was the saddest occasion he witnessed, and he had to joke in order to keep from losing his control. Men like Vance are needed badly today. They knew the difference between oratory and bombast and between wit and humor.

The Vance House in Statesville

Forty-Two
He Lit Up Our Lives

I never knew Thomas Alva Edison, of course, because the great inventor and scientist died eight months before I was born. The best I could do, and this was great enough for me, was to know someone who knew Edison.

The woman I knew was a schoolteacher. Frances Puckett in fact taught school for well over forty years, and when she left public school work, she taught privately. Her subject matter covered the entire curriculum. She taught whatever the students needed to learn, and she assumed that they needed to know everything.

She came to know Edison through no control of her own. Her parents, actually, had invited Edison to live with them briefly while he stayed in Lincoln County. Edison had come to North Carolina for one purpose: to search for cobalt. He needed something that would work in an automobile battery and still keep the weight down. While he was in this part of the country, Edison searched and dug throughout the countryside in Lincoln, Cleveland, and Rutherford counties, wherever monozite was being mined and sold. Edison in an earlier part of his life also lived in Charlotte.

The parents of Ms. Puckett became great friends of Edison, the teacher told me. She said that often she would see her father and Thomas Edison coming in from a field where they had been working, and they had their arms around each other.

"Back then," she said impatiently, "men could be great friends and not have to worry about what people said. But that was during the time when people had much nobler attitudes. My father and Edison were great friends; Edison liked people a great deal."

Thomas Edison was born on February 11, 1847, and lived until October 18, 1931. He lived to the ripe old age of 84, and during that time, after an immensely inauspicious start in life, he managed to take out more than one thousand patents on his inventions.

In a series of events that should be required learning for all students and their teachers, Edison attended public school for only three months. His miserable public school appearance in Port Huron, Michigan, led his teachers to assume that because he did not learn at the same rate as others (and probably because he colored outside the lines!) he was unable to learn. Little did they know that the child's brain had already outdistanced their own.

Edison lived at home for several years, spending much of his time educating himself, and at age twelve he went to work as a railroad newsboy. At age fifteen he became a telegraph operator in a series of cities, and during his spare time he studied or conducted his own experiments in science. Part of his early life was spent in Charlotte, where he lived at the old Buford Hotel. He earned his living by working at Western Union Telegraph across the street from the Buford on South Tryon Street.

Arthur Talmadge Abernethy of Rutherford College worked with Edison in Charlotte, and by this time the Western Union building adjoined the Charlotte *Observer* building between Independence Square and Fourth Street on South Tryon. Like so many pranksters today who loved to play with the Internet and fax machines, Edison loved to have his fun with the telegraph equipment, and it was one of his pranks that got him fired.

But it didn't matter; Edison was on his way. At age nineteen he had already secured his first patent, this one for his invention of an electrical vote recorder. After that, he turned out inventions the way most Yuppies crank out dumb-blonde jokes on the 'Net.

It was in the late 1800s when Edison came to the South and spent time in Charlotte (again), Gastonia, Lincolnton, and surrounding towns and cities in this part of the nation. By this time he had spent $40,000 (a princely sum in those days and not chicken feed by modern standards) in his efforts to develop an incandescent lamp or light.

The story persists that Edison was not dismayed by his failures. He said he had found a huge number of ways that were not workable. That sentiment echoes those of Arthur Conan Doyle, the creator of Sherlock Holmes.

Doyle said that when we have exhausted all impossible solutions, whatever is left is the answer, no matter how improbable.

When Edison came South again, after his aborted Western Union career, he arrived with his son and a chauffeur in a huge automobile that scared the daylights out of livestock and horses pulling carriages or wagons down the main streets of town. Edison liked to wear a duster, the large coat made popular by its ability to protect the riders' clothing from dust and other grime when the occupants of the vehicle had to travel the hot, dusty roads.

The loud automobile arrived in Lincolnton in 1906, and it is said that Edison lived in the old Carolina Hotel there for a while. Then he moved into the Puckett house and spent several weeks with them.

The man, according to those who knew him, had an uncanny memory that refused to let go of a fact, a face, or a name, once it became a part of his mentality. He also wrote in beautiful penmanship, his acquaintances said.

When he was in this part of the country, he spent time in McAdenville, where he helped to install one of the generators at one of the mills there. But when he was finally ready to leave, the mother of the teacher asked Edison, who was rapidly losing his hearing, about some of his inventions and future plans.

He told her of the invention that would enable people to hear the voices of loved ones or notable people who are in different parts of the town, in another city altogether, or even in another country or state. He added that even voices of dead people could be heard.

The mother told Edison that he was a brilliant man who had done wonderful things but he was talking crazy now. When Edison returned to New Jersey to his Menlo Park home, he sent the mother an early version of the phonograph, along with 150 cylinder recordings. When I visited in the home, the phonograph was still a part of the household furnishings.

Frances Puckett inherited the phonograph and recordings; unfortunately, however, she told me that someone dropped the box of 150 of the recordings and broke exactly half of them.

Edison gave up on the cobalt. He also gave up on North Carolina generally. But he remained in contact with the friends he had made here, and it was my privilege to know someone who actually knew Thomas Edison. That was my nearest brush with greatness.

At one of the mills in McAdenville there is Generator No. 31, which was installed by Thomas Edison. Chaplain Billy Miller examines Edison's handiwork.

Forty-Three
The Squire of Huntersville

W hen I first met LeGette Blythe he had already devoted many years of work as a journalist at the Charlotte *News* and after that at the *Observer*. He left the latter paper in a rather bitter dispute over the terms of a sabbatical and never returned.

He didn't need the work. He had plenty of other responsibilities and privileges in his life. I caught him on that first visit during a rare respite from his life's work, and he was eager to talk.

And talk he did. In that space of perhaps two hours I learned more about the general writer's life and work than I'd have dreamed possible in two weeks.

"Back in those days," LeGette told me in the den of his cool and comfortable house in Huntersville, just north of Charlotte, "there was a real appreciation for the writer. That day has gone, and I am and always will be grateful for the fact that I could become and remain a part of it."

Make no mistake. He was not some garrulous old man droning on and on about the good old days. He was, and remained so until the time of his death, a brilliant human being, a man whose respect for other human beings towered above that of lesser men. He was not only brilliant and hospitable; he was insightful, quick, perceptive, and helpful.

"I started my writing career almost on a whim," he told me. "Not at first. I had, of course, been educated with an eye to writing for a newspaper as a means of earning a living. I was happy to land a position at the old Charlotte *News*, and even happier to move to the *Observer* three years later. I stayed there twenty-five years." Here his writing career began.

"I knew I wanted to write a novel, he said, "but how that novel came about was unthinkable by today's standards."

He went on to relate how he sat at his desk at the newspaper when, one unusual night, the news was slow.

"Much of the time we needed four hands to keep up with what was happening," he said, "but on this particular night it was very slow in terms of news. So I slipped a piece of paper into my typewriter and pecked out the first five, or maybe it was ten, pages of a novel. At the time I didn't have any idea of how long the book would be or whether it would ever be written in its entirety, but I wrote the first few pages, slipped them into an envelope, and shipped them off to a publisher in New York. It was an impetuous thing to do, as I look back on the changes in publishing, but at the time I didn't see that any harm could come from it. I mailed them, and only days later I received a letter from the publisher who offered me a contract to complete the book. Best of all, there was an offer of an advance payment of $10,000 to be paid when I signed the contract."

Now, folks, if you think that this is a standard practice in the world of publishing, it's time for you to get an education. Keep in mind the adage from the New York circle of publishers. If you have forgotten it, read it again.

According to the adage, out of every hundred people who say they are going to write a book, only one will ever start. Out of every hundred who start, only one will finish the book. And of every 10,000 who finish the book, only one will find a publisher.

It's enough to make you decide to keep the daytime job at the local butcher shop. But in LeGette Blythe's day, publishers were begging for good writers.

Again, to pull you up short, today you would not get your first five to ten pages read by many publishers. You'd have to submit through an agent, not over the transom. This last term is, in case you don't recognize it, a reference to the old days when writers took their materials by the editor's office after closing time and slipped the manuscripts through the small window, or transom, over the doorway. The modern reference is to anything submitted cold, or without first clearing the submission with the editors.

More quick education, in light of the kindness of LeGette Blythe in educating me over a period of several sessions: Getting an agent.

This is a real struggle because it's easier to get a patent, in some cases, than to get an agent.

The upshot of it all is that getting a good agent is like getting a huge bank loan: you can get one when you can prove you do not need it. And you do not want an agent who isn't good.

The good agents, incidentally, would like for you to have earned about $200,000 by writing during the previous year. Needless to say, it takes a little pull and a lot of luck. But many publishers who will not read anything that is not submitted through an agent are in effect closing their doors to dozens, perhaps hundreds of good writers.

A personal note here: I have been able over the years to receive contracts for more than thirty-five books, and counting, all of which I obtained without the help of an agent. During the time that I did have an agent, I did not sell a single book or even a single word to a publisher of any sort.

So it is highly remarkable that many years ago publishers were so hungry for good material that they would pay a huge advance (in those days an enormous one, and not too shabby today) to writers who have never proven themselves to be money-makers.

LeGette Blythe was born as the old century faded into the past and the twentieth century was starting its long road. When he went to work at the Charlotte *News*, he was twenty-two years old, and when he signed his first major book contract he was on the shady side of his mid-twenties.

What this means, if anything, is that he was writing when a group of kids from around the country were making their voices heard: William Faulkner, Ernest Hemingway, Eugene O'Neill, Lawrence Stallings, Maxwell Anderson, Carl Sandburg, Sinclair Lewis, Pearl Buck, John Steinbeck, and other writers of that caliber. But once you get past the leading names, the second-string writers lacked the prestige that history has afforded these major authors.

Keep in mind that Hemingway during his rather long career wrote only a handful of novels and a few short story collections, as well as a small number of nonfiction books. He was not a prolific writer by any stretch of the imagination, and the reading public could devour books much faster than these authors could produce them.

So the appetite was there, the customers were ready, and the authors lacked the time and energy to meet the needs. So publishers turned to newcomers in the hopes that the next new kid on the block would become the next bestselling author.

"The publishers were in constant competition with each other for the services of the writers," Blythe told me on one occasion. "You could have a book appear in print on Monday and by Friday you would get offers from other publishers, all of whom promised better contracts, higher advances, better royalty payments. There just weren't that many authors who could turn out quality works within a short time framework, and those who could might find themselves in great demand."

Blythe did what more and more writers have started doing, partly because of desire, partly because of increased profits, and partly because of necessity. He wrote books sponsored or backed or produced by interest groups. But not in his heyday, not when he wrote books like *Bold Galilean, Alexandriana,* and *A Tear for Judas.* These books were best-sellers not only in this country but in foreign countries as well.

Several of his books became Book-of-the-Month Club selections, and as such were guaranteed a huge chunk of the literary market. Such successes also informed the world that LeGette Blythe was one of the major voices in contemporary fiction.

Sadly, because he came too early or too late, he was neglected by the *Oxford Companion to American Literature* and various of the other reference books that included less-than-notable writers simply because they were early in this nation's history or because they were among the most recent of the bestselling authors.

One day when I was in his home, Blythe proudly showed me the various translations of some of his books. Memory does not serve well here, but I think that there must have been more than two dozen languages involved.

When he began to write regional biographies, Blythe perfected (and virtually created) the genre in this part of the country. He wrote of the mountain doctors Mary Martin Sloop and Eustace Sloop; he told the story of Penland founder Lucy Morgan; he wrote about the life of William Henry Belk; and he chronicled the life and times of textile magnate Robert Lee Stowe. There is a real need for books like these, and Blythe did us all a real service in popularizing the genre.

But I suppose the highest compliment that I could pay to LeGette Blythe, other than the fact of his fine writing, was that his doors were open to the younger writers trying for a slice of the pie. That, plus the fact that he served notice that Tar Heels can write!

The Concord Weavers of the 1940s

Forty-Four
Baseball When It Was Fun
or
Contributing to the Delinquency of the Minors

H ere is where we put the X-Rated label on this book. If there are kids in the room, get them out before you start to read aloud. And if they stay in the room, don't move your lips while you read. This is a small part of the story of the seamy side of baseball, and I am not referring to the seams of the baseball itself.

This is a story (or series of stories) reaching back to the post-World War II years when the great ball players came back from military service and resumed their careers in the majors and when the has-been or never-was caliber of player who had played in the majors while the real ball players were away slipped silently into the shadows of time.

First, however, you may need a few reminders.

Think, if you haven't done so lately, about what World War II and the Korean War did to the careers of some of the truly great baseball players.

Start with one of the records that people thought would never be broken: Babe Ruth's all-time career home run total that later Henry Aaron eclipsed. Baseball fans know that the Babe hit 714 home runs, a mark that, they said, would last forever.

But keep in mind that Aaron hit 755 or some such figure, and now they say that his mark may never be broken. In order to break the record, a hitter would have to stay in the game for thirty-seven or thirty-eight years and hit slightly more than twenty home runs each year. Put another way, the player could hit forty homers each year and need to stay in the big leagues only nineteen or twenty years.

Think about it: you play from the time you reach the majors at, say, age twenty-three, and then you must play until you are forty-two or forty-three years old and still manage to hit forty homers each year. If it sounds like a superhuman feat, that's because it is.

Now go back to World War II and consider the plight of Boston Red Sox slugger Ted Williams, who managed to hit a career total of 521 home runs. Williams lost more than six full seasons (actually there were times when he made only token appearances at the park) because of World War II and the Korean War. The years he lost were the peak years of his life, and one can only wonder what he would have accomplished if he had been permitted to play during those seasons.

For instance, if Williams had played during the lost seasons, and if he had hit forty home runs each year, he could have beaten Aaron's all-time home run mark. Could he have hit forty home runs each of those seasons? No one knows. But if he had hit slightly fewer and had been within a dozen or so home runs of breaking records (Ruth's, in this case, because Aaron had not yet set his own record), he'd have perhaps stayed in the game for another year or so.

Remember that he hit .388 near the end of his career, and if he had chosen to stay around as a pinch-hitter or as a designated hitter (if the position had been a part of the game at that time) he'd have set records that perhaps no one could have approached.

The same is true of pitchers. Warren Spahn did not win his first game until he was 26 years old and he went on to become the winningest left-hander in the history of the game. All this is not to argue statistics but to set the stage for what was to happen. For one thing, young ball players may have a real future in the major leagues. If they are lucky and good!

Remember: there were only sixteen teams in the major leagues at that time and your odds of making the majors were about 3000 to one, as opposed to three to one today, and when players went off to fight for their country, and they came home either too old, too shattered physically and emotionally, or too battered by the horrors of war to think of earning a living by playing a kid's game.

There were returning veterans who managed to produce astonishing feats on the baseball field: some of them hit as high as .430; some hit fifty or more home runs each year for several seasons in a row, back when thirty home runs for a minor league player was a superb year; some won twenty games or more each season for ten or more years in a row.

And they never had a chance at the major leagues.

Why? One of them, a man with whom I played, had his feet frozen while fighting in Germany, and he could no longer run or play his position well enough to play in the big time. So he slogged (and slugged) his way through years of minor league baseball. Another led the entire nation in hitting and could not play major league ball because he had lost the use of some of his fingers. Others lost major parts of their skills by the enforced layoff.

When these people played minor league ball, many of them felt that they had been cheated out of their careers, and they opted to have as much fun as they could during the twilight years of their careers. And they made their mark, in their own way, if not in a way that baseball would have smiled upon.

For instance, if you attended a ball game in the old minor leagues back in the late forties and early fifties, when the public address system scratched out the National Anthem at the start of the game, you might have seen a row of players standing in front of the dugout.

Every member of every team stood respectfully, hats off and over their hearts, while the National Anthem played. Today the players stand and talk, chew gum, scratch themselves in places that should never be scratched in public, turn and stare into the stands, kick the dirt, and in general act bored. It is a rare and welcome occasion when the players stand and sing along. Some classy ones, happily, still do it.

One of the best players in a Tar Heel league was a thick-chested, short, and squat man who could run like a deer and hit a baseball out of any park in the world, including Yellowstone. He loved the game dearly.

ROBERT L. WILLIAMS

He knew, however, that he would never have his chance at the majors, but that fact did not keep him from playing his heart out as long as he could make it onto the field and play the game as it should be played.

Today, unfortunately, we see players in the major leagues who have more talent than imaginable. So how do many of them use it? By getting involved with drugs, gambling, bashing of girl friends or wives or even children, nightclub fights, insane driving, rude behavior toward the media and the fans, and other means of showing disrespect. Not too long ago a flashy and cocky young player had been told that a commentator had made an uncomplimentary remark about the player, who had a terrible habit of goofing off.

So the young punk made his way to the broadcast booth and poured his cup of soft drink into the lap of the commentator. Nobody seems to object that such behavior occurs. Many accept it, others grin about it, and still others think it's hilarious. But keep in mind the television man was fully two decades older than the player, who would have never had the courage to perform a similar act against someone who was in a position to fight back.

Back to the National Anthem for a moment. Part of the blame for the disrespect goes to the front offices who invite people to sing this very special song in their own inimitable way. So they twitch, writhe, wiggle, and howl as they make up their own words and much of the time their own tunes. Someone, in this writer's humble opinion, should make it a rule that if the singer can't sing the song the way it was meant to be rendered, then the invitation should go to people who will show the song the honor it deserves.

The fans come in for their share of the blame, too. They carry the idea of rooting for the home team to deplorable lengths, and in the end they throw bottles and cans and fruit and whatever else they can lay their hands on at the players. The irate fans do not seem to understand that one missile could end the career of a man who might be well on his way to shattering records and entering the Hall of Fame. Fans who are caught throwing anything onto the field ought to be arrested and clapped in jail for a week or so. And then fined about a week's salary for a good worker .

The Hall of Fame is another fiasco. Originally intended for players who were truly exceptional, people like Babe Ruth, Lou Gehrig, Ty Cobb, and other undeniably great performers. Not any more.

Now it seems that anyone who hangs around long enough will eventually be voted into the Hall of Fame. There is one pitcher, for example, who won a grand total of one game, and he is in the Hall of Fame.

And Shoeless Joe Jackson, one of the greatest players who ever lived, is kept out of the Hall because of allegedly accepting a bribe to throw the World Series. It doesn't matter that he was found not guilty; he is still guilty in the eyes of the baseball moguls.

On the other hand, players with a half-dozen felonious crimes tagged into their names will continue to play the game and will wind up in the Hall after their career ends.

This lengthy preamble is to set the stage for the real part of this chapter: the great and not-so-great players who spent their lives in the minors, because for various reasons the majors were closed to them. Or, in some cases, the players actually made the majors but too late for them to show their real abilities.

The tag line of so many stories is the oft-repeated alibi, "You had to be there to see it for yourself." That's the way it was with some of the classic North Carolina minor league baseball players. You had to see them to appreciate them fully.

The home field where the Statesville Owls played was known far and wide for its awkward layout. It was 285 feet down the right field foul line to the fence, and there was a high screen wire atop the regular fence. Long pop flies sailed over the fence with regularity.

Left field was a different matter. The fence was 418 feet from home plate, and no one had ever hit a ball over that barricade. Even when barnstorming major league teams came to town, none of the Big League players ever cleared the fence. Even Hall of Famer Jimmy "Double XX" Foxx, who managed to hit one over center field fence, never accomplished the feat.

Ted Williams hit one over the center field fence, too, a ball that cleared the wall at the 410 mark and landed half a mile, or so it seemed, on the other side.

But no one ever hit one over the Monster in left field. No one, that is, until Len Cross came to play for the Owls. We had, in fact, given up the hopes and dreams that anyone would ever clear the monster fence. No one, in fact, had even come close. No one had even hit the fence. That historic night the Concord Weavers were in town.

The Weavers were one of the greatest baseball teams ever assembled in the minors, but their glory days were fading fast. Now the team was left, after the owners sold all the prime players, with a few hangers-on. These aging athletes could still play ball, and some of the rookies had yet to prove themselves, so the team was uneven at best.

In the late innings of the game Cross caught a pitch just right, and it left the infield as if the ball had been shot from a cannon. It never did arch; it simply kept going on and on until it cleared the top of the fence by about two feet.

The game went into extra innings, and in the bottom of the thirteenth, as I recall, Cross came to bat again, this time against Lefty George Hatley, who had been around for ages. Ahead in the count, Hatley tried to fool Cross with a change-up, and the huge third baseman timed the ball perfectly and hit it with all his strength, which was more than considerable.

The ball almost went into orbit. It was as high as the lights when it left the park. Some fans said the ball cleared the road behind the park, too, which would have made the drive at least 600 feet.

There was great baseball everywhere you turned. Each team had players who were great if not legendary. But there was also tragedy. One man, happily married as far as the world knew, had a girlfriend on the other side of town, a dangerous situation. But the player was safe because he always went to the back of the house, raised the window, and slipped into the bedroom where the mistress waited. She was married, but her husband had been in jail for weeks, so the player was safe again: or so he thought.

On the tragic night, however, the husband was out of jail and was in bed with his wife when the lover arrived. The player raised the window, and the girlfriend had the awful choice of either warning the player and thereby letting the husband know her secret, or remaining silent and letting the scene play itself out.

The wife chose silence, and as the player stepped into the bedroom, the husband opened fire. The player died instantly, and someone had the sad duty to go tell the player's wife and three children not just that the husband was dead but also how he died.

If some of the players were bad, some of the owners were worse. They were, in fact, unbelievable. One owner hated to pay the players so badly that he would close his shop and leave town in order to delay payday as long as possible. One player foolishly gave the owner a loophole.

The player had a bet with the owner that the player would hit .300 or better for the entire season. And, going into the final weeks of the season, he was indeed batting about .340. The owner could not bring himself to pay off the wager, and he ordered the manager to release the player.

The manager screamed in protest, and he explained that the team was in the middle of a pennant race and that the player was the most valuable man on the team. But he couldn't win. The manager fired the player, the team lost the pennant as a result of losing the key player at the most critical part of the season, but the owner kept his money.

This same owner refused to hire another infielder to replace the released man. He told the manager to play one of the pitchers at second base or shortstop. His rationale was that if pitchers can catch balls hit back to the mound, they should be able to catch balls hit to the infield.

Happily, these incidents, which will be treated in full in another book, were overshadowed by the great game the players saw. They saw Norman Small of the Mooresville Moors and Hickory Rebels. They saw Ross Morrow, Pud Miller, Ernie Johnson, Chief Bennett, Earl Campbell (who was an outstanding third baseman with a rifle arm and, when needed, a superb pitcher), who kept lens makers in business as he stomped his glasses into the dirt on repeated occasions.

There were Jimmy Gruzdis, Al Jarlett, one of the greatest minor league pitchers ever, Stuffy McCrone, Pete Treece, Radio Jaynes, Boger McGimpsey, Red Mincey, Bus Huffstetler, Jim Miller, Eddie Yount, and a rosterful of great ball players who could have played in the major leagues if circumstances had been different. Lacey James was one of the finest pitchers ever to play in the Carolinas, and at one time the Mooresville Moors had both Hoyt Wilhelm and Dave Jolly on the same team. Both of these men later had super major league careers. Fred Daniels was one of the slickest fielders who ever played infield, and he was a steady and dangerous hitter.

The list is endless. This was an era when the players took the game seriously, and they played it with all their heart. They were loved dearly by the fans, and they gave their best all the time.

Best of all, they stood at attention during the National Anthem.

From the Civil War to the present, this nation has known few years without wars looming on the horizon. The gun above is located at Fort Sumter, where the Civil War started.

The Vietnam Wall reflects the anger and pain of a disastrous war.

In this section of the Vietnam Wall you can see the name of my friend Ardrey, whose death more than that of any other person brought the war home to me painfully and unforgettably. His name is in the sixth row of names of young men who would never see homes or loved ones again.

Forty-Five
Five Wars That Touched Me

S tephen Crane may have been a great writer and a fine poet, but he had it all wrong about war. War is not kind; war, as Sherman said, is hell, and he ought to know. He created as much of it as he possibly could. War is, to many, particularly the ones who don't have to fight them, the most deadly and useless disease ever to afflict mankind.

In this book I have written about doctors, athletes, writers, and men and women from so many walks of life, and up to this point I have very carefully avoided war when possible. But I have lived long enough that five wars, six if you count one of them as a real war, have touched me.

And I have now reached the point that the war is too much with us for me to avoid it. I could have left this chapter till the very end of the book, but I wanted to close with two married couples who have by their lives and their wisdom shown us how the good life can be lived. I refuse to end the book with the story of carnage and death and destruction.

Unfortunately, many–too many!–of my childhood memories have to do with wars and the people who fought them.

For starters, there is my grandfather, dead these many long years, and his participation in the Civil War. I wrote earlier of the pleasure I have derived from knowing someone who knew Thomas Alva Edison. I have also known someone who was in the UnCivil War. But I would not write about my grandfather if I knew anyone else in that war.

I don't know many of the details. All I know is what he told me, which was relatively little. When I first came to know him, he was already very old, having been born about 1850, which made him just old enough to be able to sneak into the war, if only for less than patriotic purposes.

The war had come to North Carolina and, worse, to the part of North Carolina that I have called home nearly all of my life. Yankee troops occupied the only college near our home. Officers used the offices of the dean and president for their headquarters, and the foot soldiers camped on the campus lawn.

And my grandfather, Blackdaddy, everyone called him, though I never knew why, wanted to become a soldier and fight the Damn Yankees that had come to change our way of life. So he went to the proper people and told them what he was prepared to do, if it proved to be necessary.

The men he talked to agreed, but first, they said, he must make a quick trip for them to the other side of town, where he could find necessary supplies to bring back to the officers and the enlisted men. Blackdaddy did it, even though he felt less than heroic in his efforts.

He made the trip repeatedly over the next few days and weeks, and while he never had the opportunity to shoot a single Yankee, he felt that he was doing his part in the effort. He made the trip on foot, on horseback, on a mule's back, and in an old farm wagon, and each time he successfully delivered the goods needed to keep the war effort going. He never knew the men were only local bums.

Then one day another man in another uniform made the same request, and Blackdaddy obeyed. Soon he was making the trips regularly.

"I never asked questions," he told me in the slow drawl that seemed to require half an hour per sentence. The entire family was that way. Everyone would utter a single word or, if you were lucky, a phrase, then pause for at least ten to fifteen seconds before adding the next couple of syllables.

"I did what they told me to do," he added. "I never really knew what good my hauling liquor did any of them, but if that's what it took to fight a war, I did my part."

And that was it. He sold liquor to both sides.

In his entire military "career" he never heard a shot fired in anger, he saw no violence, and he committed no acts of heroism. He carried liquor to both sides, and that's as much as you can make of it.

And for his service I am proud of Blackdaddy, who learned that if the soldiers on each side could pause long enough to sip a little whiskey now and then, the next step often was talking, then singing, and finally settling down to a peaceful night's sleep. In the morning there were a few headaches, but nobody bled. Nobody died, and nobody had to lie helplessly while typhoid, smallpox, or gangrene ravaged what was once a healthy, strong body. One could do much worse for his country.

Oddly enough, I knew one person who witnessed a small and insignificant part of the Civil War, but I never knew anyone (at least to my knowledge) who endured the horrors of World War I. The next war in my memory was World War II, and I'd give virtually anything if I could find a way to remove that war from my memory. Great-Uncle John, however, spent time in uniform then and later whipped a man who said we'd lost.

December 7, 1941, was truly a day that will live in infamy. I was splitting the kindling wood I was supposed to split the night before when I heard the news. Our neighbor to the north side of us came out into the yard and she was flapping a soiled white apron and calling out at the top of her voice that the Japs had bombed Pearl Harbor.

Soon the entire block had joined her in the near-hysterical awe that pervaded the entire neighborhood. No one seemed to know where Pearl Harbor was or who was damaged by the bombing, but it seemed to be tacitly understood that the Japanese had done a terrible thing by bombing the place.

It took hours before we finally understood a little of what it was about: that the United State had been attacked and this nation was at war.

The first reaction to the war was that everyone rummaged through the family's Christmas decorations and promptly discarded everything that was made in Japan. I never knew how not having a decorated tree in any way hurt the enemy, but I knew not to ask too many questions.

Then the real horror of the war set in. Our part of town became a ghost town, almost, as person after person disappeared. You'd see Shag Lapish on the street corner talking with Lizard Howard, and the next day they'd be gone. One by one the fine, strong, healthy, happy, and exuberant boys were transformed into frightened, awed, forlorn, lost, and miserable men who were dragged away from their homes.

The entire community became a ghost town, in a sense, as all male residents between the ages of eighteen and twenty-nine seemed to vanish into thin air. Only weeks earlier the streets had been filled with strong, active people, and now only children and middle-aged folks moved listlessly down the narrow lanes. A pall of gloom hung like fog or smoke over the entire town.

At once the square or rectangular pennants appeared in nearly every window in our part of town. The flags hung from the window frames and each contained a star for every member of the family now in military service. Many houses had only one star showing, while others had as many as four or five stars, which changed colors ominously for reasons we did not understand at first.

The mystery had a tragic solution. Each time a son or daughter from the house died in action, the color of the star changed, and it was possible to read the history of grief that marked the houses in the town, a town that only recently had known nothing worse than the occasional fender-bender, the arrest of the town drunk, or an outbreak of measles or mumps.

My oldest brother, Johnny, was a superb baseball player who seemed to be infallible at shortstop. Whatever was hit his way struck his glove and, almost faster than the eye could follow, was on its way to first base or to second to start the double-play.

He never told us when he received his draft notice. All I knew was that one day when I was in the fifth grade there was a knock at the door and the teacher told me that I had a visitor. It was Johnny.

"They told me you needed lunch money," he said, handing me thirty-five cents, which probably represented all the money he had. Like most young and unmarried men, he worked all week to help support the family.

He kept one dollar for himself and gave the rest of his salary to my parents to help support the group that lived in our house: eleven of us.

I didn't know what to say, and neither did he. He dropped the coins into my hand and walked away. I did not know until I reached home that afternoon and found my mother in tears that my brother had wanted to say good-bye, in his own way, to me. I knew that he did not trust himself to say what was in his heart, and he chose the easy way out, which was probably the hard way for all of us. He had never been able to show emotions well, and he didn't want to start then.

My second-oldest brother simply rose one morning, dressed, and told us all that he was leaving for the army. Next my uncles who lived in the house entered military service, and suddenly the huge house with all the people became as quiet as a graveyard at midnight.

Not far from us a kid named Bid Burgess went into the army. I had never known him well; in fact, I was the kid-brother hanger-on for all the young men who left our part of town. I knew Bid Burgess only because he loved two things inordinately: he loved to play baseball morning, noon, or night, and he loved to shoot a .22 rifle. We would see him on late afternoons as he carried his rifle into the woods to shoot at targets. We could hear the sharp popping of the bullets as he practiced until he became an expert.

How could any of us have known that he knew he was going into the army and wanted to be ready when it was time to aim the rifle at moving targets wearing uniforms?

How could we know we'd never see any of these people again? How could we know that their lives ended the day they left home and boarded the bus to take them to the reception center?

Oh, they came home on leave, but their time was so precious that it was heartbreaking to see them dashing madly from one house to another in their frantic efforts to say their good-byes to all the people they needed to see one last time. And some people with the same names as the ones we watched as they boarded the bus for the army came back to our town.

But the names were the only real similarities. Boys went into the military, and men returned. Some of them, at least. But they were not the people we knew. They came home filled with excitement and fears that had no names and no identities. They rushed headlong into jobs and into marriages, as if these precious institutions would vanish, like other values.

They had seen these standards disappear once before, and if they did not clutch them with all their might they might vanish again.

Many of them began to job-hop as soon as they accepted their new employment. They could not be confined, and they could not be still, lest something also nameless and horrible should engulf them, and obliterate them from the face of the earth.

Nearly all of them had learned to drink, gamble, curse, and fight while they were in the military service. They lived wildly.

Or they were sullen, angry, and silent.

Johnny decided to try out for a professional baseball team, and he played one game. During that game he handled all of his fielding chances flawlessly, and on the two times he came to bat he hit a home run each time.

And never played another game.

The old excitement, joy, and verve had disappeared. The game was mechanical. They hit the ball, he caught it. They threw the ball, he hit it. The players might as well have been plastic figures rather than human beings.

My second-oldest brother came home, too, and he immediately took flying lessons; he enrolled in college; he worked every minute of the day, in one way or another. It was as if he did not dare stop or some menace would leap from the shadows and devour him. He did not stop the remainder of his life.

He was in his mid-fifties when he learned that he had lung cancer and had less than a month to live. He died within little more than a week.

As he breathed his last, he continued to fidget, as if still afraid of the Thing that had pursued him since 1942. The doctor asked him where he was, and he replied in a voice filled with tragedy and defeat, "At Fort Bragg, getting ready to go fight Germans."

Moments later his lips moved again. "Mama," he said. "Swing me."

He was back on the front porch of our house, asking a mother who had been dead for years to swing him in the swing that was a part of the front porch furniture of every house on our street.

Then he died, and I shall always be grateful that his last moments on this earth were spent in a swing shaded by the huge chinaberry trees that grew in our front yard. I still rejoice that he did not leave this world while preparing to fight Germans.

We don't know how Johnny died. He and his wife separated, then divorced, and when she died, he wept inconsolably, like a child, although they had not been man and wife for more than a decade. But he loved her with the passion he could never voice and the emotions that he dared not recognize. If he could have seen her one more time, he may have dropped thirty-five cents into her hand.

Johnny was found dead in his apartment, the victim of an apparent heart attack. For the first time since his induction into the army, he, too, was at peace.

Bid Burgess was one of the ones who did not come home. His mother received the telegram stating that he was missing in action, and she told everyone that he'd be coming home soon. She knew her son was not dead. He *could not die* on some battlefield in Germany. Her son was an excellent marksman, and he'd get them before they got him.

She kept his baseball glove, three baseballs, and two bats, one of them broken and with tape around the handle, against the day when he would again walk up the sidewalk, sweep her into his arms, and then gather his rifle and baseball equipment and head toward the old baseball field and then into the woods for target practice.

When the next telegram stated that he was still missing in action and presumed dead, she did not waver in her faith. She kept his rifle and baseball equipment throughout the remainder of the forties and into the fifties. Boys around her grew into puberty, then into young adulthood, then departed from home for college or for another war, and still she clung to the baseball glove, bats, and balls. It perhaps never occurred to her that her son would now be almost forty years old and that he might not relish a ball game the way he once did. All she knew was that her son, when he came home, would not be like the others, changed and transformed into an entirely different human being. He would be the same boy who promised her that when the war was over he'd come back to be with her.

Then one day I saw our paperboy coming down the street with the basket of his bicycle loaded with baseball equipment. He had not been born until several years after the war had ended, and his face was wreathed in smiles.

"Look what Mrs. Burgess gave me!" he said joyously. "What do you think she was doing with all this baseball stuff? She couldn't play ball, not as old as she is."

By this time a small crowd had gathered. Housewives had emerged from their houses, and some of the men, already off work and heading home for a few hours of rest before the next day's work, stopped. No one spoke, not even when the boy asked why everyone was crying. We couldn't explain to him that the woman's son had just died.

My high school class prepared for graduation in the spring of 1950, and as we rehearsed our trip down the aisle to collect the long-awaited diplomas, the newspapers daily carried stories of the bitter conflict that was spreading in Korea. As we entered our final days, we noticed that some of last year's class seemed to disappear the way the boys did in 1942. The newspaper printed brief announcements of the departure dates of some of the nineteen-year olds in our community.

One of these was a bashful, tall, gangly kid who was the tallest boy in school but one who never played any sports. He was simply too uncoordinated for basketball, and he had too many feet for baseball. A gentle, totally sweet person, he'd have snapped like a twig if he had ventured onto a football field.

In class he never distinguished himself. He was simply there, the never-absent smile greeting every joke, every question from the teacher, and every comment anyone made to him. He never dated, and he never seemed to belong anywhere. But there was not a person in the school who didn't like him. It is doubtful that he ever earned a distinction of any sort during his lifetime thus far.

He entered basic training, and I am certain that there he smiled at every insult, every degradation heaped upon raw recruits. He made all the twenty-mile marches, smiling all the way, and when he came home on leave he stood awkwardly, still smiling, as he stood on the periphery and watched life passing him by.

His orders after basic training were for him to fly to Korea as an infantryman. He smiled, I'd bet my last dollar, as he boarded the plane and flew across the Pacific Ocean. On the flight, you can be sure, he smiled at everyone who spoke to him and those who didn't. He took meticulous care of his uniform and equipment, and he stood, or sat, on the outside, always on the outside, looking in, as the other soldiers tried to sleep, joke, read, or daydream as they sought ways to block out the harsh reality of where they were and where they were going. The plane landed in Korea, and the first man off the plane was a tall, lanky, smiling kid.

He had too many teeth and he had a gentle smile for everybody he met. He unquestionably smiled at the officers and NCOs who ordered him to keep moving forward. He was still smiling, no doubt, when the sniper's bullet caught him between the eyes and he fell forward. He never set foot on Korean soil. And he was, almost certainly, smiling as he died.

Then it was my turn. My brother just older than I joined the Navy, and I waited for the draft to take me away from my new career as a professional baseball player. Uncle Sam did not disappoint me. One hundred of our high school class and members of classes of other schools traveled to Charlotte for our physical examinations. Half of us passed.

The others, either intentionally stupid for a day or retarded in some unseen manner, flunked the intelligence test. A few, including the shortstop for a major league baseball team, failed the physical. I never understood how a man could play one of the toughest sports in history and still could not march and do calisthenics.

Of the fifty of us who passed both mental and physical tests, twenty-five of them managed to secure a deferment of some sort between our first physical and our induction dates. Some rushed into marriages, some felt a sudden calling into the ministry, and others persuaded bosses or influential citizens to intercede on their behalf with the draft board.

Just before I left for the army, I rented rooms in a house near the high school where I had graduated. An elderly woman rented small apartments, two downstairs and two upstairs. In one of the upstairs apartments there lived a mother who had received a telegram only weeks earlier that her son had been killed in Korea. She had gone into mourning and into understandable deep depression.

Then one day she screamed so loudly that I thought a madman was slaughtering her. Rushing upstairs, I saw her pointing in horror at the man who had backed across the hallway from her. She stood in the doorway of her apartment, pointed, and screamed again and again as we tried to calm her down.

The man across the hallway was her son, the one who had been "killed" in Korea.

When he could get her calm enough to listen, he explained that he and some other soldiers were in a tent in a small clearing beside a river. Sweaty and grimy, he decided to take a quick bath in the river before the nightly mortar attack started. He took soap and a towel, nothing else.

He removed the chain holding his dog tags from around his neck and laid his belongings on his cot. Then he went to take his bath.

He had just reached the river when the mortar attack began. Too terrified to return to his tent, he swam the river and entered the jungle.

Everyone in the tent died in the attack. Body parts lay in every direction. When rescue teams arrived, someone found his dog tags, and he was listed among the dead. When the newspaper printed the casualties from our area, I saw his name on the list, and I thought of him as he, a year ahead of us, stood in the high school glee club and belted out Sigmund Romberg's "Stout-Hearted Men" in the spring concert. He had a deep, rich solo voice, and he owned the audience when he sang "I Got Plenty of Nothin'" from George Gershwin's *Porgy and Bess.*

Then he, like the others we read about, was dead. Or so we thought.

When his mother had calmed herself sufficiently, he explained that as he bolted into the jungle, he lost all contact with his unit. He alternately ran and hid until he located some other American troops.

His new commander informed him that he was scheduled to return to the States within a few days, and he decided that he would drop in on his mother and surprise her.

He did, very nearly fatally.

He never knew that he had been reported killed in action. Within a few days he was on a plane headed back to the United States. Once here, he did not bother to write or call, and his surprise party worked better than he had ever imagined.

He had not simply come back from Korea; he had returned from the dead.

Shortly after the son came home, I was on my way to Fort Jackson, where I was trained as a tank mechanic. Then, as I was carrying my orders to head for Korea, someone changed my direction because there was a hot spot in Trieste and tank mechanics were needed there.

So I went to Europe, rather than to Asia. In Germany, the commanding officer changed my orders again, and this time I headed for Salzburg, Austria, the best place in the world to fight the Korean War.

And that's where I spent my Korean War days. There, in the city where Mozart lived and in the country of so many great composers and performers, I learned to love the Bavarian Alps.

And there I read a book called *The Old Man and the Sea*, and that book started me writing, and I've done it ever since. So blame Hemingway. I was a product of local education and had never heard of Papa before.

By the time the Vietnam War had grown into a full-scale global conflict, I had begun teaching on the college level. But during my last year on the high school campus, we had a kid in class named Ardrey, a whale of a nice student who had no civilian future at the moment. He wasn't ready for college, so he enlisted in the Marine Corps.

There he found a home. He became a model Marine, and he loved every aspect about the Corps. Those of us who had taught him rejoiced in his great new career, and we were as proud as if we were his parents when he moved up in the ranks so rapidly and so well.

Then one morning as I drove to the college, I turned on the radio and heard the casualty list. Among those killed was my friend Ardrey. I fought tears all the way to the college, and the first person who spoke to me there was a genuine slob. He was bug spit. His mother was undoubtedly a fine woman, but he was a self-made SOB.

"I want to do some extra credit work to pull up my grade in your class," he whined. He had flunked every test, plagiarized on his term paper, and scored 32 on his midterm exam and pulled his average *up* five points. I told him that if he was perfect on his final exam, he'd still fail.

He began to plead. "They're going to draft me and send me to Vietnam, I'll wash your car, mow your grass, give you money."

"Get out of my office," I said, my voice rising in disgust. "Just what in hell makes you think you are any better than my friend Ardrey?"

He left my office and barged into the departmental chairman's office. The chairman, incidentally, had been a Marine officer in two wars and wasn't sympathetic. He had also heard my outburst.

"Just what in hell makes you think you are any better than Ardrey?" he asked the wretched slob.

The snail trail lurched into the hallway and bumped into another former military man, who had also overheard. He pleaded his case only to hear the same reply: "Just what in hell makes you think you are any better than Ardrey?" the professor asked.

"Who is this Ardrey?" the slob moaned. "Everybody keeps talking about him. What did he do? Who is he?"

"Something you'll never be," someone said. "A hero and a man."

Frazier "Slow" Robinson was one of the great athletes in the old Negro League. He was catcher for legendary Leroy "Satchel" Paige, one of the greatest pitchers of all time.

Forty-Six
The End of a Great Road

With April comes the major league baseball season, and with baseball comes the barrage of information and arguments about the highest salaries, the greatest teams, and the greatest players of all time.

But in a modest neighborhood just outside Kings Mountain and in a room dominated by photos of great black baseball players and uniforms from a bygone age of glory and greatness, Frazier Robinson will not take part in the debates, and with good reason. First, he was unquestionably a great baseball player, but because of the times and because of his race he was never among those blacks who broke the color barrier in an age when not only the ball but all of the players were white.

And Frazier Robinson will not debate the greatest players of all time, not because he was denied the chance to see the greatest white players in history but because he was privileged to play with the greatest baseball players, regardless of race or salary or position, of all time.

If you ask him to name the greatest player he ever saw, he will smile modestly and say something like, "Oh, there were so many great ones, so many. I can't pick just one; they were all great."

Robinson knows what he is talking about. For years he was battery-mate to the man some proclaim as the greatest pitcher who ever played the game: Leroy "Satchel" Paige, the legendary athlete who reportedly pitched two games a day at times and who enjoyed the reputation of doing just about what he wished on the baseball diamond. He was known to walk the bases loaded, then call in the outfielders and have them sit down on the edge of the infield grass: and then he would proceed calmly to strike out the next three batters. He was one of the true legends of the game.

Robinson doesn't buy the publicity. "Satchel was a fine pitcher," he says, "and it was as easy to catch him as it is to sit here and talk with you."

But, after a moment of reflection, he adds, "I honestly think that Satchel would have won 95 per cent of his games, if he had been allowed to play in the major leagues during his prime. He had perfect control, not because he was born with the talent but because he worked at it hour after hour, day after day, and he was a smart ball player. If you got a hit off him, you'd be lucky ever to get another. I saw him beat Dizzy Dean, Bob Feller, and the other great ones, but if you want to know what Satchel Paige was like, think of Nolan Ryan at his best and then add perfect control and perfect command of all his pitches, and then you would have Satchel Paige."

Known in his heyday as "Slow" Robinson, Frazier played with some of the great teams ever assembled, the Kansas City Monarchs, the Satchel Paige All Stars, and the world-champion Baltimore Elite Giants, as well as, near the end of his career, the Canadian Winnipeg Buffaloes.

He played with or against such great performers in the Negro Major Leagues as Jackie Robinson (the first black baseball player to crack the color barrier), Larry Doby (the second), Monte Irvin, Don Newcombe, Sad Sam Jones, Cool Papa Bell, Hank Aaron, and a list of other players that reads like the Major League Baseball Hall of Fame.

In a career that started in the 1930s, Robinson found that playing baseball was far superior to the other opportunities offered by the Great Depression era. He says, "Playing ball was a great deal better than picking cotton or digging ditches."

He doesn't watch much baseball today. At age 83 he was still quick of mind, agile, and the picture of grace and strength, but the game has lost a great deal of the power it once had over him. He said, "Last summer some of us from the World Championship team of the Baltimore Elite Giants were taken to the major league All-Star game as special guests of honor. We sat at banquets with the great players of the past and the great personalities of the present, but when the game started I watched about two innings and then went back to my hotel room."

He doesn't apologize for his attitude. He is, rather, indignant about the sloppiness of modern players.

"We couldn't get by with the mistakes they make today," he said. "The message was to play professionally or go home. We had to be professional in every game, all day long. We played for the game, not fame."

He added, "We had the love of a game that will never die, not in our minds. It was great to live then, to play with the greatest players of all time, and to experience the thrill and the excitement of going to the park every day to compete with and against the best that ever will be."

So Frazier Robinson can be forgiven for walking out of the major league All-Star game. He has his own all-stars. All he needs to do is open his scrapbooks or his memory bank and they all live again in his personal Field of Dreams: the best that the world has seen.

And he is intensely proud to have been one of them.

Or he was. A few months ago Frazier "Slow" Robinson died, after a lengthy illness which he faced as courageously as he faced the other obstacles in his life.

It would have been so easy for him to vent his anger and sense of injustice toward everyone he met, but Slow Robinson was much too big a man to let that happen. He rose above the petty and sometimes enormous elements of racial prejudices and concentrated on the nobler aspects of life. He played the game of baseball hard and well, and he played the game of life with equal dedication. He came out of nowhere in a sense and rubbed elbows with some of the greatest athletes of all time, and he came away ennobled himself.

It was a remarkable experience to sit and talk with a man who had known personally and well some of the finest athletes this nation has ever produced. It was almost like entering a time machine and making the trip back to an age when life was simpler than it is now and people were more interested in their performance on the field than in the latest stock reports.

But Slow Robinson did not see himself as a legend. He viewed his performances in terms of the happy times he experienced and the joy he brought to those who came to see the great players take the field. Or perhaps it was that he was surrounded by legends and, as Shaw said, in heaven an angel is nobody in particular. When all you see is excellence, then the best tends to become average in your mind. Except that no one would see the players in Robinson's league as average. They were stupendous.

Naturally, he felt that he was entitled to a shot at major league baseball, but the color barriers were still firmly in place. But he never spent his time lamenting about what never happened. He prefers to talk about the old-time great players it was his privilege to know and the great game it was his joy to play.

Christopher Bechtler, the man with the golden touch

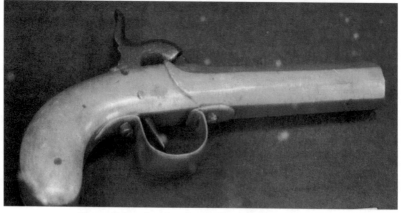

One of the classic pistols Bechtler created

Forty-Seven
The Nation's First Gold Rush

When Spanish explorers ranged the mountains of Western North Carolina, their search for gold was largely fruitless. Little was found that would be sufficient to attract settlers and prospectors into the wild terrain.

If DeSoto and his men had lingered longer, they might have stumbled on what was to become the first gold rush in the history of the United States. One of the primary gold sites in the state was in the mountains of Rutherford County, where the nation's first private mint operated.

There was gold to be found not just in Rutherford County but in several counties in the Piedmont. At one point there were fifty-six active gold mines in the Tar Heel State, and people with gold fever arrived from nearly every state and from several foreign countries. A simple mining town was almost like the United Nations, with languages and cultures from around the world. For a period of several years, North Carolina was indeed the Gold State. The simple fact is that this state led the entire United States in the production of gold, and the ancillary industries that invariably follow the gleam of gold swelled the state's employment in gold production to more than twenty thousand people.

It was not altogether a pretty scene. People with gold fever do not always live the purest of lives and attract the nicest of humanity. The gold fields were, in fact, filled with prospectors, gamblers, preachers, and politicians, to list only a few who arrived with eyes for gold.

One of the new arrivals was Christopher Bechtler, a German immigrant who was an artistic jeweler and watchmaker. When he settled in Rutherfordton, one of his first acts was to take out an ad in the closest newspaper and announce that he was settled in and ready to do business.

Bechtler opened his business office at first at the Twitty Tavern neighborhood. On July 28, 1830, Bechtler announced that he had with him a stock of fine watches and clocks and that he was prepared to create or repair watches and clocks of all sorts. All kinds of jewelry could and would be repaired at modest cost and with prompt work from the master craftsman from Germany.

Like many artistic people of his day who worked in metals, Bechtler also repaired or made guns and worked as a goldsmith. At the time of his arrival in Rutherford County, Bechtler found a small town that offered neighborly people, good climate, dozens of streams that were clean and beautiful, wild life of all sorts common to the mountains and foothills, a growing town, and a tavern.

He found that gold was the primary source of excitement, and one fact that intrigued him was that more than $250,000 worth of gold had been shipped from the Rutherford County area to the United States mint in Philadelphia and other major locations. But to his shock and dismay there was no money to be found anywhere.

This was an era of trade. Europeans traded with Native Americans for furs and other desirables, and local people traded with each other for shoes, leather goods, clothing, guns, horses and mules, seeds, plows, tools of all sorts useful in the mountains, and land.

Trade, however, no matter how profitable and handy, is not always a solution to a problem. For one thing, unless you were a skillful trader, you might wind up giving away much that you had worked for. Traveling traders, like gamblers, do not spend their lives in pursuit of breaking even. They want a profit, and they want it fast and unencumbered.

The word *barter* in itself means "to trick," and people who worked hard for what they had could not afford to be bilked out of their goods. And that's where Christopher Bechtler came in. At that time there were no laws prohibiting any individual from creating their own gold coins, and that laxity in the law allowed a legend to appear. The Bechtler mint and the coins created there also became legendary.

Up until Bechtler made his appearance there was great discord concerning money, or gold. Gold, like many other commodities, was not always pure, and the standard was highly flexible. A nugget of gold used to buy a sack of flour and other useful items might now be worth as much, in reality, as one half that size, depending upon quality.

People who moved from bartering goods to trading gold for goods ran a constant risk of losing their values or properties along the way. And Christopher Bechtler came onto the scene and pretty much solved the problem. He took the gold people brought to him and carefully tested the gold for impurities and settled only for the gold that was comparable to the quality he used in his watches or other forms of jewelry. Then he created the stamps and molds, and he was in business.

The Bechtler coin press came into use in the same year that his mint started operations. Bechtler offered and delivered on his promise of honesty in all respects. He maintained a variation on the open-book policy: his was an open-assay policy in which he let other assayers double-check on him so that the owners of the gold could be assured that their precious metals were treated with an open and honest business format.

The procedure went very simply: people who had found gold brought it to Bechtler, who weighed it in the presence of the finders, and later he made the assay reports available to them. For those who had brought gold in earlier, he turned over to them their gold coins with the karat value and weight prominently in view.

The results were astonishing. Within a few months Bechtler had minted close to the $3 million worth of gold coins, and before he had finished his minting work the tiny operation had turned out almost twice that much. The story is that in one year Bechtler minted more gold than the other minting operations combined.

For more than twenty-five years Bechtler operated his mint, despite efforts by the United States mints to close him down. They succeeded, finally, in the 1850s as the mint at Charlotte was set up and Bechtler could not continue in the face of such formidable and permanent opposition. The $1, $2.50, and $5 gold pieces bearing the name of Bechtler would soon cease to exist.

The mint closed, but the value of the Bechtler coins became more valuable than ever before. Some of them are worth $19,000 each.

How important were the Bechtlers, and how valuable were their products? Keep in mind that the tiny little mint in Rutherfordton operated between 1830 and 1852,. The man in charge for many of those years was Christopher Bechtler himself, and he was later joined by his son August and Christopher, Jr. Keep in mind also that Rutherford County was the major source of gold in the United States between 1790 and 1840.

The Spencer Mountain scene at Christmas

Forty-Eight
Half a Million Points of Light

When you visit Gaston County, you will find that the county, one of the largest in the state with 363 square miles, has more towns and cities than any other county as well. Gastonia, the current county seat, was established in 1877; Stanley, earlier known as Brevard Station and then as Stanley Creek, existed as early as 1843. Lowell became an official town in 1850, Cherryville and McAdenville followed in 1881, Mount Holly, earlier named Woodlawn, dates back to 1889, and High Shoals became a town in 1893. Belmont was established in 1895, and Cramerton began in 1906. Tiny Dellview became a chartered town in 1925. Dallas, the first county seat, was organized in 1843.

If you look at a history book, you will see that many of the towns changed names at least once. Cramerton began its existence as Mays Mill.

The town of McAdenville was known as Spring Shoals Manufacturing Company. Cherryville was White Pine, and Belmont was Garibaldi, named after the famed Italian hero. Bessemer City, only a stone's throw from Gastonia, first was known as Wooten Station and then as All Healing Station.

The county and county seat were named for William Gaston, who was for many years an associate justice of the Supreme Court. Dallas, the first county seat, was named in honor of George Dallas, vice president of the United States under President James K. Polk. One small irony of the names is that, according to local history buffs, neither man ever set foot in the county.

For many years the county boasted "a mill per mile," while others pointed out there were more stills than mills. But keep in mind that Gaston County was also the scene of the first major gold rush.

Cowboy wit Will Rogers once commented that, because of the huge number of illicit moonshine stills in the state, "North Carolinians will vote dry as long as they can stagger to the polls." One of the long-lasting jokes in the county targets a local man who later became governor of the state. When someone asked for the name of the best lawyer in the area, the local resident replied, "Lawyer X when he's sober." The visitor then asked for the name of the second-best lawyer in the county. "Lawyer X when he's drunk," the local man said.

There is much to do in Gaston County, but if you happen to be there during the Christmas holiday season, all roads lead to the town of McAdenville, known throughout the nation as Christmas Town, USA. Starting around the first of December, the town's residents put up one of the most impressive displays of Christmas decorations you can find anywhere in America. The lights stay on, for the most part, through New Year's Day, although in the past the town's leaders, for various reasons, turned on the lights a little later and turned them off a little earlier. You best bet is to get there around the middle of December or at the latest a day or two after Christmas.

To get to McAdenville, exit I-40 onto the Lowell-McAdenville exit a few minutes east of Gastonia. Follow NC 273 into the tiny town with nearly half a million Christmas lights, if you count those inside homes and those on the outskirts of town, with about 400,000 downtown.

There are thousands more lights, give or take a few, along the main street and at the lake at the edge of town.

For years the Christmas lights have been under the auspices of Stowe-Pharr Mills, and you will have no worries that the various people will decide not to decorate. It is a given that McAdenville will have Christmas lights, and it is a rare house or yard that is not fully decorated with red, green, and white lights. The fact is that you cannot look in many directions without seeing beauty.

Try to arrive just at dusk, if possible, and find a place to park. Then get out of the car and walk through the town. Take along a camera and a good supply of film, for there is much to photograph along the main street. You can see a lot by driving through, but you must keep moving because of the traffic backed up behind you. There will be, incredibly, one car for each light in the town!

If that sounds impossible, keep in mind that each December about 400,000 cars with about two million occupants pass through the town. So park, get out and stroll up and down the streets, and take pictures at your leisure. If you must arrive late, you may find that it takes a very long time to make the drive. However, the slow-moving traffic allows you and yours to have unhurried looks at the decorations.

One of the top spots in the town is the lake, which is lined with about six dozen Christmas trees ranging in height from ten to twenty feet and decorated with thousands of brilliant lights that are doubled in number because of their reflection in the lake. In the center of the lake there is a fountain which pumps 3,000 gallons of water per minute into the night air, and the lights at the fountain base illuminate the jets of water and create a spectacular beauty. Along Main Street there is a life-size nativity scene and another of carolers who sing at the top of their voices night and day.

It isn't just the lights that are attractive. Residents of the homes along the long street decorate their doors and yards to their own taste, and there is a wholesomely fierce competition for the prize for the best yard or door decorations.

If the traffic is too much for you and you need to wait for a few minutes, or if you have seen the McAdenville lights and want still more, you can drive back the way you came and head for the even tinier town of Spencer Mountain. Stay on NC 273 and you will arrive with no problems.

On a still night you have a wonderful picture of the floating Christmas tree, the illuminated trees along the shores of the lake, still more trees in the yards of houses surrounding the church, and then as a bonus the reflections of all the trees and the church in the water of the lake.

If you visit Gaston County during the rest of the year, you can find much to see and do. The area's history is fascinating, filled with drama and heroism, and the new look in the downtown portions of town has moved the county far from its old image of a textile town and little else. Take my word for it: Gaston County is far, far more than textiles and mills. It is uninterrupted history.

Downtown lights at McAdenville

Don't assume that McAdenville and surrounding towns are impressive and beautiful only during Christmas time. Most of the towns of Gaston County have a great deal to offer. While you are in the vicinity take time to sample some of the food. There are fish camps galore and barbecue platters. Don't miss the slawburgers at R. O.'s barbecue house in west Gastonia. The story is told of a trucker from Gastonia who was driving his rig through New York City when a policeman pulled the truck over and asked the driver where in the world he was from.

"Right behind R. O.'s," the driver said. After all, what kind of hick cop doesn't know where R. O.'s barbecue restaurant is? And when you go there, don't leave without a slawburger. But they are addictive. Some people refuse to eat one for months, only to develop an obsession about them.

New River bluegrass band

Members of New River include, left to right, Horace Scruggs, Wayne Parrish, Ray Allison, Dr. Dean Jenks, and Dr. Bobby Jones. Missing is Dean Davis. The group performs regularly throughout the region.

Forty-Nine

Living in the 'Rock Candy Days'

D r. Bobby Jones, while studying at East Carolina University, had little time for the music he had enjoyed as a member of the Shelby High School band. His only active musical energy was devoted to the mandolin he played to provide respite from the rigors of his medical studies.

But when Doctor Jones returned to Shelby, he picked up the mandolin again and found that the pleasure in bluegrass music was still there. Soon he made his way to Leatherwood's Courtsquare Opry in Shelby, which was a legend in its own right. Jones began playing the mandolin during open mike time, and soon he was joining others with similar tastes.

It was not long before the general pickers and singers formed a loose-knit group that met at some member's home where they played until they realized that they had a unique sound and style. That's when the idea of forming their own band struck them, and as they discussed the idea more and more, it seemed evident that everyone in the group was in favor of the move.

"I didn't really intend for any of this to happen," Jones said. "It was just a few of us picking and singing, sometimes to only five or six people, but we had fun, and one thing led quickly to another. I don't know when it registered that we were essentially perfect for each other."

The other "things" included the formation of the New River bluegrass band and a series of appearances at smaller bluegrass gatherings. And in July 1998 New River released their first recordings: a CD and tape called "Rock Candy Days."

July, the month of Independence and Democracy in the highest senses of the words, was a perfect time for the release, because New River typifies the form of democracy that Andrew Jackson and poet Walt Whitman would have loved.

In addition to Dr. Jones, the band includes Dean Davis, a professional studio photographer in Boiling Springs, a ten-minute drive from Shelby; Ray Allison, lead singer and guitarist who drives a truck and works on the loading dock for Yellow Freight trucking company; Wayne Parrish, an employee of Duke Power Company in Rock Hill, just across the South Carolina border; Dean Jenks, who was head of Crawley Memorial Hospital in nearby Boiling Springs; and Horace Scruggs, a retired college maintenance man and brother of Earl Scruggs, legendary master of the banjo.

New River is democratic in more ways that diversity of members. "No one is in charge," says Bobby Jones. "I do some of the business end of the work simply because I have organizational skills that are helpful. When it comes to making decisions, we all agree or shelve the discussion."

"We get along fine," says 76-year old Horace Scruggs who has played the guitar for more than seven decades. "The younguns mind me pretty well. If they don't, I hit them."

Horace Scruggs is one of the reasons "Rock Candy Days" was recorded, and he is one of the reasons the CD is one of the best-selling recordings in the Tar Heel bluegrass scene. The record was dedicated to Horace Scruggs, whose timing, Jones said, is flawless.

"His playing always hits my ear just right," Jones said, "and all of us have spent years learning as much as possible from him."

"We actually wanted to accomplish two goals," Jones added, "and we have accomplished both of them. The first was to document one of the relatively unknown giants of bluegrass music and one of the best rhythm guitarists in the business, a man who has lived most of his life in the shadow of his more famous brother. The second goal was to introduce Ray Allison, a superb vocalist, to the world and the world to Allison."

Jones and other members of the band agree that Allison is a giant in the world of bluegrass vocalizing. "Ray is, without a doubt, my favorite bluegrass singer in the nation and in the world," Jones said. "His 'high lonesome' delivery combines all the elements of American grassroots, of tragedy and hope, of despair and victory, of the man on the farm and the man in the mansion. He is a masterful singer who has sung for many years but who at the same time is relatively unknown. I hope and believe he will not be unknown for much longer."

Jones is not alone in his enthusiasm. Steve Leatherwood, the bluegrass impresario from Shelby, considers Ray one of the top artists on the scene.

"Ray Allison is not only an exceptionally fine singer," Leatherwood says, "but he is a masterful song writer. He wrote four of the songs on 'Rock Candy Days,' and his interpretation of the songs of others is astonishing."

"We like to showcase the best of the old and the new at the same time," said Larry Cline, host of South Carolina Educational Public Radio's Bluegrass Sound, "and I am really excited about the new sound I hear from New River."

Similar responses have been evoked from Russ Jordan, himself a well-known bluegrass musician and also host of "Going Across the Mountain" radio show heard throughout western North Carolina.

"Rock Candy Days" is a mixture of bluegrass music from all ages as well as songs written by members of the band. Some of the songs were written by Bill Monroe, the father of bluegrass music, Earl Scruggs, James Randolph, Freddy Hart and Howard Harlan. Such traditional tunes as "Angel Band" and "White House Blues" lend an air of authenticity while original music by Ray Allison and Wayne Parrish provide new sounds. The New River sound is at least as harmonious as the stage lives of the performers.

Their principles are as one. New River has one incredibly rare talent: They are perfectionists who at the same time can be relaxed, funny, and as comfortable as an old wool sweater on a rainy November day.

Horace Scruggs is one of the reasons for the perfection. He admits that he had a terrific teacher and partner when he was a child.

"Earl and I when we were just children would start back-to-back on one end of the house, and we'd play a tune like 'Sally Goodin' as we walked away from each other and keep playing until we met at the front of the house. If we were not perfectly synchronized when we met, we'd put our backs together again and start all over and go around the house until we got it right." The Earl Scruggs legend continues to grow rapidly.

Horace says he couldn't avoid music when he was a child. "I don't know exactly what got me started," he admits. "But Dad played the banjo, and so did my brother. I picked up the guitar, and I've played it ever since, except for three years during World War II when I didn't have much chance to play. And I still love to play, especially with these boys."

Dean Jenks is a Shelby native who plays the banjo, bass, guitar, and mandolin. A self-taught banjo player, Jenks also studied classical guitar with Ray Ledford, a local musician who studied under Segovia.

"I won a talent contest in the third grade," Jenks said, "by playing the guitar and singing 'Your Cheating Heart.' After I finished my masters and doctorate work at the University of South Carolina, I came back to Shelby, and one night Bobby Jones called and asked me to come over to his house to play a little Bluegrass music. I went, and we've been playing together since that time."

Jenks adds, "In one of my few music lessons I learned something very important: I found that I'd been wearing the picks backward."

"At least you had picks," Scruggs challenged. "I used to break teeth from combs around the house. At least, I did until my Mama caught me."

Dean Davis, who has played the bass fiddle for more than 25 years, finds a satisfaction in bluegrass music that is missing elsewhere.

"Bluegrass music is it for me," he says. "It's not just relaxing: it gets in your blood. I appreciate where it comes from, and even more I appreciate its purity. You've got to love it to play it. I listen to some gospel music and some country, but bluegrass is where country was born. One of the greatest sights for me is to go to a music festival and see kids with a banjo around their necks. I know that they are going to keep the party going."

Ray Allison is a triple-threat musician: he plays guitar, sings, and writes some of the music New River plays. He also acts as master of ceremonies and mixes homespun wit and humor to keep the act loose.

"I grew up on bluegrass music," he says. "Living in Cleveland County kept me close to what I love best in music. One of the first things I learned is that in country music if you are not young, personable, and pretty, you aren't going to make it. In bluegrass, if you have talent, people are going to appreciate it. If you don't have it, you can't fake it."

Allison can't recall when he wasn't playing and singing, often in church with family members. And he can't imagine a life without music in it.

"I drive a truck and work on the dock," he said, "and when I go home, dog-tired, I need my music. It never fails to surprise me with the high energy it provides. Music is my valium, my medicine. I can be physically worn out, and when I pick up my guitar, I'm well within five minutes. It truly is the universal language."

Wayne Parrish has played the fiddle, mandolin, and guitar for most of his life.

"*This* is roots music," he says. "It's what I was brought up on. My uncle, brothers, and cousins all played, and it's easy to know why so many people love bluegrass. People look for clean, acoustic sound and songs that have genuine soul. These days so many people don't get to hear live bluegrass music, and when they get a chance to experience it they are amazed by the feel and the energy of it."

"Rock Candy Days" is not only the title of the new CD; it is also Allison's favorite song that he has written. The song is a lament for the lost innocence of an earlier age, and Ray, a nostalgic glint in his eye, admits that he wishes he were still living in those Rock Candy Days.

New River's sound is a blend of the ancient and modern style as well as unadorned simplicity and ornate complexity, New River is at first hearing another good bluegrass band that will attract a healthy following. On second hearing, the CD and the band compare favorably with the best in the South and in the nation. This is not careless exaggeration: this group is real; New River is not just good but terrific. It is also an anticipation of the new wave in old music.

"Public response has been surprisingly good," Dr. Jones said. "When we started, we played six to ten gigs a year. Now we are turning down offers. I think we have surprised ourselves. And that's better than good."

Fifty

North Carolina's "Friendly" Governor

Clyde R. Hoey was indeed a legend in his own time, but somehow, no one seems to know just how, he was relegated to a place in dusty antiquity by many North Carolinians. During the writing of this book I had occasion to mention Hoey's name to people with a better-than-average education, and the vast majority of them had never heard of the "Friendly Governor."

One such person said to me, "Well, I wasn't even living when he was governor, and I don't see how I'd have known about him." My response, probably unfair, was that Caesar and Napoleon were dead long before I was born, but most modern people have heard of them. Hoey was not, of course, a Caesar, Napoleon, or Charlemagne, but he was a man who deserves more than to be forgotten. He played a vital role in numerous North Carolina matters of importance that will continue to affect this state. He set some incredible examples for successful living. For example, he was, at an incredibly young age, a businessman whose influence was felt across the western Piedmont and perhaps across the state. And the work he did has a rightful place in state history.

By the time he was twelve years old, because of his father's failing health and family needs during the Reconstruction era, he had to give up his formal education in order to help support the family. He took a job as a printer's devil, or apprentice, in the office of the Shelby *Aurora*. In one of many ironies, once Hoey became governor of North Carolina, one of his primary concerns and one of the laws he urged the legislature to pass was the regulation of child labor.

Governor Clyde R. Hoey

When he had been employed for four years, he had his first chance to go into business for himself. Hearing rumors that the Shelby *Review* was about to collapse, he rushed from one creditor to the next and asked if the creditors would allow him a little time to pay the bills for the *Review* if he could work out arrangements to buy the paper.

His appeals worked, and at age sixteen he became a newspaper owner and publisher. He changed the name to the *Cleveland Star*, and local history was made. The paper, under another name, is still enjoying a wide readership and popularity in Cleveland County.

The teenage Hoey became an ardent supporter of the Democrat Party in Cleveland County and in neighboring counties, and he used his newspaper to campaign for candidates for office. Because of his outspoken editorial views, he was often asked to speak at political rallies, and almost immediately he found himself the favorite potential candidate for the North Carolina Legislature.

The incredible part of the story is that Hoey won the election, although he did not get to vote for himself (or for anyone else, for that matter). At the time of the election, Hoey was not old enough to vote, and yet he won.

At the same time the youngster was leading an active professional and political life, he somehow found time to read law on his own, and one summer he took off enough time to study law at the University of North Carolina, the first formal educational training he had received since he was twelve years old. He packed all his energies into the study, and in 1899 he was admitted to the bar, and for many years he practiced law in the area.

To say that he was a good lawyer would be like saying Milton was a good poet. Hoey was a hypnotist in the courtroom, a mesmerizer who could lead a jury into whatever direction he chose. He was startling in appearance (some compared him to an old-time riverboat gambler), and his attire was almost always the same. Some insisted that he bore a remarkable resemblance to western legend Wild Bill Hickok. He wore a long and dramatic cutaway coat know as an English walking coat, high and incredibly stiff collars, and the inevitable carnation in his lapel. For years his hair was long and flowing, and the effect produced incomparable drama, particularly when jurors heard the amazingly well-modulated voice. It was a rare person who could resist it. His oratory impressed all who heard it, clients, judges, juries, and opposing attorneys alike.

One of the favorite stories told about Hoey the lawyer was that one day he was defending a man accused of stealing chickens. During the defense Hoey offered a long and eloquent statement of the sterling character and unquestionable honesty and integrity of the accused man. Later, after the jury acquitted Hoey's client, the freed man walked out of the courtroom and one of his "associates" approached him.

"Tell me the truth," the friend said. "Did you steal those chickens?

The acquitted man looked at the man, his face filled with awe and bewilderment. "To tell you the truth, I *thought* I did," the man said. "But after hearing what that man said about me, I can't be sure any more. I just don't think I'm the kind of man who could do something like that."

Hoey's courtroom reputation spread across the county and then across the state. In 1913 he was appointed the Assistant United States Attorney for the Western District of North Carolina. It was said that Hoey for his living practiced civil law early in his career and for recreation he practiced criminal law. In 1929 he had the opportunity to have the recreational time of his life.

The case was the infamous trial of Fred Beal and the others of the Loray Seven who were accused of having murdered Orville Aderholt, chief of police in Gastonia. The case was sensational from numerous points of view, and every leading newspaper in the world headlined the progress of the trial, no matter how insignificant the events of the day's testimony might be. (The story of the Loray Trial is described in detail in another chapter of this book.)

To review briefly, the Communist Party supported a labor union called the National Textile Workers Union, and the avowed purpose of the union was to take over the Loray Mill in Gaston County and then move on to control every mill in the county, then in the state, then in the South, and finally in the nation. When the communists owned and controlled all mills, the party would then concentrate on food production and transportation until they actually controlled the United States. Hoey and others were facing formidable opposition in the form of fame civil defense attorney Arthur Garfield Hays and the entire staff, except for Clarence Darrow, from the so-called Monkey Trial in Dayton, Tennessee. The irony of the child labor laws has been mentioned already, but there were several additional ironies on the way. The trial was also the first time that Clyde Hoey was in far over his head. He was not extremely keen as a labor lawyer.

First of all, Hoey brought considerable prestige of his own to the trial. In 1919 he became one of North Carolina's Congressmen, filling the seat vacated by Edwin Webb. Hoey had married Bess Gardner, sister of Shelby attorney and later Governor of North Carolina. When the Loray labor dispute began, it was Hoey's brother-in-law who as governor issued the order for the militia to rush to Gaston County to prevent rioting. Gardner, who earlier had been defeated in his bid for the governor's mansion, won without opposition in 1928, just as Hoey had entered Congress without opposition earlier.

At the time of the trial, Hoey became a member of the State's team of prosecutors while brother-in-law Gardner watched carefully from Raleigh to see that the smouldering labor struggle did not erupt into open warfare. The trial proceeded relatively smoothly, and the defendants were found guilty and sentenced to many years in jail. They jumped bail, however, and took refuge in Russia, where some of them died. Fred Beal, the leader of the union organization, chose to return to the United States after he found conditions in Russia to be intolerable.

Hoey later, after his brother-in-law left the governor's mansion, sought the position himself. His campaign record at home had been a stupendous success (with Hoey receiving 100% of the votes cast in several precincts), but he had not tested state-wide waters fully. After a bitter fight, Hoey was elected by a margin of 50,000 votes (in Cleveland County he won by a margin of 3,369 to 34) and in 1937 he was inaugurated as Governor of North Carolina.

That was about the time Fred Beal had sneaked back into the country and had been discovered and arrested. Hoey, after having worked so hard to convict Beal, had an abrupt change of heart, at least to a degree. He wrote on November 21, 1940, that he had given full consideration to the Fred Beal case and that he could not pardon him, because he felt that Beal was guilty of the crimes with which he was charged. (Beal, incidentally, was apparently not guilty of the crimes, but Hoey did not know this. Almost fifty years after the case had been tried, a man in North Georgia confessed on his deathbed that he had killed Chief Orville Aderholt.) Hoey also wrote that it was too early to consider a parole.

However, Beal had written a book (*Proletarian Journey*) in which he bitterly condemned communism, which Hoey hated with a passion. This repudiation of communism was the evidence that swayed Hoey.

Beal had been arrested in Massachusetts but he had refused to leave the state to face North Carolina justice. However, on the advice of his attorney, Beal came here and entered the New Caledonia prison on February 17, 1938, and as he entered the prison he declared that he would prefer to be a convict in the United States rather than a free man in Russia.

Hoey cited the fact that Beal's conversion from communism must be genuine, because the party, which energetically defended Beal during the trial, made no effort whatsoever to defend Beal against the prison sentence. Still, Hoey reasoned, he could not recommend clemency for Beal simply because he turned away from the Red Menace, communist; he was not convicted because he was a communist.

(Many people remain convinced that Beal and others were convicted for one reason only: the fact that they *were* communists. The supporters noted that the first jury was ready to vote unanimously for acquittal before they ever heard the first defense witness!)

Hoey continued that he had reviewed the case and had found no evidence of miscarriage of justice. The final decision was that Hoey would commute the sentence from seventeen to twenty years to ten to thirteen years. By doing so, in essence he made it possible for Beal to receive a parole almost as soon as Hoey's successors came into office. Hoey's decision was written on November 21, 1940, and a short time later Beal was paroled. He died of a heart attack in Massachusetts not long after he was released from prison.

In 1940, the same year that Hoey made it possible for the man he had worked hard to convict could be freed, Hoey in a speech at North Wilkesboro stated that one communist holding office in this country is one too many and that Congress should pass a law outlawing the Communist Party and the German Bund and any and every other party that holds allegiance to foreign governments.

How will history treat Clyde R. Hoey? One friend and co-worker with Hoey said that Hoey entered the governor's office better-liked than any other citizen in Cleveland County. He left the office better-liked than any other citizen in North Carolina.

And that is high praise!

Egg battlers on Easter morning at Sugar Hill

Fifty-One
The Great Sugar Hill Egg Fight

Every Easter Sunday morning, starting before the Great Depression and continuing into the present, the Sugar Hill Egg Fight has been one of the strangest customs in America, from one point of view. From another, it's just a new version of the old shell game, as well as a batch of bad yokes.

Once each year, before the roosters are awake, hard-boiled characters and members of the community gather in the tiny community of Sugar Hill, near Fallston. There they "fight" until one of the egg-wielders chickens out and takes his loot and scurries for safety in parts unknown.

The rules are simple: contestants will bring a basketful of hard-boiled eggs, still in the shell, and you challenge another yegg to a fight. The fight consists of one person holding his egg so that one end faces the opponent. Then the two bump the eggs together gently until one of the eggs breaks. The "victor" then captures the other person's egg and puts it into his basket, bucket, box, or whatever he brought to store his trophies.

If you visit the scene of the titanic struggle, you will find it hard to believe that a few hundred years ago the people of England participated in such a sport or recreation. Actually, it may have started in ancient Greece. And while the egg-fighters are trying to prove their mastery over the eggs of others, they are unwittingly engaging in some of the oldest practices known in the history of religion. In fact, they are combining ancient customers, blending the oldest with the most modern of Easter celebrations.

The origin of the Easter Egg as such may stem from the early Christian habit of forbidding the eating of eggs during Lent. Only when Easter arrived could eggs be eaten, and people made certain they had a plentiful supply of cooked eggs ready for the feast.

There was an ancient belief that on Easter Morning the sun actually danced for joy in the sky as the church celebrated the triumph of Life over Death, and people rushed to the hilltops, taking their eggs with them, at dawn in an effort to see the sun perform the amazing dance spectacular. The hilltop vantage point explains why the Sugar Hillers hold the mock battle (Life versus Death) at the top of the ridge Easter Sunday morning. The fighters are the first to see the sun rise as the symbol of Immortality.

Another symbolic element of the custom is that of viewing the egg as a symbol of life in that the whole egg contains the potential Life Force, while the broken and cooked egg symbolizes death. In ancient Greece the combatants, armed with their supply of eggs, met each other at dawn and rapped their eggs together.

"Christ is risen!" one of the fighters said, and the other replied, "He is truly risen!" Each person carried eggs dyed red for the battle. And this is only the beginning. As the ritual progressed throughout the years, more and more modern aspects appeared.

The ancients realized that the egg, if it was to produce life, must be fertilized, and they looked, accordingly, for the proper symbol of fertility. They chose, naturally enough, the rabbit, or hare, which was a fertility symbol in early Egyptian history and culture.

It required very little modification for the hare to become the Easter Rabbit or Bunny, and this magical creature scurried through the predawn darkness and laid eggs for the children to find, or the rabbit after daylight had arrived hid the eggs for the children to seek and gather for their celebratory baskets. In nineteenth century England the habit of egg-fighting included yet another tradition, which follows.

The bishop and other high-ranking officials of the church engaged in an egg-throwing battle, sometimes against children, with the breaking of the egg again symbolizing the invasion of the fertilizing cell which could eventually produce life, or it could symbolize a rebirth. When the egg was laid, one "birth" occurred; when the egg hatched, the rebirth was evident.

At Sugar Hill the battlers resort to all types of efforts to produce the hardest shells imaginable. Some feed their chickens gunpowder or metal filings. Some boil the eggs much longer than normal, and some reboil the eggs for increased hardness.

What happens to the eggs once they are broken? "I take mine home and the family will eat some of them," one fighter said. "What we don't eat we'll feed to the dogs."

"I feed mine to the hogs," one man said. "That is, if I win any. My eggs are like the girls I take to a dance: they usually go home with somebody else."

One man who has participated every year for the past eighty Easters, explained why he was there. "I just like to do it," he said.

As you might expect, the event is carried out each year in a true spirit of fellowship. No one wants to argue or dispute the outcome of the fight, which is not a fight at all but simply egg-cracking. After all, it doesn't require a referee and instant replay to determine if an egg is broken.

The participants compete in surprising silence. There is very little cheering or good-natured bantering. Nor is there disappointment. The winners and losers are good sports. If there are children engaged in the contest, by some fluke of luck they always seem to win, which is as it should be. Everyone is determined that the kids will leave with a basketful of Easter eggs.

The super fight, which has outlasted hula hoops, eight-track tapes, all kinds of clothing fashions and political movements, shows promise of lasting for centuries. The grandchildren of earlier battlers now rush to Sugar Hill on Easter morning to carry on the tradition.

One curiosity is that on the occasions I have attended the fight, I have talked with many of the participants. To date, not one of them had ever heard of the Greek and English traditions. All they knew is that it was good enough for Grandpa and, by gum, it's good enough for them. And that's good enough for anybody. The fight is nothing to crow about, but it assuredly is all it's cracked up to be.

Fifty-Two
The Biggest Gold Strike of Them All

This story is technically not located in North Carolina; in fact, it is not located in any land in the world, unless you count the bottom of the sea. And this story is not about gold only, although the gold does in fact figure prominently in the story. In addition to gold there is a hurricane, a sinking ship, and hundreds of people willing to give away all the treasures they had in this world, and a drama emotional enough to chill the hardest heart in the world.

This is also the story of two birds and the lives they saved. And it is also the story of a door that saved a life.

The story begins properly in California. The gold rush had erupted into a frenzy almost from the moment a prospector found gold at Sutter's Mill, and thousands of people rushed headlong toward the gold fields and the fortunes they believed in their hearts that they would find.

Most failed miserably; some found a little dust and a nugget or two. Hundreds returned to their homes, heartbroken, broken in spirit, and broke in the financial sense. Some died on the arduous trip across the continent, and others never made it to their destination because they chose to stop along the way and settle down in a foreign part of this mighty land.

Some, however, did in fact find their fortunes. They planned to return, wealthy, to their homes and families.

People traveling to California had a choice of going along with a wagon train, riding a bumpy stagecoach at least part of the way, rocking and swaying on one of the few trains heading west, or sailing around the tip of South America. The final alternatives were to stay in the West or travel across Panama and catch a ship there bound for home.

But first they had to make the gruelling trip home across a continent. And that was no easy accomplishment.

Trains were slow; wagons were bone-breaking in their discomfort, and cumbersome. They were expensive in terms of the supplies needed along the way. There were also the dangers of Indian raids, disease, and terrible weather. The stage coach was only a slight step upward. The costs were rather high for the amount of convenience involved, and the slow-moving vehicles were easily victimized by holdup men and Indians.

Railway travel offered considerable advantages over the first two means of transportation, but again expense and danger were prominent factors.

People who chose to sail around South America witnessed some of the most horrible weather imaginable. Waves fifty feet high were reported by captains who made the voyage, and there were the added problems of time, cost, and discomfort. The ships were small, unsafe, and susceptible to tragedies of all dimensions.

Those who chose to cross Panama did not fare much better. They had to contend with heat, insects, malaria, endless delays, miserable accommodations, and betrayals by the people they were forced to trust. But once the adventurers had found their gold, they were bound and determined to return home with it and live the life of their dreams.

So it was with the passengers of the ship *Central America*, so named because it picked up California travelers in that part of the world and delivered them to ports up and down the East Coast. The vessel also carried passengers to Central America from which point they could embark on the second leg of their journey to the land of gold.

The passengers returning from California had reason to celebrate. They had conquered the West and were returning with their trophies.

To a large extent, these men and women were millionaires. They carried immense sums of money on their persons or stored it in their luggage. The *Central America* was, in fact, laden with about all the cargo it could hold, all gold.

It's now time to tell you how I happened to become involved with this particular story. I had started my free-lance writing career in 1963 and had worked steadily at it while continuing to teach school. One day I received a call from one of the personnel at Expeditions Unlimited, a seagoing salvage business that specialized in finding sunken ships.

The company also salvaged the cargoes, preferably treasures. Going on the expedition were writers from all of the prestigious publications. I was to be the only freelancer on the trip, and I was predictably interested.

It was an exciting prospect. One of the workers there had called me earlier and had submitted my name and some of my modest credentials, and now I had the opportunity to see how the story would play out. The top people at the firm had already located what they believed to be the *Central America*. All they had to do was sail to the general location, relocate the wreck, and start to work.

The work, I should add, was not a piece of cake. The major problem was that the deep currents of the Atlantic Ocean kept piling tons of sand upon the wreckage, and the crew had to use what amounted to a gigantic vacuum cleaner that moved the sand. It was obvious that the sea that had kept the ship for more than a hundred years had no intention of releasing it now.

You need to understand about the ship. It left Cuba on the way to the East Coast harbors, and for the first day or two there had been smooth and uneventful sailing. The departure date from Havana, Cuba, was Tuesday, September 8, 1857. By Thursday, September 10, the storm hit.

The *Central America*, a side-wheeler, didn't have a chance. She was over-matched from the outset as the hurricane-force winds tossed the ship about like a wood chip and thirty-five foot ways swept across the decks. The swells grew higher and higher, and as the ship crested a swell, it fell into the canyon of water below.

One of the crew members called up to Captain William Herndon to warn him that the ship had sprung a leak and the engine room was filling with water. As the sun sank on that fourth day of the voyage, the crews in the engine rooms worked in water that was waist-deep and climbing by the minute.

During the night the engines ceased; the side wheels were motionless. The ship was at the mercy of the waves.

The human drama now became unbearable. The ship wallowed helplessly, and it was common knowledge that it could not remain afloat much longer.

Passengers who had been millionaires only days earlier now offered to give their money away. They dumped gold nuggets onto the deck of the ship and announced that anyone who wanted it was welcome to it.

There were no takers. Everyone knew what would happen if they were dumped into the sea: the gold would be the anchor that dragged them to what the old salts referred to as Davy Jones' Locker.

No one wanted the gold, which was now a curse.

Women and children were herded toward the few lifeboats. Men bade tearful farewells to their wives and offspring. They all knew they would never see each other again.

One man in a panic ripped the door off his cabin, and despite the efforts of several other men who tried to force him to release the door, he clung to it tenaciously as if the door would be his complete salvation.

On Friday night the ship shuddered violently, then slipped beneath the waves, sucking Captain Herndon and three hundred men along with it. In the midnight-black waters the ocean was dotted with the bodies of men, women, and children.

At this point the first bird made its appearance. Miles away, a Scandinavian vessel sailed in the now-calm waters. The captain had no idea that only a short distance away men and women were dying in the warm Atlantic waters.

Then, inexplicably, a small bird flew up into the face of the captain of the vessel. The captain stood at the helm and gazed out at the peaceful waters as the bird again fluttered into his face and then flew out to sea. Again and again the bird returned, fluttered in the captain's face, and again flew away.

Finally the captain gave orders to sail in the direction the bird had flown. A short time later he spotted the people floating on whatever they could find. Some had managed to tread water for hours. Others had died as they lay on their flotation devices.

In the distance someone spotted a man who waved and yelled at the crew. The man was floating on a cabin door. As the crew rescued the man, the second bird made its appearance.

As the ship's crew rowed the bodies of the dead men and women to the ship, the men on board had begun to carry the obviously dead people to a special area of the ship. They pulled the apparently lifeless body of a woman from the sea and carried her to be placed among the dead. Then someone noticed a quick movement inside the dress of the woman.

They thought it was the woman's heart beating. They carried her to the area where the living had been taken and began to administer aid to her.

When they unbuttoned her dress, they saw that the movement had been caused by the woman's pet parakeet, which she had refused to leave behind. But by this time someone had detected a faint pulse in the woman's wrist, and they realized that she was, indeed, alive! The bird had saved her, for surely she would have died if she had been placed, in a light coma, among the dead and had been left there without any treatment of any sort.

The rescue vessel carried the survivors to port. Of the total six hundred passengers who had left Havana, only forty-nine were saved. More than four hundred people, plus crew members, died in the hurricane that hit the *Central America* just off the North Carolina coast. The ship sank in water eight thousand feet deep. The ship's location, and this includes drifting along the bottom of the ocean, was two hundred miles off the coast of North Carolina.

Ironically, the initial efforts to salvage the ship had to be abandoned because of the sand at the bottom of the sea. In 1989, several years after the aborted attempt, Tommy Thompson and his Columbus-America Discovery Group, relocated the *Central America* not long after another deadly and powerful hurricane had lashed the coast of North Carolina.

This was the year that the tornado of May 5, 1989, destroyed the house where my family and I lived, and we of necessity had to involve ourselves in trying to put our lives back together when the new expedition was launched, even if I'd been invited to go. And this time I hadn't been.

In September 1999, almost a decade to the day from Hurricane Hugo, the group found the ship and successfully salvaged a cargo that included gold coins, clothing owned by passengers in 1857, books, diaries, journals, and newspapers still preserved enough to read.

They found steamer trunks filled with possessions of the passengers on the ill-fated ship and its tragic voyage. They also found twenty-one tons of gold bars, worth a massive fortune even in today's inflationary times.

Imagine gold, which sells for more than $100 per ounce, in such vast amounts! The discovery of the *Central America* was easily worth billions of dollars in gold alone. The discovery has been labeled by prestigious publications as the greatest treasure ever found in the history of mankind. And the wealth cannot be counted only in terms of dollars.

But the joy of the discovery cannot equal the tragedy of the people who perished in the hurricane. In many ways the voyage was comparable to that of the *Titanic*. There were obvious differences, of course.

The two vessels were filled with passengers who were in a celebratory mood. They were the people who struck it rich and were celebrating their luck. They were exhilarated by their fortunes, and they were now going to party all the way to the East Coast.

On board the gold ship there were people from twelve countries and from thirty-one states in the United States. The tragedy has been called the greatest peacetime disaster in American history.

Aside from the obvious, what makes the story so tragic is that these people had risked their lives repeatedly as they crossed the continent, sailed through treacherous waters, endured hardships of many varieties, survived sickness and calamities, and they had made their way to the gold fields of California. Their fortunes made, these same people endured the hardships again as they made their way to Panama for the trip home.

This was to be the easy part. They could spend several days and nights at sea, and the entire voyage would consist of great food, fancy dresses, pleasant talks, and plans for the future.

For months, years even for some of them, the passengers had endured extreme discomforts and survived dangers. They had used years of their lives, perhaps, in the search for the gold that would make their declining years comfortable and secure.

Some had failed totally in their quest for gold. Others had found their fortunes. Those who failed in many cases could not afford the expensive trip home and elected to remain in California. Some took the longer and more uncomfortable wagon trains back east.

These were the lucky ones, although none of them knew it at the time. The unluckiest of all were the ones who found the gold and tried to bring it back home with them. Or perhaps the least fortunate ones were the crew members who earned their meager salaries and endured hardships every day of every voyage. They presumably did not bother to dream of gold and lavish lives. They knew they would be lucky to stay alive long enough to see their retirement years arrive.

They never dreamed that their futures would be at the bottom of the sea for more than 130 years, until someone found the wreckage of the ship and brought its cargo to the surface. But the most precious cargo, that of human lives, would forever belong to the sea.

As a famous author once wrote, "Man proposes, but God disposes."

Doug Pruett, left, and Joe Wright

Fifty-Three
Art in Poetry and Poetry in Art

Poetry, we are told, is virtually impossible to define. Edgar Allan Poe ventured a definition by saying it was "the rhythmical creation of beauty." Wordsworth called it "the spontaneous overflow of powerful feelings. It takes its origin from emotion recollected in tranquility." Perhaps that says it, but other writers offer divergent opinions.

To Samuel Taylor Coleridge it was simply a matter of "the best words in the best order." Leigh Hunt saw poetry as "...the utterance of a passion for truth, beauty, and power...." Carlyle said it was "musical thought." Shelley defined it as "the record of the best and happiest moments of the best and happiest minds."

Edwin Arlington Robinson tells us that poetry is "language that tells us... something that cannot be said. All poetry, great or small, does this." Emily Dickinson sneaked up on the topic by saying, "If I read a book and it makes my whole body so cold no fire can ever warm me, I know that it is poetry. If I feel physically as if the top of my head were taken off, I know that it is poetry." So poetry, then, is art. But what is art?

Here's a definition of both poetry and art: it is what Doug Pruett and Dr. Joe Wright, both of Casar in the South Mountains, do in their studio in the reborn community of Shade.

You will find, almost as soon as you enter the studio, which is as unpretentious as the two men are, that this partnership is on the one hand bewildering and on the other hand the most natural thing in the world. It is bewildering in that Pruett is a trained artist who happens to be an outstanding teacher (you can judge that appraisal in light of the many honors he has won everywhere he has taught and in light of his widespread recognition as a superlative artist and teacher), a fine singer, an active church worker, and a devout and dedicated family man and Christian, and definitely not in that order, and he still finds time to create.

He holds a bachelor of science degree in Art and Art Education. He is a former Cleveland County Teacher of the Year and a semifinalist in the state Teacher of the Year competition. As an artist, he works in nearly every medium but prefers water colors and clay to all others.

Dr. Joe Wright completed his baccalaureate degree at North Carolina State University and completed his veterinary studies at Tuskegee Institute in Alabama. He has been a practicing veterinarian for twenty years. He is the writer in the partnership, and this second career or avocation had lain dormant, for the most part, for years. It was an accidental discovery that truly impelled him into serious writing. His son Joseph entered the house one day, and in his hand he carried an old watch. Dr. Wright asked where he found the timepiece, and the son led him to the spot where, amid a huge cluster of flowers, the watch had lain, apparently for years. Wright was impressed by the discovery and knew that one day he'd write the story.

Not just write the narrative but interpret the story, add to it a poetry and a deeper meaning that transcended the mere loss of a timepiece. He wanted the story to be not only about time but also timeless. But the poem needed a visual impact as well, and Wright pondered for a long time the best medium through which the narrative could be presented.

But it had to be more than narration, and when he met Doug Pruett, the idea of painter-writer collaboration was born. The story had actually been written twelve years earlier, but it had been only a private and personal creation. Wright called the work "Validation." The prose-poem could easily stand on its own, but the proper combination of circumstances created the partnership with Pruett, and the two men proved that the whole is greater than the sum of the parts.

"My writing had always been sporadic at best," Wright said, "for the past several years. I always wrote for my own pleasure, and I never really had any plans to publish what I write. At least not until Doug and I began to talk about a possible collaboration. That possibility is now fact." He added, "I never had any idea what to do with the writing except to enjoy it and share it occasionally with family and friends."

Wright describes his writing as vignettes, which he calls snapshots. He enjoys the camera imagery, partly because he is now a dedicated camera buff and loves to photograph animals, nature scenes, and people.

"I think it's actually easier to paint a scene, if you have Doug's talent, than it is to photograph it," Wright said. "You can create your own colors and light and dark areas when you paint, but when you shoot the photo you have to use what's there. So with my writing I try to create my own colors with words, since I cannot do it with the camera. I don't come at a story directly. I like to let it build and then provide the reader with a conclusion that he can appreciate but one he never saw coming. One instance is the story I did about the person who brought me a dog to treat. I never let the reader know until the very end that the dog is a dead animal."

Every writer and every artist at one time or another has attempted to define art, and they have been no more successful than those who attempted to define poetry. One possibly useful definition (but one woefully inadequate in reality) is that art is "the conscious use of skill and creative imagination in the production of aesthetic objects."

There's no doubt that Wright and Pruett utilize their skill and creative imagination in a conscious and aesthetic way. Their success is amazing.

Doug is unique and individualistic. One of the marks of his teaching ability is the number of former students who are now either art teachers or professional artists who win national honors as well as respect of peers.

So is Wright, who in addition to being a veterinarian is also a super singer, artist, community leader, deacon in his church (at this writing), and, like his partner, a devoted family man and Christian.

It is remarkable that two men could pool such remarkable talents in such a rewarding way. But you need to see what they do before you make any judgments of your own.

Start with Pruett. He has been drawing or painting virtually all of his life to this point. Like many children, he drew pictures on the backs of brown grocery bags, on scrap paper, and on any other surface that was not out of reach or taboo. After completing his studies at Appalachian State University, he began his teaching and art careers on highly successful notes.

"I try to do something of a highly subjective nature in my paintings," Pruett said. "I do some realistic works, but my major aim is to paint something that you can't see with your eyes but you can perceive it with all of your senses, in a way. When I visit a place where I'd like to do some serious painting, I take photos to capture the reality of the scene, and then I wander through houses and gardens, I talk with people who know the scene and understand it, and then I return home and feel that I can do six or eight legitimate paintings that incorporate more than the physical attributes of the visit."

Both men spend their working days in a very realistic set of circumstances, but when their time is their own, they work, each in his own environment. The creative spirit cannot be contained.

"Being creative is miserable," Pruett said. "You are miserable when you are so tied up with mundane duties that you can't work, and you are miserable when you are working and you find all the frustrations of trying to get the work exactly the way you want it."

"Try doing your painting with words," Wright added. "One of our most popular collaborations was a work called 'Tapestry.' Doug painted the picture and I wrote about it. I had little or no emotional investment. Yet when people saw the painting and read the short essay, many wept."

"And there is a story behind everything I paint," Pruett said. "But the story is not necessarily the one I wanted to present. Instead, it is the story the viewer perceives, as though he were reading a book."

He added, "I sometimes visit a special scene, go to the nearby grave-yard, and put myself into the scene as much as I can, long before I start painting," he said. "I leave the interpretation to the viewer. You know how it is with some people. They look at a painting and feel compelled to have some sort of interpretation. All I want them to do is look, find what they cannot avoid finding, and then reflect however they wish. I don't want to lead them into my viewpoints."

"It's the same with writing," Wright said. "When you write some-thing, you take a greater part in it and you want the reader to take a greater part as well. People like having thought provided for them. I only open a door and extend to them an invitation. It's like entering a room. You are on your own from that point."

Wright says that he likes to create a story that comes equipped with its own colors; I let the reader provide his own mental images."

Doug Pruett has won numerous honors for his teaching and for his art work. He has been named Teacher of the Year at the high school where he taught for years, and he has also won the same honor at Casar Elementary School, in addition to being the Cleveland County Teacher of the Year. Recently he was named semifinalist as the North Carolina Teacher of the Year. He lives in Casar in the South Mountains, where he does the major-ity of his painting. His subject matter includes tiles, sculptures, water col-ors, and oils.

Wright captures a scene with the intensity of a Thomas Wolfe or Walker Percy. He seems to unearth the exact word for the scene or narrative flow, and inevitably the final impact of one of total naturalness. There is not a contrived word or feeling anywhere in his work, which is at times as lean as that of Steinbeck or Hemingway or as complex as Dreiser.

"It would not be accurate to say that I misdirect the attention and the comprehension of the reader," Wright says. "It's more like coming at the reader with indirection that eventually leads him into seeing what I want him to see. I sometimes think that I am writing with a camera and that I am producing photography rather than words. I create the colors with language and emotion."

The work of Pruett and Wright cannot be described; it must be seen and read. If art is "the conscious use of skill and creative imagination in the production of aesthetic objects," then these two men are without doubt or question artists.

Better than their talent, in one major sense, however, is their deep and profound interest in their fellow man, in their community, and in their God.

"Timeless" is the first collaboration between Wright and Pruett. The origin of the idea came when Wright's son Joseph found an ancient broken and rusted watch in a flower garden at their Fallston home. Wright cleaned and restored the watch as much as possible, and later Doug Pruett incorporated the watch into a painting he was doing.

Lon Canipe and some of the decorations he won during World War II

Fifty-Four
From the South Mountains to the Apennines

It's a long way from the South Mountains of North Carolina to the majestic and awesome peaks of the Apennines in Italy. And when the trip is made the way Lon Canipe made it, the distance is more important than the circumstances surrounding the visit.

For Lon, it was not a matter of choice. As a child growing up in the virtual shadow of Benn's Knob, the highest point in the South Mountains range, Lon had a gun in his hand from the time he was able to handle one, and he was an accomplished hunter by the time he reached his teens.

Life in the South Mountains was not a picnic for the Lon and his parents and eleven brothers and sisters. Lon's father, L. A. Canipe, came along at a time when education was not a fact of life. In fact, L. A. Canipe could neither read nor write.

But do not assume that the man was uneducated; he was simply unschooled. Put him in the mountain forests and he could tell you the names of all the trees, wild flowers, animals, and birds. On his small mountain farm he could make with his own hands the items he could not afford to buy in the stores, even if there had been time, energy, and money for shopping. Put him in a cotton field and he could figure out how many bales the crop would yield; or put him in a lumber yard and he'd tell you how many board feet of lumber the truckload of logs would produce and what dimensions could be cut. No, he was far from being uneducated. He knew his world like an expert. And he taught his children how to survive in the woods and in the world.

L. A. Canipe's family grew cotton, wheat, rye, and corn. Lon's father kept twenty-two hives of bees and the family made molasses for more mealtime sweets. On the farm they grew fruits, nuts, and vegetables.

There was a need to find an honest if not luxurious life-style for themselves. And Lon Canipe, Jr., grew up with a strong will to live and a great strength of character and disposition. But nothing, or so it would seem on the surface, had prepared Lon for what was on the way.

Shortly after he reached age nineteen, Lon, like so many other young men during this time period, received his draft induction notice, and he became a soldier on October 7, 1942. He spent his basic training period at Camp White and Camp Adair, near Medford and Eugene, Oregon. After training with G Company of the 362 Regiment of the 91st Infantry Division, he sailed for North Africa. He and his outfit arrived in Algiers in the spring of 1944., and shortly afterwards became part of the massive landing force at Anzio Beach

Quickly–far too quickly!– Lon began to move upward in rank. On his second day in combat he became platoon sergeant despite the fact that he was several years younger than many of the people under his command.

"We were caught in German shelling and in the second day of the battle the lieutenant in charge of our outfit was wounded, and that same day the technical sergeant was hit as well. I was next in line in our company, and I became the technical sergeant," Lon said in an interview at his home not far from the South Mountains. "On that day I turned twenty-one years old. That was in June, and on September 16, 1944, we encountered a nest of Germans, and that day was one I will never forget."

What happened is that one of the high-ranking officers, basing his judgment on reconnaissance reports, concluded that the mountain ahead of them held only a few Germans and only two machine guns.

"Boy, was he wrong!" Canipe said. "I was moving ahead and carrying a walkie-talkie when the officer asked if my unit could move around the edge of the mountain ridge to scout the enemy. We began to move, and the Germans opened up on us. Bullets came from everywhere, the way it seemed to me, and our men began to lob smoke shells at the Germans. We couldn't see ten feet ahead of us."

Canipe recalls that the troop movement began shortly after midnight, and the men stumbled across a German in a foxhole and captured him. As they continued their assault on the hill, the long night ended and the sun came out.

"The day was beautiful," he said. "It was sunny and was warm."

He added, "It was like a North Carolina autumn day, but the smoke was still thick. In one of our tents we had the bodies of two Germans who had been killed only hours earlier and two wounded Germans. We had decided earlier that we'd try to rest if we could, but I told the men that someone had to stay awake and remain alert. I even said that the Germans might kill me, but they would never take me captive. It wasn't long after that when I heard voices. I knew that the soldiers were Americans because they spoke perfect English. That was when I learned that some Germans spoke better English than we did. The next thing I knew German soldiers stepped into view, and we had no choice but to surrender."

Canipe earlier had been given an officer's watch, and one of the Germans grasped Lon's hand and pulled the watch up to eye level. Lon jerked his hand away in anger, and the next instant there was a knife blade at his throat.

"I shoved my hand out to the Germans then," he said. "They were welcome to look at that watch all they wanted to. But my real fear was that they would look inside the shelter and see the dead and wounded Germans and come back and kill us. But they never bothered to look, and some of us were marched away as prisoners. After that we were herded into a boxcar where we stayed four days and four nights as the train took us across Austria and to the German town of Moosburg. We were placed in Stalag VII A, and that's where I stayed for the next eight months."

Life at the Moosburg Stalag was precarious at best. "The Germans fed us boiled potatoes with the peelings still on them," he said, "and we'd peel the potatoes and later we'd use those tiny stoves we made from empty food cans and boil the peelings for more soup. We stayed hungry all the time. In the first three months I was a Prisoner of War I lost fifty pounds. I know the amount because we had to work in a building that had scales, and we weighed ourselves. But we didn't need scales to tell us we had lost weight. Our clothes were like tents."

The imprisonment was an ordeal of horror as many of the soldiers died of starvation or disease. For those who survived their lives were filled with constant discomfort.

"I did not change clothes one time in eight months," Canipe said. "The shirt and pants I wore when I was captured were the same ones I wore every day and night that I was at the Moosburg Stalag. The stench inside the prison barracks was bad beyond belief; it was unbearable."

He added, "We couldn't even take off our clothes at night because it was so cold inside the barracks that we couldn't bear to be exposed to the temperatures."

Each barracks had a wood stove in it, but fuel was a major problem. The men when they were out on a work detail managed to pick up scrap wood and carry it back to the barracks, and someone had to stay awake all night to feed the stove. Even so, the prison was a cold and cheerless place.

Moosburg, located in the Bavarian region of Germany, was only a short distance from the Austrian border, and in winter the weather was brutal. Canipe recalls that there was so much snow that he did not see the ground for more than three months. "And on the occasions when we could take a hot shower–both times– we had to stand out in the snow for hours, and by the time we were in the showers our clothes were soaking wet and we had to wear them that way until they dried on our bodies," he said.

Morale was low much of the time, and the men became, as Canipe said, "ill-tempered." "If someone talked too loud, some of the others would yell at him to shut up. We were too weak to fight, but the men could crawl around and scratch and yell at each other. The German guards loved to see us brawling. They'd laugh and call out to us that brothers were fighting brothers."

There was fear each time the SS Troopers came to the barracks for inspections. "They would grab our bedding and throw it into the floor, and if anyone was near, the guards would lash out at them and hit them as hard as they could," Canipe said. "The beds, by the way, were only burlap sacks filled with shingle shavings, and the sacks were working with bed-bugs that feasted on us each time we tried to get a little sleep. The Germans gave us a powder, but it seemed to fatten the bugs rather than kill them."

Because he was a noncommissioned officer, Canipe did not have to go out on work details the way the lower ranks did, but whenever one of the enlisted men was too sick to work, Canipe volunteered to take his place. He'd work all day for the reward of a single bowl of barley soup.

"As if the poor food, cold barracks, and filthy beds were not enough," he said, "the Germans would steal the food that came to us through the Red Cross, and there was nothing we could do about it. The Germans did not pay much attention to the rules of the Geneva Convention. They made it clear that we were the enemy and would be treated like enemies."

He continued, "In fact, when we traveled by boxcar to Moosburg, every other car was filled with chickens or cows the Germans had stolen, but every boxcar on the entire train, including the ones hauling the chickens and cows, had a Red Cross painted on the top so that our planes would not bomb the trains."

Canipe recalled that the German officers enjoyed brutalizing the POWs. "When the captain entered the barracks, which held 400 men, if we didn't leap to our feet and salute we'd be ordered out into the snow and forced to stand there for hours at a time, until we were soaked to the skin and nearly frozen," he said. "But the cold weather did not seem to bother the lice and bedbugs that afflicted us night and day. And to make matters worse, the Germans would tell us that we were going to be taken to Austria where so many people were killed and buried in mass graves. It's little wonder that so many people went out of their minds. Many of them never recovered, not even when they were finally released and taken back to their homes. My old company commander called one day and said he was coming by for a visit. When he arrived he told me that he had visited five other members of our outfit, and none of them could carry on a conversation."

One morning after he had been in prison for eight months, Lon Canipe heard a noise that he couldn't believe. It was the sound of an M1 rifle.

"I had spent my boyhood around guns," he said, "and I know one gunshot sound from another. I yelled to the people in the barracks that I had heard the M1 rifle, and they yelled at me to shut up. I heard it again and again, and the men told me I was out of my head. But I knew what I had heard, and soon the others knew, too."

He recalls the morning with unabashed joy. "The shots came closer and closer, and I knew that the American forces were near the stalag. Then I saw two tanks come rolling up to the prison, and not long after that I saw a jeep. Inside the jeep I saw an officer who was dressed in his trademark fancy uniform, and he wore pearl-handled pistols on his belt. It couldn't be anyone else, because no one else had that flair. It was, of course, General George Patton. We were saved!"

"Was there a happier person on earth at that moment?" I asked him.

"Couldn't have been," he said. "Patton was so close to us we could see and hear him perfectly. Then two of his men ran to the flagpole and took down the German flag and ran up the Stars and Stripes. I was weak and almost unable to walk. But I walked up and shook that man's hand."

He was not unfamiliar with Patton, and his reaction to him was mixed. "He was the easiest man I ever saw to love and hate at the same time. But on that day we all loved him," Canipe said.

The next few hours and days were a blur as the men were taken to a tent and deloused, given the first real meals they had enjoyed in months, and dressed in warm and comfortable clothing. At about the same time the Russians had arrived from another direction, and soon there was a stack of German bodies that looked like cordwood, Lon Canipe remembers.

"We didn't grieve because of the deaths," he said. "We all could remember how the Germans would call the roll and then send the dogs after the men who were missing. No one had escaped. The men had simply died in their beds. And the Germans would watch the bodies of the men hauled off behind horses, and they'd salute until the body was out of sight. It was another one they didn't have to feed."

He can't recall how many of the prisoners died before Patton and his men arrived to liberate them. "There is a huge cemetery only a short distance from the stalag," he said, "and it was filled with the bodies of prisoners who died. It's a wonder any of us lived to see freedom and the United States again."

At his neat and attractive home on NC 18 not far from the South Mountain peaks where he grew up, Lon Canipe keeps scrapbooks filled with the stories he will never forget. The stories are simple and hard.

Among the mementos are the telegrams that told his family the bad news. One message from the war department told the Canipe family that Sergeant Lon Canipe, Jr., was missing in action, and for weeks Canipe remained a MIA soldier. Another telegram informed the family that Canipe had been reportedly taken prison. A follow-up message verified that Canipe had been taken prisoner by the Germans.

"I never thought I'd make it back," Canipe admits. "I thought with all the polluted air I'd come down with tuberculosis, or maybe a heart attack would get me. Or the Germans might decide I'd lived long enough. Or starvation might be the cause. We were in a compound that was intended to hold about five thousand people at most, and here we were with more than ten thousand, and all of us were undernourished. We lived in horrible conditions, and many of the people there had almost given up hope. But we made it back. At least, some of us did."

He is still concerned about those who did not make it back.

Lon Canipe saw more of life's tragedies, its cruelties, and its potential for disaster by the time he was twenty-one years old than most people will see in a lifetime. But the horrors did not leave him a bitter and frustrated man. He maintains his circle of friends and fellow church members; he is well-respected in his community and among the POWs who gather each month in Shelby for the purpose of keeping their organization and their memories alive.

The former POWs assume, in many instances, a leading role in taking the war to the people who are too young to know about it. Some of the POWs speak to school groups and to social organizations concerned with the fact that some real Americans and their contributions are fading into oblivion. Lon Canipe wants the nation to remember.

And that's an important consideration. Too many people see the POW license tag on Canipe's car and wonder what it means. Others tend to dismiss the service of men like Lon Canipe as less important than who wins the Super Bowl or World Series.

But to a nation that was reeling in shock and disbelief at the German aggression in Europe and the sneak attack by the Japanese bombers on December 7, 1941, the legacy of Lon Canipe and his fellow POWs is not just important: it is crucial. They served their country honorably and well, and they made sacrifices that most of us never dream about making. We owe Lon (and the others he symbolizes) a great debt, and perhaps we should thank them each time we see them.

Why not say, "Thanks, Lon. I owe you big!"

Make that Mr. Canipe, not Lon.

Better yet, make it Technical Sergeant Canipe, American in every sense. A hero who answered his county's call, and would do it again if the occasion demanded. It takes a big man to do that!

It is almost impossible for us to begin to imagine what it would be like to be held captive by an enemy that had demonstrated to the world that cruelty was only one part of the war equation. We cannot begin to understand what it would be like to wonder if we'd be killed the first time we irritated some guard. We can't know the agony, the heartache, the hunger, the loneliness, and the sense of desperation that filled the lives of the POWs daily, for weeks and months without cessation.

Lon Canipe and other POWs are concerned that we don't really appreciate what they did. Maybe it's time to tell them that we truly do.

One of the Cherryville Shooters fires an ancient weapon in the town's observance of an equally old custom. No one is quite certain how the ritual originated, but Cherryville residents want it to continue.

Fifty-Five

A Town Without Witches

It's a no-brainer to find a town without witches–or so they say! But how many towns do you know of where there is an annual and public exorcism of all the witches past, present, and future, and while the townspeople, or part of them, at least, are ridding their home land of witches, they also take the recommended methods of preventing late frosts from damaging their gardens in the spring. The town or small city is Cherryville.

Some of the old muskets, which have been handed down from parents, grandparents, and great-grandparents, are taped tightly to prevent accidents, and each year, almost without exception, the shooting goes ahead without incident. As the Shooters make their rounds, they visit certain houses that open their doors to them, and they go in and enjoy coffee, cake, and other light refreshments. The Shooters agree that these nourishment stops are welcome during the long and cold nights.

The shooting continues through the night and into the daylight hours of New Year's Day. On occasions the Shooters travel through Cherryville and on to Dallas, Shelby, and other neighboring towns and communities.

For years there was only one group, but as membership grew, some of the former members of the original group splintered off and formed their own group. The groups also generally agreed not to compete with each other territorially. A peaceful coexistence had been the rule. Actually, some feel that the growing number of houses to be visited is too great for one group to make all the requested stops. Yes, there are homeowners who invite the Shooters to their homes!

What about the witches and the prevention of late killing frosts?

The Cherryville Shooters open the New Year with a bang rather than a whimper. Dozens of shooters, armed with old black-powder guns, proceed through the town and deliver their chant and black-powder welcome to the New Year. Despite the long years the ceremony has been observed, it is not weakening; in fact, it seems to grow stronger year after year. No one seems to know exactly how or why the ceremony began, but that is not important. What really matters is keeping the tradition alive and well.

No one seems to know where the idea originated, but some students of the historic event suggest that the idea actually came from Germany, along with some of the settlers that crossed the Atlantic Ocean and eventually made their way to the Carolinas and to Cherryville in particular.

One version of the story is that the noise from the guns was enough to frighten away witches. The prevention of frost is essentially anyone's guess.

Does the chanting work? Something in Cherryville does. For years there were two major industries in Cherryville, and in recent times the town lost both of them. But, despite the predictions of the doomsday prophets, Cherryville has continued to prosper. Newer businesses have come to town, municipal and community spirit has remained high, and people generally reflect a happiness that comes with good health and good fortune.

Would good fortune have come if there were no Shooters? No one, it seems, is willing to take the chance.

The ancient Cherryville Shooters as seen decades ago

Remember that Cherryville is the town that "adopted" the infant who died the first day of her life and was thrown into the creek that runs through the town. That story was told earlier in this book. Formerly known as White Pine, Cherryville has held the annual New Year's Shoot for longer than anyone can remember. And they do it with considerable flair and a great deal of noise. It's no wonder the witches refuse to hang around. Boilermakers might be persuaded to leave, too.

Here's how it happens. On New Year's Eve (actually, at one minute past midnight and on special occasions in mid-afternoon) the Shooters, groups of men who travel from house to house and spend the early morning hours and often the rest of the day in their "duties," arrive at homes of friends, climb out of cars, and begin a chant that is part of the ritual of assuring good fortune for the coming year.

"Good morning to you, sir," the chant goes in part. "We wish you a Happy New Year, good health, long life, which God may bestow as long as you stay here below.

"May he bestow the house you are in where you go out and you go in.

"Time by moments steals away, first the hour and then the day. Small the lost days may appear, but soon they mount up to a year."

The chant goes on in the midnight stillness.

"This another year is gone and now is no more of our own. But if it brings good of our promises as the year before the flood,

"But let none of us forget that it had left us much in doubt,

"A favor from the Lord received, since which our spirits have been grieved.

"Marked by the unerring hand thus in His Book our record stands.

"Who can tell the vast amount placed to each our account? For the old year's gone and the new year's come, and for good luck we'll fire our guns."

At this point the Shooters, one by one, walk to the center of the irregular circle and they fire their ancient guns, which range from old rifles to muskets to blunderbusses, some of them as old as 160-170 years or older. Before the night is over, the Shooters will stop and chant the poem at a large number of houses, where the Shooters will be offered refreshments and a chance to rest their eardrums. When you visit Cherryville, remember that you need not take along any witch-repellent. The witches are gone!

The statue of the Shooter is a recent addition to downtown Cherryville.
You can visit the small park and see the statue just south of Main Street.
The park is open daily during daylight hours.

The first Cherryville town hall, shown above, still stands. It is located just outside the main shopping district in the town. While you are in the vicinity, you can see the old city jail and the highly interesting C. Grier Beam Truck Museum. Call before making the trip, because the museum is open on a part-time basis. The same is true of the Cherryville Historical Museum, which contains a huge number of interesting items relative to the early days of White Pine, or Cherryville. The new museum is located at the site of what was once the more modern jail, which was closed many years ago and sat empty for decades. Don't get confused: there are two old jails. One of them is a log structure used to incarcerate the occasional drunk, who was a rarity in Cherryville. The other was on Main Street.

Judge William Gaston was one of the first staunch defenders of religious freedom in the young nation. He contributed to the building of the first Catholic church in the area and also wrote the North Carolina State Song. Gaston's law office can still be seen in New Bern.

In New Bern, if you visit the restored Tryon Palace, you can see historical reenactments like the one shown above. In this photo you can see the back of Tryon Palace, which is a wonderful place to take the family.

Fifty-Six
The Bard of New Bern

Much has been said throughout this book about the connections that exist between and among so many of the stories, although the narratives may be separated by great distances in time and geography. In this brief chapter there are connections that may not seem obvious from the outset, but they are worth pursuing.

Start with Tryon Palace, the luxurious residence in New Bern, the second oldest city or town in North Carolina. Here in the palace lived Governor Tryon, whose opulent life-style clashed dramatically with those of the farming and merchant classes of people so far removed from the town of New Bern. Many of the so-called backwoods people resented the governor's palace more than words could express, and in the minds of several historians it was the obvious display of wealth and status that enraged many North Carolinians to the point that they were ready to rebel. Many people of the mountains were unaccustomed to stories of opulent living; they had a hard enough time just feeding their families.

At least one historian has gone so far as to state that the rumors and eyewitness reports of the lavish palace was the greatest machine for propaganda devised to encourage the men and women who worked hard for their living to add their support to the growing and restless movement toward making this nation free of British rule. It is difficult to imagine how this ostentatious building so far away could have been such a powerful element in the growing tide of democracy.

And there are other connections less tenuous. The first involved the New Bern Fire Department and its need for fine horses to pull the heavy wagons used as fire trucks.

The heavy weight of the water and equipment meant that only the finest horses could be used, and this is where Fred the Firehorse made his appearance. And he came from Gaston County, having been purchased from the Craigs of Gastonia.

Fred was not only a willing worker; he was also a highly intelligent animal that seemed to realize how important he was to the safety of the town. When the fire alarm sounded, Fred became excited and restless, and when he was harnessed and taken to the streets, he did not need guidance. Fred knew, somehow, where the fire was. He had either memorized the signals or he had an uncanny instinct that led him directly to the fires.

Whatever the gift was, Fred was the only horse in the New Bern fire department that possessed it. When the alarm sounded, Fred did not merely plod toward the emergency: he raced as fast as his legs and strength and the weight of the fire wagon would permit. It was his enthusiasm, in fact, that led to the death of Fred.

One day he was responding to a call, and he overtaxed his great heart. Fred suffered a heart attack and collapsed and died en route to the fire.

What made his story more tragic is that some thoughtless person had turned in a false alarm, and the noble horse died as the result of a thoughtless and stupid act. But the fire department personnel and the people of New Bern decided that Fred would be immortalized in a sense, and a taxidermist preserved the head of the horse and later it was mounted and given a place of honor in the New Bern Fire Museum.

At this point we see the start of a connection. Fred was born and raised on a farm in Gaston County, far from the North Carolina coast and the town of New Bern. Fred grew up among the rolling hills of the Piedmont, not far from the South Fork and Catawba rivers, in an area that was at the time largely agricultural.

The connection continues. In New Bern there was an attorney, a distinguished judge, a poet, and among the most important Catholic in the state. His name was William Gaston, and the county of Gaston where Fred was born was named after Judge William Gaston, the bard of New Bern.

Now try to name one poem written by this renowned jurist and religious leader. The typical reader seldom if ever heard of William Gaston. It is unlikely that many North Carolinians could quote one line of a William Gaston poem. Neither could they tell you why Gaston County was named after him. Or why the county seat was named Dallas.

To add to the depth of the question, keep in mind that William Gaston never set foot in Gaston County. He never wrote the name of the county in any of the documents he penned. He never spoke the name of Gaston County, and he never heard of the county during his entire life.

But William Gaston was a dynamic and honorable man who was a distinguished statesman, a scholar of great reputation, and a civic leader who worked for freedom of religion for all people in the true sense of democracy. As indicated earlier, he also served as a judge. Not just as a judge, mind you, but as a State Supreme Court Justice.

In the 1840s in the area to become Gaston County there was a move to build a Catholic church to serve the spiritual needs of the Catholics who had moved into the area. Father Cronin had come to the land adjacent to the Catawba and South Fork rivers and had worked untiringly to see that the church was built as quickly as possible. One of the donors who contributed large sums of money was Judge William Gaston of New Bern.

Judge Gaston died in 1842, nearly three years before Gaston County was formed, and this explains why Judge Gaston had never heard of Gaston County: it did not exist until after his death. The generosity of Judge Gaston was one of the reasons the county was named after him, but this was not the sole reason. One of the major reasons was his poetry.

But first look at other connections to other parts of the nation. In Rutherfordton there lived for a while General Lew Wallace, who spent his time at the Esmeralda Inn while he completed the stage script for his classic work, *Ben-Hur: a Tale of the Christ.* Later Lew Wallace became the first governor of New Mexico. When the Mexican War broke out, Pinckney Henderson and friends rushed to Texas to fight for the independence of Texas and its inclusion in the United States. Henderson became the first governor of Texas, and he later returned to North Carolina and was buried alongside Adam Springs, who many people think was the father of Abraham Lincoln. Springs, according to local legend, was buried standing up so that he could "watch" his fish traps on the South Fork River.

But this still does not explain the connection, other than that of the Catholic Church, to Judge William Gaston. The rest of the answer lies in Gaston's poetry.

The poetry comes in just a moment. But first consider this brief stanza from a poem that is, or should be, well known by every man, woman, and child in this state and, for that matter, in the nation.

The tune, written long before the poem, is well known. Entitled "To Anachreon in Heaven," the tune served as a tavern beer-drinking song. Here is the quote:

> On the shore, dimly seen, through the mist of the deep,
> Where the foe's haughty host in dread silence reposes;
> What is that which the breeze, o'er the towering steep,
> As it fitfully blows, half conceals, half discloses?

Ready for the rest of the quote? It goes like this:

> Now it catches the gleam of the morning's first beam
> And in full glory reflected now shines in the stream;
> 'Tis the Star Spangled Banner, long may it wave,
> O'er the land of the free, and the home of the brave.

Don't jump to conclusions. William Gaston did not write this poem. Francis Scott Key did. But Gaston's poem should be almost equally well known by Tar Heel residents. The words are by William Gaston, and the tune was composed by Mrs. E. E. Randolph.

> Carolina! Carolina! Heaven's blessings attend her!
> While we live we will cherish, protect and defend her;
> Tho' the scorner may sneer at and witlings defame her,
> Still our hearts swell with gladness whenever we name her.
> Hurrah! Hurrah! The Old North State forever!
> Hurrah! Hurrah! The good Old North State!

There's much more, but you get the idea. "The Old North State" is the official song of the State of North Carolina, and the poem by William Gaston is one of the reasons for the fact that Gaston County was named after him. Incidentally, if you visit New Bern (and I strongly urge you to do so), you will find that the small house that once contained the law offices of William Gaston is still there and in excellent repair.

Try not to rush through your visit to New Bern and to the many superb attractions there. Sample the cuisine and enjoy touring some of the old and beautifully maintained houses where the atmosphere is pure History and the Past is tangible in every room. There are many tour offerings if you don't trust yourself, but I strongly recommend that here, as in most of the other locations you might visit, you take the downtown walking tours. By walking, you can spend as little time–or as much–as you wish at each stop. Obtain a city street map with the major historical attractions and saunter to your heart's content. Advice: mid-summer can be hot there!

On your walking tour of New Bern you can visit the old law office of William Gaston. Not far away are some of the most beautiful and fascinating churches in this part of the state. Or, if you are interested in more mundane attractions, you can see where Pepsi Cola was born.

The entrance to Tryon Palace in New Bern

ROBERT L. WILLIAMS

Samples of the von Schweinitz helianthus

Fifty-Seven
Blowin' in the Wind

Sometimes the shortest stories are the best. This is one of the short ones, but it has a meaning all its own. It's also a personal one, and your indulgence will be appreciated.

The story started on May 5, 1989, when a devastating tornado ripped our pre-Civil War house apart and either destroyed or badly damaged over one hundred houses in the South Mountains area. In the months after the tornado, our lives were ripped apart as badly as our house had been, and for what seemed like an endless period of gruelling labor, we used the logs uprooted by the tornado and built a log house near where our previous house had stood.

As we worked all winter, we took little notice of the vegetation that grew around our house, but in the spring we stopped work long enough to till a small garden plot so that we could have a variety of fresh vegetables to add a little joy to our lives. It would do us a world of good, we reasoned, if we could create a semblance of order to our fragile lives.

While we were planting the garden we noticed that some strange plants had started to peep through the soil. We did not dig up the plants because they were far enough out of the way so that they would not be a problem with our veggies.

As the summer heat moved into our part of the state, the strange and new plants grew taller and taller. Soon they were well over six feet tall, and by midsummer they were up to a height of eight feet or even more.

In early September the first flowers appeared. They were small gold-and-white blossoms that resembled miniature sunflowers. Each had thirteen petals radiating out from a small golden center. We noticed that the stems were covered with a bristle-like coating.

On the back of leaves there were tiny dark spots barely visible. Curiosity got the better of me and I dug up one of the plants. The roots looked like the lower half of the human body, with two extensions that looked like legs. A few days later I read a newspaper account of a rare plant that had been thought extinct for many years. The flower was the von Schweinitz helianthus, which once grew in profusion in the North Carolina mountains and literally in the autumn covered meadows with the sunflower blossoms.

Ages earlier, when bison and elk roamed the mountains and the foothills of the Tar Heel State, these flowers retreated to the fringes of fields and meadows, and even when the settlers came in with their plows and saws and farming equipment, the helianthus retreated even more until it grew only on the thin ribbon of soil between the fields and the forests.

Then it disappeared altogether. The tiny sunflower had gone the way of the ivory-billed woodpecker and the eastern mountain lion and the passenger pigeon. But the article I read informed me that in South Carolina a small colony of the flowers had been found and that the miniature sunflower was now classified as the rarest flower on earth. The description in the article was a perfect match for the flowers in our garden.

We invited experts to examine our flowers, and we came away from the discussions with a conviction that our flowers were indeed the rare von Schweinitz helianthus. But where did we get them?

Then it dawned on us. The tornado, followed by Hurricane Hugo, swept up from the south of us and dropped debris of all sorts on our property. We found half a bike, bits of furniture, and other indications of damage to property. And, we reasoned, the high winds that toppled trees also could have carried seeds into our property and dropped them there.

Whatever the reasons, we have the flowers, and they seem to thrive in our garden area and they proliferate each year. So while we might not have traded our house for the flowers, we nevertheless would not part with them. Not if we can help it.

To us the miniature sunflowers will always represent the incredible power of Nature coupled with the intimate, delicate, and invaluable beauty and will to live of a tiny yellow flower with a core like a tiny sun and thirteen petals radiating from the center.

There might even be a more celestial meaning behind the flowers, one with which we have no argument whatsoever.

An up-close look at the rare sunflower clusters

One of the few national honors accorded Sidney Lanier

Fifty-Eight
The Final Days of a Fine Poet

Many a school child, back in the days before good writing and good literature were forsaken so that our students could be politically correct instead of educated, grew up reading the works of Sidney Lanier, generally regarded as the finest poet to come out of Georgia and one of the best poets the South ever produced. Lanier was born in Macon, Georgia, in 1842 and died in 1881. So why is he in a book about North Carolina stories?

He's here for one major reason: he died in North Carolina. To be more precise, he died in Polk County; in fact, he died in the tiny town of Lynn, just outside Columbus. Lanier, you have already noted, lived a very short life, but his poetic output was prodigious.

He wasn't simply a poet. He wrote one novel, and he possessed a great musical talent. He played the flute masterfully, and for a while he had a musical career planned. However, the Civil War interrupted his music studies, almost permanently.

Barely nineteen years old when the Civil War broke out, Lanier entered military service and was taken prisoner and was sent to Point Lookout prison in Maryland. He spent four months in the deplorable conditions there, and when he emerged he was deathly ill with life-threatening tuberculosis.

To the health problems he added an economic one. Unable to work for a living, he lived in near-abject poverty for years after his release from prison. His physical constitution was almost totally wrecked during this time.

So bad was his health that after his release from Point Lookout in 1865 until 1872 that, as he wrote, "...pretty much the whole of life had been merely not dying."

Earlier trained as a lawyer, Lanier wrote a novel entitled *Tiger-Lilies* about his experiences during the Civil War, and the publication of that book convinced him to abandon his future as a third-rate lawyer (his description of his career in law) and turned back to his music and poetry.

His musical career soared as he became flutist for the Peabody Orchestra of Baltimore. To add to his income, he presented a series of lectures, which in turn led to his appointment to the faculty of Johns Hopkins as lecturer on English literature.

Health problems persisted, however, and he resigned himself to writing more poetry. Among his most successful and best-known works were "The Song of the Chattahoochee" and "The Marshes of Glynn," both of which were once as familiar to high school students as the latest mystery or romance novel is to many modern readers. The two poems were celebrations of two of the favorite spots on earth for a poet who would not live to see his fortieth birthday.

His name could be added to the list of writers who were forced to do their life's work within a few astonishingly productive years: Byron, Shelley, Keats, Chatterton, Stevenson, and other excellent writers lived very short creative lives, and now Lanier would join the group.

If you wish to see the inspiration for one of Lanier's works, travel to the delightful city of Brunswick, Georgia, and view the gorgeous Marshes of Glynn. You can sit where Lanier sat and enjoy the superb scenery, and you can reflect on Lanier's words that are as beautiful as the marshes along the highway. There is even an oak tree, fittingly called the Lanier Oak, where the poet sat as he wrote one of his major poems.

"The sun is a-wait at the ponderous gate of the West," he wrote in "The Marshes of Glynn," and the line is fairly obviously his own premonitions of his entrance through the Gate of the West. He added, later in the poem:

> "Tolerant plains, that suffer the sea and the rains and the sun,
> Ye spread and span like the catholic man who hath mightily won
> God out of knowledge and good out of infinite pain
> And sight out of blindness and purity out of stain."

He added that he would later become a part of the Great Plan.

"As the marsh-hen secretly builds on the watery sod,
Behold I will fly on the Greatness of God as the marsh-hen flies
In the freedom that fills all the space 'twixt the marsh and the skies.
*   *   *   *   *   *   *   *
Oh, like to the greatness of God is the greatness within
The range of the marshes, the liberal marshes of Glynn."
If you prefer north Georgia, try this:
"Out of the hills of Habersham
Down the valleys of Hall,
Downward the voices of duty call–
Downward, to toil and be mixed with the main,
The dry fields burn, and the mills are to turn...."

Lanier never lost his love for music and God. Near his death, he wrote, "Music is love in search of a word." In one of his best-known religious works he added, "Into the woods my Master went/ Clean forspent, forspent. Into the woods my Master came, /Forspent with love and shame."

When his health failed alarmingly, Lanier moved to Polk County and into the attractive house outside Columbus. The house is not open to the public, but you can see it from the highway. Honor the privacy of the owners and at the same time honor a great poet and gentle human being.

The Sidney Lanier house in Lynn, outside Columbus

Dr. Richard Maybin and Louise Maybin

Fifty-Nine
Making the World a Better Place

Robert Frost once observed in a poem about a tuft of flowers that men worked together, whether together or apart. He could as easily have said that some men and women work together and apart at the same time, and by doing so he would've described the lives and careers of Louise Maybin and her husband, Dr. Richard Maybin, longtime residents of Lawndale, North Carolina, no more than a few minutes' drive from the South Mountains.

Louise and Dick Maybin were married, prior to his death in the mid-1990s, for more than half a century, and during this time they forged a relationship that makes them unique to North Carolina and beyond.

For decades Dr. Maybin served his community from his clinic in Lawndale, but over the years he was far more than a medical doctor. He was in every sense a missionary, a pillar of the community, and a speaker in constant demand at churches and social groups statewide. He did not treat the body only; he believed firmly that the body and soul form a union that is inseparable.

Louise Maybin, like her late husband, is uniquely energetic and dedicated to God and his people, no matter where they happen to be, whether in this country or abroad. She is a church worker, also an acclaimed speaker, a teacher, a social worker, and a lover of humanity in the highest and broadest sense of the word.

And that is why the Maybins are in this book. Like some of the other stories here, they did not perform wonders for their own glory, and they did not seek for money, fame, or adulation. They sought to serve their God and their church and its people. Someone in the Lawndale community once said that the Maybins wore enough hats to stock a clothing store.

In a very large sense this book is dedicated to the Maybins and to the people like them who have devoted their lives to making the world a better place. And they have succeeded beyond their wildest dreams. They, and the people like them, are the forces that over the long haul prevail; they are the forces of peace and love and helping hands and generosity. Louise Maybin and Dick met at a church gathering at Lake Junaluska. Louise grew up in Southern Pines, where her father was a grocer. When she graduated from high school and enrolled at Queens College in Charlotte, her ambition was to become a director of Christian education.

"Or an aeronautical engineer," she added, smiling. "I was a Bible major, and I knew early in life that I wanted to work with the church, but I also knew that my work could take me in any number of directions."

After she completed her studies, Louise became director of the Lake Junaluska playground, and she worked for the late J. B. Ivey, founder of a chain of clothing stores and also a native of Upper Cleveland County. It was at the camp that she met Dick Maybin, and their paths soon became one afterward.

Does she regret that she never became Christian education director? Not at all; in fact, she is confident that she became one early in life and has never wavered from her course. Her entire life has been one of leading and directing and guiding.

"I feel that I've done Christian education works since we came to Lawndale," she said. "I have directed the Loy White camp, served as a counselor since 1968, played the organ for church, worked with youth programs at St. Peter's United Methodist Church, and also worked with youth at the Lawndale United Methodist Church."

She worked closely with Tyner Ivestor, wife of the late Carl Ivestor, one of the legendary veterinarians in the area, one who came in under the grandfather clause and practiced until his death. Mrs. Ivestor and Mrs. Maybin were subdistrict counselors under the former youth education structure. She also taught classes at the old Piedmont, Belwood, and Burns public schools.

These classroom experiences were not always predictable. "Once at Belwood School we were planning a special meal, and we asked students to ask their parents to donate certain foods, among them dressed chickens," she recalled. "And, believe it or not, one child brought a chicken to class, and the bird was dressed in a bonnet, cape, and other clothing."

She added, "After that, we learned to be more specific with what we requested."

For years, Louise Maybin in her spare time has been a tutor for students with special needs, and in countless other ways a source of help and information needed by her church and community.

Among her major work outside the community is the mission work she has done in foreign lands where poverty and need are the rule, rather than the exception. Her husband spent much of his own time working side-by-side with her in these countries.

Dr. Richard Maybin, a native of Ware Shoals, South Carolina, made his way to Lawndale by a circuitous route. After completing his medical classroom studies, he served a 15-month internship at Baptist hospital in Winston-Salem, and for two years after that he served in the United States Air Force.

While still in the Air Force, he agreed to help Dr. Forrest D. Edwards, who had started the Edwards Clinic in Toluca, only a few miles from Lawndale. While still on active military duty, Maybin traveled from his Air Force assignment base to perform tonsillectomies on weekends for Dr. Edwards. He then became a full-time doctor in the clinic while Edwards was in Mexico on a church trip.

The Edwards trip to Mexico was for the purpose of dedicating a church he'd been instrumental in building in the Mexican town of Toluca, and when Edwards returned, he helped the local residents to decide to call their community Toluca, after the Mexican town.

When Edwards returned to Upper Cleveland County, Dr. Maybin moved to Lawndale in 1949 to open his own practice, and he remained there until his death. Maybin, like his wife, served as youth counselor in Cleveland County church work, and the husband and wife team worked as a team at Lake Junaluska for fourteen years. He also conducted health and wholeness seminars at Pfeiffer College.

In 1970 Dr. Maybin started what was to become a series of trips as a medical missionary. The first trip was to Bolivia, and after that initial trip he served as medical missionary to Haiti, Antigua, and other sites where medical help was desperately needed. In 1985 Dr. Maybin, like his medical colleague in Belwood, Dr. Cecil Barrier, won the prestigious Jefferson Standard award for his unselfish dedication of time, energy, and expertise in helping the unfortunate and needy.

But the lives of Louise and Dick Maybin were not about winning awards: their work was helping people. Dr. Maybin was one of the first practitioners in the area to use medical hypnosis in the treatment of some health problems, and he was among the first area physicians to provide a health counselor as part of his services.

In many other ways, too, Dr. Maybin went far above and beyond the traditional methods of treating patients. For instance, he kept a mattress in the back of his station wagon in the event he had to transport seriously ill or injured persons to the hospital if there were no emergency vehicles available.

He made house calls virtually as long as he was able to maintain his practice. He delivered babies as part of his much-needed service, and he was immensely pleased with the fact that in all his years of medical practice he never lost a baby.

"Both Louise and I came from poor beginnings," Maybin said, "and we feel a special need to help those in need. We feel honored to have been here for half a century, to serve and to be served. I plan to keep active as long as possible."

Only death stopped him, and his widow, Louise, is still carrying on the Christian work as she has done all of her adult life. She spends a part of each day in the service of others as she works, as her husband did, to make the world a better place. And they succeeded beyond belief. Louise still plays the organ for the Lawndale United Methodist Church. She began playing as soon as the church was organized, and she has no intention of slowing down.

During the last conversation I had with Dr. Richard Maybin before his death, he said, "I know one thing for a certainty: part of me is immortal, and this life is only a preamble to the life to come. We live here and hereafter, and it is the second life that counts most."

Patients who consulted Dr. Maybin for medical treatment the first time were likely to come away surprised by the doctor's values and medical judgment. Never one to prescribe medications in a cavalier manner, Dr. Maybin advocated preventative medicine almost as much as the curative part. He was a great believer that we can take control of a large part of our body's health simply by eating properly, taking good care of ourselves through exercise and good judgment, and by having a healthy mental and emotional outlook.

A friend told me that once he went to see Dr. Maybin in his office because of a persistent bronchial infection that he could not shake. "I came away with a prescription for my congestion," he said, "and a great deal of advice that will last me long after the medicine and the illness are gone. I heard one of the best sermons I ever heard in my life, and the best part of it was that it didn't take Doc more than five minutes to deliver the message. I'll never forget that visit. It changed my entire outlook on life."

Someone once observed that no matter how much you pay a good preacher, a good teacher, a good lawyer, and a good doctor, it's never enough. Whatever you pay a poor preacher, teacher, doctor, or lawyer is too much. Nobody ever complained about paying Dr. Maybin too much.

Dr. Maybin, like all dedicated professionals, had his priorities, and they were duties to God, his church, his wife, his friends, his community, his patients, and the world. If you wonder what order he gave to these priorities, the answer is simple: it was a seven-way tie for first place. The Maybins could not separate the duties, which were also privileges for them, because they were one and the same. Dr. Richard Maybin worshipped God and cared for his wife and patients and all the others at the same time. In his medical office he was never too busy to see a patient without an appointment, and if the patient was an emergency case, he went to the front of the line, no questions asked.

A man who could be at home in a conversation at the neighborhood hardware, at a church social, or in a medical convention, Dick Maybin possessed an amazing ability to be himself no matter what the conditions. He was a quick man with a joke, a wonderful story about the foibles of human nature, and a sympathetic ear and voice; he served his community, his church, and his God wisely and well.

Another doctor, a quiet-spoken Yankee, had a comment that suited Dick Maybin well:

"You hear that boy laughing? You think he's all fun;
But the angels laugh, too, at the good he has done;
The children laugh loud as they troop to his call,
And the poor man that needs him laughs loudest of all."

Oliver Wendell Holmes did not know the Maybins, but he'd have been proud to make their acquaintance. After all, they fit his poem perfectly.

Fred and Lillian Mintz have been married for nearly seventy years, and they were as happy when the photo was taken as they were on the day they were married. What is their recipe for a glorious marriage? They advise others to work together, share their lives in every way, and, above all, love the Lord and pick good parents. The two decided to be married on the flip of a coin; they stayed married through unselfish love and devotion.

Sixty
Still in Love–In Delight!

This is not a story about people who discovered new lands, masterminded military victories, wrote award-winning novels, starred in epic motion pictures, or led nations to new heights of glory. This is, instead, a story about a man and a woman who grew from childhood into adulthood, fell in love, and at this writing, almost seventy years later, are as much in love as they were when they tied the knot back in 1931.

This is a story about human goodness, generosity, love, loyalty, respect, and helping hands. It is a story about people who found their heart's desire in one another, and neither strayed from the look of love in the other's eyes. When they tied the knot, it was a good one.

That knot was not a loose bow knot or slip knot. It was one that was meant to stay tied for as long as the two lived. And it hasn't even started to pull loose. These two people, if ever any two people were, were meant for each other.

Lillian and Fred Mintz of the tiny community of Delight on the fringe of the South Mountains remember as if it were yesterday a trip in a Hudson automobile. Actually, Fred was the one in the Hudson. He was headed to a birthday party for a pretty fourteen-year old girl whom he had known for a few years. He could not have foreseen what the rest of his life would be like because of that pretty young girl. If he could have, he'd have been the first to arrive and the last to leave, and he'd have been back the next day.

The girl who celebrated her birthday the day Fred Mintz arrived in the Hudson may have been only fourteen, but she already had a pretty good idea of what she wanted out of life. One of those items was the good-looking kid in the Hudson. Like Fred, she didn't know what was coming.

It took four years for that early affection to blossom into a permanent love. It also took the flip of a very special coin that Fred Mintz carried wherever he went.

It was his lucky coin. He wasn't a gambling man, but the coin won him many a good-natured wager with his friends. And on this day it was to win him a wife.

Four years had passed since that birthday party, and the pretty young girl had become a pretty young woman of eighteen. Lillian now lived in Polkville, a crossroads town in Upper Cleveland County, and she and Fred had made a date to work at the Cleveland County Fair in one of the booths. They never made it to the booth, partially because of the Show Train and partly because of Fred's lucky coin.

The Show Train, as the name implies, was the string of railroad cars that delivered the Fair to the county. Today the county fair is simply a variation of the entertainment that surrounds us every day of the year. But in those days the Fair was the highlight of the year for many people. Even watching the Show Train come in was a treat not to be found in the typical day's activities.

When Fred and Lillian reached the railroad crossing, the train was too close for them to cross the tracks. So they parked and watched the Show Train grind past them. As they waited, there was a slight lull in the conversation, and Fred abruptly asked Lillian if she would do him the honor of becoming his wife.

The Mintzes recall vividly that the day was a Sunday, and they have ample reason to recall all of the events of the evening. After Fred asked Lillian to marry him, she, shocked by the suddenness of the question, hesitated before replying. Fred took the hesitation for indecision, and he pulled out his lucky coin.

"Let's decide it this way," he said. "I'll flip the coin, and if it comes up heads, we go get married. If it's tails, we'll stay here and when the train passes we'll go to the Fair booth to work."

Lillian agreed. Fred flipped the coin, and it landed heads. They made a change in their direction and in their plans, and hours later, in a day when it was a simple matter to get married, the two were spliced.

The marriage ceremony cost Fred Mintz $5, a full week's pay. And if you ask him about it, he'll tell you today that the marriage license and fee represented the best money he ever spent in his life.

When Lillian was growing up, she was to be baptized at the First Baptist Church in Shelby and she wanted a new dress, a special dress, for the occasion. The one she received was a bargain.

"My mother bought the cloth for five cents a yard. She decided that three yards would be plenty of material. She already had the thread and other needs, and when the dress was finished it had cost a total of fifteen cents," she said. "Imagine that! You'd have a hard time buying the thread for that much money today."

As for her life with Fred Mintz, she had this to say: "Times were hard back then and everybody worked hard. You never had time to fuss and fight. People lived a Christian life and helped and loved one another. And wives and husbands stayed together."

She grinned, and suddenly the eighteen-year old girl emerged from the brilliant and beautiful smile. "I told Fred we were together for life," she said. "I also told him that if he ever started running around on me, he'd better keep running and not even stop to look back."

She has advice for young people today. "Be happy. Find a way to live a good life. Don't be afraid to work hard. Love one another. But the main thing is to pick good parents." It worked well for her and Fred.

The truth is that both of the Mintzes have a great deal of useful and entertaining knowledge for the world. They know the rigors and the rewards of hard work. They know the desperation facing people during the Great Depression. They have witnessed crops being ruined by the insects and poor growing seasons.

He added, "It was a good life back then. The work was fairly hard, but back then people didn't mind hard work. A man was expected to work, if he was able to do so. There were no programs to pay people for not working. People were honest in those days, too. Nearly everyone you met was a good and sincere person, and you could believe what he said. You could do business on a handshake, which was more binding than a written contract is today. It was also a good time to bring children up."

Lillian and Fred Mintz were blessed with four fine children, two of whom at this writing live in Greensboro, one lives in Fallston, and the other lives in the Polkville area.

Fred and Lillian Mintz were in love when they were married, and they remain devoted to each other today. Their children love their parents and respect and honor them. Some of the grandchildren of the Mintzes attend church with them, but the entire family, the nuclear one as well as the extended one, is in church somewhere nearly every Sunday of the year.

How did all this happen? How can one man and his wife have such fine children and in turn their children have wonderful children and grandchildren?

"God has blessed us wonderfully," Fred says. "He has given us health, a roof over our heads, opportunities to better ourselves, and wonderful children. We love our God, our church, our children, our community, and our country. And the more we love others, the more we love each other."

"You have to cooperate," Lillian adds. "You have to work together, stay in church, teach your children right from wrong, live right and set a good example for them. And you have to have Goodness in you."

As far as Fred is concerned, Lillian says, "I wouldn't trade him for anything. I've got him spoiled just right and wouldn't want to train another one."

But all these wonderful aspects of their lives did not just happen. Nothing simply happens; everything, in one way or another, is caused. The Mintzes have worked all their lives to make their marriage and family a success. They work to make the world around them better.

Lillian, for example, worked out of her home when she was the telephone operator for the Polkville area. "I was in charge of the switchboard," she says, "and I had to know all the rings back then. We had sixty to seventy customers on the switchboard, and whoever operated it had to know each and every one of them by their rings. We still have that phone."

"Back then people could not be particular about where they worked, what hours they were on the job, or how much money they made. Most of us were lucky just to have a job," Fred said, concerning their marriage.

Their initial plan was not to tell anyone they were married. On the Sunday they tied the knot, they returned to Upper Cleveland County and Fred left his bride, as usual, at the home of her parents.

"My plan was to visit her again on Wednesday, our usual agreement, and tell her parents at the proper time that we were now man and wife."

Fred points out that in those days the idea of a honeymoon was something that the very rich enjoyed. The working man in the middle of the Great Depression simply could not afford to take time off from work and then spend extra money to take an expensive trip to some romantic part of the world.

"We never even thought of a honeymoon," Fred said. "We decided to have one for the rest of our lives. In the Depression there wasn't any money to be had. Buying a house was out of the question, and getting a job that paid a lot was just a dream. A man was lucky to have a job at all."

In those days Fred delivered the Charlotte *News* (the same paper for which this writer worked for several years as a special assignment writer while he taught school) in his Ford Roadster that he had bought with his earlier savings.

"He was the second person in Shelby to own one," Lillian says proudly. "He delivered the papers six afternoons a week and then on Sunday morning. His route was sixty-five miles, which meant that in a year he drove more than twenty-three thousand miles delivering those papers."

"We decided to have some lumber cut for the house we planned to build," Fred recalls, "but by the time the lumber was ready to use, the government had shut down most of the supply houses and we couldn't buy the materials we needed to finish our house. I was driving up from Shelby to see Lillian, and that's about the time she made up her mind that I'd be much happier in the country."

Lillian nods in firm agreement. "I decided that the best thing for Fred was to bring him up here and put him to work on the farm. I didn't know how he'd get along, being from the city and used to city life, but the country seemed to agree with him pretty well."

Fred agrees with his wife of nearly seven decades. He liked the country from the start, and he has no regrets whatsoever.

In addition to farming "until the boll weevils ate us out of house and home," the Mintzes found time to become energetic members of their social groups, and they somehow managed to find time just to enjoy being with each other.

When she was not working the switchboard or working on the farm, Lillian Mintz, working alongside her husband, helped to organize Polkville Baptist Church, where they still attend, and assisted with the Sunday School. She was active in the Missionary Society and the Woman's Club, Parent-Teacher Association, the Dairy Association, and the North Carolina Farm Bureau Women's Organization.

Fred, too, kept busy. He served on the school board for twelve years and was director for the Agricultural Stabilization Board. He found time to be a director for the Volunteer Fire Department, serve as an instructor for veterans returning to civilian life, acted as precinct chairman for Delight, and remained active in the Masons. Both participated in Gideon work.

He worked as a deacon in the church, as a magistrate, and as director for the Rutherford Electric Membership Corporation. During World War II he helped to build Camp Croft. As a young man he and a friend built a real working airplane that they flew briefly.

"It's been a good life," Fred says, "and we are grateful for each new day. It all came about, incredibly, as the result of that coin toss."

But don't let him off that easily. Get him to admit the truth about the coin toss. "I couldn't lose," he said. "It was a two-headed coin."

The Mintz family had long been known for their tenacity and their endurance. Fred's great-grandfather was Captain John B. Mintz, who saw considerable action during the Civil War. He was also in charge of the iron works at Iron Station and the one near High Shoals in North Carolina as well as the Cherokee Iron Works near Gaffney, South Carolina. He died at age 85 while living on the Broad River near the tiny town of Blacksburg, South Carolina. The iron works died much earlier, having been destroyed by Sherman on his march to the sea.

Another Mintz ancestor was William Decatur Mintz, who joined the army led by General Hood and they marched to Franklin, Tennessee. As they entered the rolling hills around Franklin, Major General Cleburne, a native of Ireland who found himself in this country fighting for Southern rights, said that it would not bother him to be killed and laid to rest in such beauty. He repeated that he had no family and that he could easily lay down his burdens at this point and never pick them up again. His one ambition, it seemed, was to reach the breastwork erected a short distance from them to provide cover for Federal gunners.

Suddenly, the general made his wishes come true.

Cleburne spurred his horse forward, exposed at every turn to enemy fire. Nothing slowed him down, not even when the hail of bullets ripped through his body. When his horse finally collapsed and died, its head was lying across the Federal breastwork. Cleburne himself had been shot more than thirty times. His wishes were granted, and he was buried nearby in the family plot of Andrew Johnson's family.

Decatur Mintz himself did not fare well in the battle. He had traveled many hundreds of miles with his outfit, from as far away as Arkansas.

When he reached the rolling hills of Tennesse he, too, was struck by the beauty of the terrain.

But there was a battle to be fought, and as he was passing through a low growth of bushes, a rifle ball struck him in the side of the head, even with his eyes. The bullet passed through his head, taking out both of his eyes but leaving him alive. He stumbled into a ditch where he lay unconscious for hours after first drinking deeply from water at the bottom of the small gully. When he woke later and tried to drink again, the water was too bloody to drink. He knew that the blood was his own.

A fellow soldier found him and helped him to a nearby house, where he was nursed until the Federal troops arrested him and took him to a prison camp up north. When he was released, he returned to North Carolina and eventually studied at the School for the Blind in Raleigh. Later he studied law, passed the bar, and practiced law in western North Carolina.

He left his law practice because he could not gauge the veracity of a witness without seeing the man's face. He said that a lawyer can learn a great deal and make far more valid judgments about a man's testimony if the lawyer can look the man in the eye and observe his body language and facial expressions.

Fred's other grandparents lived just outside Hiddenite at Linney's Grove. Their home was near the present site of the Lucas Mansion, earlier described in this book. Fred Mintz describes an incident in which Federal troops approached the Mintz house in search of a runaway soldier who, as it happened, was hiding in the attic. The head of the Mintz household walked into the yard, carrying his shotgun, and ordered the Federals off his property. Surprisingly, the men retreated, but as they reached a bend in the road, some of them turned around and fired at the house. The bullets are still in the wood, Fred says.

Ironically, Big John Mintz, who stood well over six feet and weighed more than three hundred pounds, lost his wife. Years later he met, courted, and married the widow of Christopher Bechtler, the man who founded the mint in Rutherfordton. Incidentally, when Fred lived in Shelby he walked to work with a gentleman who had a law office nearby.

That man was Clyde R. Hoey, later the governor who, after he helped prosecute and convict the Loray Seven, commuted the prison sentence of Fred Beal, who had returned from his Russian exile.

To establish one more link, when the author's house was destroyed by a tornado, it was Fred Mintz who helped to make equipment available to pull logs from the woods for the construction of the new log house.

But what about Lillian? What is her story?

"My father was David Barrett Whisnant, a farmer in this area of Cleveland County," she said. "He was also a school teacher. He lived in Shelby not far from where Fred grew up. Whisnant Street there is named after him. He also owned land around Benn's Knob in the South Mountains. My mother was Lela Maude Eaker before she married my father." The area around Benn's Knob is where Knobby, the South Mountains bigfoot, reportedly wandered through forests and farmlands.

Lillian recalls when she was a girl growing up in Upper Cleveland County and later as a young wife helping her husband make a living, times were hard. There was little money, and they worked long hours in order to make ends meet.

But they do not dwell on hardships. They have a contagious and wonderful attitude of hopefulness and faith. They have devoted their lives to each other and to their God, and their faith has not been misplaced. They learned long ago to rely upon each other and to strengthen and help each other in times of crisis.

It would be difficult, indeed, to find anyone who knows the Mintz family who didn't also like, admire, or love them. Their story was placed at the end of this book for one major reason: all the other stories simply paved the way to this one. Fred and Lillian Mintz never set out to change the world or to gain fame and fortune. They simply wanted to love each other and God and share that love with the people with whom they shared their lives. They never shied away from hard work, and they never shirked their duties as parents and neighbors. They loved each other constantly and faithfully, reared their children to be credits to themselves and to their families and to their communities, and worked endlessly to make their world a better place.

Theirs is a story of all the love and faith and trust and goodness that is so necessary in all of our lives. Matthew Arnold wrote one line that summarized their lives: "Ah, love! Let us be true to one another." The Mintzes put that thought into action. And they did so much more. At this writing they are still setting examples that will be difficult to follow.

They truly taught us how to live richer, fuller, better, and greater!

William Decatur Mintz

Young Fred and Lillian
Mintz

Big John Mintz

More Titles from Southeastern Publishing

100 Practically Perfect Places in the North Carolina Mountains

A book that guides you to the best mountain peaks, the best waterfalls, the finest museums, the most taxing and relaxing hiking or walking tours, the most scenic drives, the superb lakes and streams of the Tar Heel State, the most interesting private homes of some of the state's finest leaders in all social spheres, the most interesting and historical churches, the graveyards where some of the South's most fascinating people rest, the most rewarding towns and cities, and much, much more: 456 pages of legends and stories, plus striking photos. Retail price $15.

Faces of the Snow

A mystery/suspense novel set in the North Carolina Mountains, *Faces of the Snow* is the story of a killer whose victims are all women who have given birth before their marriages, who graduated in the same high school class, and who belong to a frivolous club based upon the fact that all the woman were united in a morganatic marriage. And the sheriff finds himself more deeply involved than he would have ever imagined. Retail price: $9.95.

To order call (toll-free) I-877-LAND.

Mad Dog's Tooth

A college professor sentenced to prison for what should have been a simple misdemeanor is given a once-in-a-lifetime chance to get back into society: all he has to do is run for the office of sheriff in a small town where the worst crime is a crowd of college kids getting drunk on weekends. Elected through the efforts of his friend and personal attorney, Chester Ivy becomes the best sheriff money can buy—for one day. That's when his best friend, the attorney who bought the election for him, and Ivy's wife are murdered in a drug-and-love nest. And Ivy is named beneficiary of millions of dollars. That's when the finger of suspicion is directed at him, and he finds himself acting as his own attorney in a trial that could, and probably would, cost him his life.

Bush League Bums
The Best (and Worst) Tar Heel Minor Leaguers

So you think you know North Carolina Minor League baseball when it was the best show in town? This is your chance to find out, and while you are at it you can relive the glorious days of the thirties, forties, and fifties, or you can experience them for the first time. Here is the book you have been waiting for: the story of the players in the old Outlaw League, the Victory League, the Western Carolina League, and the North Carolina State League. These are the legendary players who lived wild and free and played the same way.

To order call (toll free) 1-877-5263